The Human
Archaeology of Space

The Human Archaeology of Space

Lunar, Planetary and Interstellar Relics of Exploration

P. J. CAPELOTTI

McFarland & Company, Inc., Publishers
Jefferson, North Carolina, and London

Also of interest are the following works from McFarland:
The Franz Josef Land Archipelago: E.B. Baldwin's Journal of the Wellman Polar Expedition, 1898–1899, by E.B. Baldwin, edited by P.J. Capelotti (2004); *The Svalbard Archipelago: American Military and Political Geographies of Spitsbergen and Other Norwegian Polar Territories, 1941–1950*, edited by P.J. Capelotti (2000)

LIBRARY OF CONGRESS CATALOGUING-IN-PUBLICATION DATA

Capelotti, P.J. (Peter Joseph), 1960–
The human archaeology of space : lunar, planetary and interstellar relics of exploration / P.J. Capelotti.
p.   cm.
Includes bibliographical references and index.

ISBN 978-0-7864-5859-2
softcover : 50# alkaline paper ∞

1. Space archaeology.   2. Space vehicles.
3. Space debris.   4. Cultural property.   I. Title.
TL788.6.C37   2010   999 — dc22   2010021587

British Library cataloguing data are available

Front cover: The lunar rover from the *Apollo 17* mission; (above) illustration from the plaque on the *Pioneer 10* spacecraft (both images from NASA)

Manufactured in the United States of America

McFarland & Company, Inc., Publishers
Box 611, Jefferson, North Carolina 28640
www.mcfarlandpub.com

For Jeremy and Jenny

Table of Contents

Acknowledgments

I grew up a space junkie. It seems almost impossible to imagine the world of the 1960s now, before the internet and cell phones and twenty-four-hour television, when a child was allowed the freedom to invent new worlds to explore largely without the interference of ubiquitous electronics and associated marketing. When one did come in from the treehouse in the yard, it was to watch Jacques Cousteau build houses under the sea or NASA astronauts walk in space. It is still vivid in my mind, the night in July 1969 when I was allowed to stay up late to watch as the first humans set foot on the moon.

Later, I learned to combine the magical word "exploration" with the even more beautiful word "archaeology." As I pursued my doctorate in archaeology, I learned about and began to correspond with the anthropologist Dr. Ben Finney, who had pioneered the reconstruction of the technology and techniques used by Polynesians to settle the Pacific Ocean. When I mentioned to him that I wanted to combine my interest in space with archaeology, he suggested that I should construct a catalog of the archaeology of aerospace sites on the Moon and Mars, "the remains or imprint of Russian and American space ventures there," as he wrote to me in December of 1993.

From this suggestion I began collecting data in the 1990s, some of which found its way into my dissertation at Rutgers University. I was grateful that preeminent archaeologists of early hominids and human behavior at Rutgers such as J.W.K. Harris and Rob Blumenschine allowed me the intellectual freedom to follow these data into archaeologically meaningful implications for human evolution. Besides Ben Finney, two others, Richard Gould at Brown and Scott L.H. Madry, then of the Remote Sensing Center at Rutgers, encouraged me to expand my archaeological horizons. From their own work at the poles and the equator, colleagues like Susan Barr of Riksantikvaren in Oslo, Norway, and Bill Thomas, now director of the New Jersey School of Conservation at Montclair State, provided intellectual templates for my own thinking.

As I finished my dissertation, the internet began to explode the possibilities of data access. What had seemed like a hill of dozens of files on space archaeology on my desk grew into a mountain of thousands of internet bookmarks on my computer. In recent years some of my archaeology students at Penn State Abington — Kevin Drew, Tyler Callum, Noah Elbahtimy, and Allen Naygauzen — and I have begun to excavate this mountain, with a goal of producing the catalog of space archaeology envisioned by Ben Finney nearly twenty years ago. At the same time, this catalog required a new theoretical framework within which to think about the human movement into space. That is the ultimate purpose of this work.

P. J. Capelotti, Ph.D. • Penn State Abington College • Summer 2010

Carlsbad City Library
Phone: 760-602-2049
www.carlsbadlibrary.org

Customer ID: ************6663**

Items that you checked out

Title: The human archaeology of space : lunar,
       planetary and interstellar relics of
       exploration
ID: 31245006150753
Due: Saturday, August 7, 2021

Total items: 1
Account balance: $2.25
6/26/2021 11:57 AM
Checked out: 1
Overdue: 0
Hold requests: 0
Ready for pickup: 0

Receipt required for lost item refund within 6
months.

Thank you for using the Carlsbad City Library.

Preface: Measuring the Monuments of the Moon

On 18 June 2009, an Atlas V rocket launched the *Lunar Reconnaissance Orbiter* (LRO) from Cape Canaveral Air Force Station in Florida. Four days later, the unmanned spacecraft entered orbit around the polar regions of the Moon. For a year, hovering fifty kilometers above the surface, it undertook an intense series of photographic surveying and geophysical mapping in preparation for future manned polar base camps on the Moon and Mars.

Passing from pole to pole and crossing and re-crossing the Moon's equator, the LRO also took pictures of the landing areas of the manned Apollo spacecraft missions, the first since the last Apollo mission in 1972. This use of the orbiter as an archaeological platform, searching for abandoned relics of the first era of human exploration of space, continues an intermittent interest by the National Aeronautics and Space Administration (NASA) in the archaeology of space exploration.

In a press release, NASA calls this element of the LRO mission "nostalgia." It is in fact much more than simple historical curiosity. In the realm of cultural oddities, even NASA admits that conspiracy theorists cling to the idea that the lunar landings were a hoax, designed to win the space race by clever use of television studio sets that simulated a lunar landing. The faked mission to Mars seen in Hollywood's 1978 *Capricorn One*, released in a post–Watergate environment of public distrust of the government, fueled such hoax theories.

Documenting these landing and research sites is impossible from Earth even with the Hubble Space Telescope. In the summer of 2009, however, in some of its first imagery returned to earth, LRO used its high-resolution cameras to document the landing areas of all Apollo missions save for that of *Apollo 12*. The resolution on the *Apollo 14* site, in particular, revealed not only the shadow thrown by the lunar module *Antares*, but the footpaths created when the mission's astronauts set up a remote research station nearby.

Later, the probe relayed images of the *Apollo 12* landing area that revealed artifacts and pathways in even greater detail. The major components of discarded expedition gear left behind on the lunar surface — such as the lunar excursion module descent stages (LEM-DS) and the earlier unmanned *Surveyor 3* probe explored by the *Apollo 12*

1

Figure 1. The equatorial landing sites of *Apollo 11–17* (because of an explosion in its oxygen system *Apollo 13* did not land on the Moon). The sites are all on the side of the Moon that faces Earth and all near the equator, which is interesting in that they were created by a species that evolved near the equator of its own planet. (Credit: NASA's Goddard Space Flight Center Scientific Visualization Studio.)

astronauts, are visible in the imagery. Equally as interesting are the complex series of foot-paths created by the astronauts as they placed an instrument package on the Moon, and walked from the lunar module to the *Surveyor* probe and then to nearby geological features.

Such imagery of walkways created by bipedal *Homo sapiens* exploring the surface of a place other than their home planet can offer interesting insights into the ways in which

Figure 2. Buzz Aldrin (left) and Neil Armstrong practice for their lunar mission on a set designed to simulate the surface of the Moon. (Credit: NASA S69–32233 [22 April 1969].)

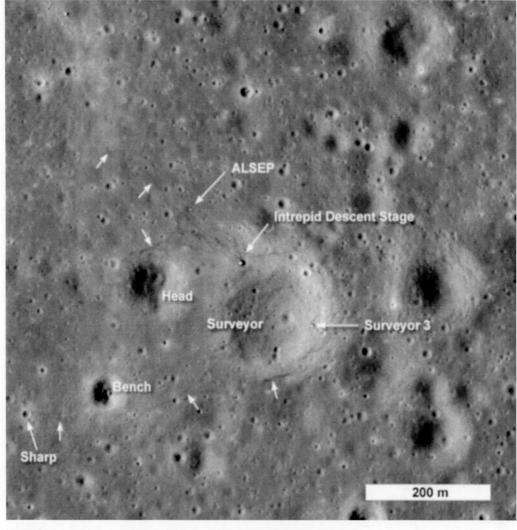

humans carry behavioral patterns into space. Given a flat, largely unobstructed surface, the walking paths are relatively straight. When confronted by a landscape of mounds and craters, the humans go around these obstacles rather that across or over them.

Numerous images taken during the Apollo series of expeditions show roadway tracks made by the lunar rover vehicles. One such image shows an astronaut walking alongside the path made by the rover. Even though the human can make any pathway he wants, he walks *alongside* the freshly created roadway, imitating the behavior of pedestrians avoiding those areas frequented by motor vehicles on his home planet.

University of Hawai'i anthropologist Ben Finney once wrote that humankind "evolved as an exploratory, migratory animal."[1] Not only might the human exploration of space supersede the movement of *Homo erectus* out of Africa or *Homo sapiens* across the Wallace Line, Finney argued that it could "be studied directly without having to reconstruct and test the vehicles involved or interpret ambiguous texts."[2]

Leaving aside the earthbound challenges of archaeological surveys of abandoned rocket gantries in Florida or Kazakhstan, what space archaeology currently lacks in direct access for the archaeologist, it more than makes up for in its sheer volume of historical, technological, and planetary data. The purpose of this book is to gather into a single source the data on the artifacts that *Homo sapiens* have discarded in space and place them into the framework of archaeology. Because, as Finney implied and as the imagery noted above reveals, nearly all of this data is directly relevant to human evolution and cultural diversity and, today, all of it is readily accessible on one's laptop, PDA or droid.

NASA alone has eight separate web sites devoted exclusively to data just on its current missions, and each of these sites is further broken down into distinct descriptive pages on human aspects of exploration, emerging hardware and other technologies, space port and research facilities, and mission goals and accomplishments. Then there are the sites for the eleven separate federal space launch, control, or research centers.

If you visit the Kennedy Space Center site, for example, you can path to the history page. There you will find this delicious little archaeological nugget: "[Scientists hope that the unmanned] Voyager [exploratory probe] will pass beyond the boundary of the Sun's influence before the onboard nuclear power supply wanes too low to tell us what's out there. *Voyager 1* is now the most distant human-made object." In anthropological terms, the artifact of human intelligence, *Voyager 1*, launched in 1977, is about to become the first tool fashioned by human hands to leave the boundaries of the solar system.

The news release remarks on this event as an interesting bit of technological trivia, rather than as the immense cultural landmark that it most assuredly is. In fact, in Novem-

Opposite, top: Figure 3. LRO's image of the *Apollo 14* landing site, showing footpaths created by astronauts setting up a remote research station away from the Lunar Module *Antares* (arrow). (Credit: NASA/Goddard Space Flight Center/Arizona State University.) *Opposite, bottom:* Figure 4. LRO's first look at the *Apollo 12* landing site with the associated *Surveyor 3* probe. The footpaths created by the *Apollo 12* astronauts are shown by unmarked arrows. (Credit: NASA/Goddard Space Flight Center/Arizona State University.)

Figure 5. As if reflexively displaying Earth behavior by avoiding the middle of a roadway, *Apollo 15* astronaut Jim Irwin walks alongside a pathway created by a lunar roving vehicle. The *Apollo 15* mission was the fourth to land humans on the Moon and the first to bring a lunar roving vehicle to the Moon. In this way, the humans could extend their range of exploration from a few hundred meters to tens of kilometers. (Credit: NASA, image AS15–86–11654.)

ber 2003, scientists began to debate whether *Voyager 1* had in fact reached the edge of the solar system and begun to encounter a new region of unexplored space, where the wind from the Sun blows against the variety of gases that are diffused throughout interstellar space. At this point, the Voyager spacecraft was more than thirteen billion kilometers from the Sun.

For the purposes of this book, it must be remembered that the two Voyager spacecraft

Figure 6. Artist's conception of the unmanned *Voyager 1* spacecraft. This artifact of human intelligence was launched on 5 September 1977 and is now crossing the boundary of the solar system on its way into interstellar space, some thirteen billion kilometers from the Sun. (Credit: NASA.)

have not yet become strictly archaeological objects. Since humans can still contact them — until late in the year of 2015 — they still exist as part of a living human cultural system. In archaeological terms, they are in their systemic context. Once that contact is broken and the spacecraft no longer responds to the humans who launched it on its way, it becomes an object of archaeological concern, a discarded artifact freighted with the attributes of the culture that constructed it.

This is the case with, for example, the *Pioneer 10* space probe, launched in 1972 on a mission to investigate Jupiter. *Pioneer 10* completed its mission and then continued on, following an escape trajectory away from the solar system. A final attempt to contact the spacecraft was made on 7 February 2003, a few weeks after a command was sent to it to shut down its final working experiment. Nothing was heard in return. After thirty-one years, the probe had entered its archaeological context, even as it was still in motion — only now as a dead satellite. It is headed towards the red star Aldebaran, the vicinity of which it is scheduled to reach in approximately two million years, or roughly the same amount of time that members of the bipedal, large-brained, tool-making and tool-dependent genus *Homo* have walked the earth.

In this example, it becomes clear how much longer a tool created by humans exists in its archaeological as opposed to its systemic context. The *Pioneer 10* continues to exist well past its original mission — the rendezvous with Jupiter. By human lights, such performance is likely at the limits of expectation. After all, thirty-one years of active life would occupy the majority if not the totality of a space scientist's active career. A young Ph.D., let's say, thirty-three years old at the start of the mission, would have been ready to retire after the final attempt to communicate had been made more than three decades later.

But *Pioneer 10* has just begun its archaeological lifespan. It will long outlive our theoretical Ph.D., and maybe even his gravestone. If *Pioneer 10* isn't intercepted by an advanced civilization or destroyed in a collision with an asteroid in some distant star system, it will likely complete its two-million-year journey to Aldebaran, where it will perhaps be caught in its gravitational pull. It will then begin to orbit that faraway star until the end of the history of the galaxy several billion years in the future. These are vast and bracing considerations. For it is the very possibility of one of the composite tools fashioned by *Homo sapiens* being studied by another intelligence in the universe that in this work ties the method and theory of lunar, planetary and interstellar archaeology to that of the archaeology of extraterrestrial civilizations.

The sheer volume and variety of anthropological hypotheses ready to be spun from the mountain of data collected by the exploration of space is enough to awaken even the most sluggish or jaded brains. "More Data Than Ever!" as the *Mars Reconnaissance Orbiter* website proudly announces, almost as if it were a grocery store. Need to visualize a multispectral scanner Earth survey from space? Check the SkyLab Mission archives at the Johnson Space Center. Want to study how the SkyLab astronauts had to be positioned to conduct their Earth resources experiment? There is a picture of that, too. How about a cultural analysis of the type of humans NASA employed for SkyLab (exclusively white male engineers with fixed smiles and names of two syllables or less)? Or look at a map of the Moon showing the distribution of unmanned U.S.–U.S.S.R. probe landings. Why was NASA fixated on the Sea of Tranquility while the Russians obsessed over the Sea of Storms? Why did both bunch their landings within a few degrees of the lunar equator? Were the lunar poles uninteresting, dangerous, or difficult, or were human explorers of the Moon simply echoing several million years of equatorial adaptation on Earth, where the poles were the last place human explorers managed to plant their flags?

Finally, there is the incomparable National Space Science Data Center (NSSDC), with its historic mission profiles and technical synopses of each spacecraft. The NSSDC technical specifications on artifacts located on moons and other planets (as well as those artifacts in heliocentric orbit and those heading away from the solar system) are reprinted herein. These appear in the "Technical Notes" sections of chapters two and three on lunar archaeology, chapters five and six on planetary archaeology, and finally in chapter eight on interstellar archaeology. These technical specifications, along with the mission histories, are edited in order to provide a format usable to future aerospace archaeologists. They are enhanced with brief notes on the archaeological relevance of each mission to create something approaching a foundational work in aerospace archaeology.

Widening our field of vision even farther, archaeologists can now see the whole of space — its contemplation as well as its exploration — as part of a new field of investigation. Just as the Scandinavian archaeologist Christer Westerdahl argued a decade ago for consideration of a "maritime cultural landscape" to encompass the study of the human use of maritime space by boat, Australian archaeologist Alice Gorman proposes a similar cultural landscape of space. This, she argues, would follow a trend in cultural heritage management away from the notion of archaeological sites as discrete locations and see them instead as "a cultural landscape forged by the organic interaction of the space environment and human material culture."[3]

The 500-metric-ton gorilla in all discussions of archaeology in space, of course, is the question of non-human intelligence in the universe. Like a sliver of space junk that becomes impossibly heavy the faster it goes, it seems that the closer archaeologists get to the question of potentially non-human artifacts of intelligence, the more they fear the career-killing consequences of embracing the subject too closely.

But this feeling, too, is beginning to fade. The idea of archaeology in space has been accepted by the World Archaeological Congress, which has even formed a Space Archaeology Task Force in 2003. And, if one accepts the idea of archaeological research on sites from the history of human exploration in space, it is hardly a giant leap to consider the potential for archaeological fieldwork on the evidence of extraterrestrial civilizations. The very fact that *Homo sapiens* has made a deliberate decision to launch unmanned spacecraft equipped with a variety of symbolic messages intended for another potential intelligence opens the door for archaeology to consider the possible forms and structures such intelligence might take, and what artifacts and archaeological features such an intelligence might create in the wake of its history.

If Darwin is, as evolutionary biologist Richard Dawkins suggests, the only game in the universe, then we should expect to find systems of increasing complexity (though without any easily predictable cultural outcomes) throughout the universe. We should also anticipate that such systems, like our own, may have advanced to the point where they have left behind artifacts of their particular intelligence in response to their individual selective environmental pressures.

The sub-field of "exobiology" is now a commonplace and consistently generates news from what were originally hypothetical undertakings but now enjoys data from moons of the outer planets that suggest plausible regions for extraterrestrial life. The icy Jovian moon of Europa, with an apparent frozen ocean similar to Earth's Arctic Ocean, is now under consideration by such biologists and intensive planning by spacecraft engineers who seek to burrow an oceanographic-style probe through Europa's pack ice in search of microbial life. The Saturnian moon of Titan has a dense atmosphere and liquid hydrocarbon lakes in its polar regions which suggests a colder version of the early formation of

9

Earth and possible microbial extraterrestrial life. (And, in true *Homo sapiens* fashion, the two missions now compete for funding.)

But what if what we eventually find in space is not life but traces of past life, not a living civilization but traces of a past civilization? Highly speculative landforms like the unexplained linear markings on the Tharsis Plateau of Mars or "The Face" and the nearly pyramidal shapes in the Cydonia region of Mars — which recent imagery suggest are likely no more than ancient mountains corraded by eons of sandstorms — were advanced by the late astronomer Carl Sagan and others as sites to be examined by future missions to Mars as potential artifacts of intelligence.

In one sense, the issue of planetary archaeology and extraterrestrial civilizations proceed hand-in-hand. In October 2009, astronomers from the European Southern Observatory announced that, after an examination of 2,000 nearby stars, they had located 32 different "exoplanets," planets that exist beyond our solar system. This raised to 400 the number of such planets discovered since the first such exoplanet was announced in 1995. Given the billions of stars in the galaxy, the odds seem good that numerous exoplanets are orbiting at the right distance from a star — the so-called "Goldilocks" distance: not too far, not too close — to allow for the formation of water, amino acids, oceans, life and, potentially, intelligent life.

One such planet — Gliese 581c within the constellation Libra — approximately twenty

Figure 7. Artist's conception of a planet with a mass six times that of Earth orbiting the star Gliese 667c. This is one of thirty-two new exoplanets discovered by the High Accuracy Radial Planet Searcher (HARPS) of the European Southern Observatory. (Credit: ESO/L. Calçada.)

light years from Earth, was discovered by a team led by Stéphane Udry of the University of Geneva in 2007. Both 581c and a nearby Earth-like planet, Gliese 581d, lie within the habitable zone where water can exist without either freezing or vaporizing. This makes them both potential waterworlds, covered entirely by oceans and, possibly, inhabited by living forms.

At the very least, these 400 exoplanets, along with those almost certainly to be discovered in the years to come, will be amongst the first locations in the universe where *Homo sapiens* will aim their unmanned Voyager-like spacecraft in future galactic exploring expeditions. If current practice is any guide to future missions, humans will send both orbiting platforms and as well as surface landers and probes to these exoplanets. This means that these planets will one day hold the most widely scattered collection of hominid composite tools that it is possible to imagine.

Sagan, who believed there were more than a million currently active galactic civilizations, once wrote an article entitled "Is There Intelligent Life on Earth?" He argued that if one viewed satellite imagery of one-mile resolution, one could stare at the entire eastern seaboard of the United States for hours and see no sign of life, intelligent or otherwise. If structures similar to the Jonglei Canal in the Sudan or the Aswan High Dam in Egypt or Hadrian's Wall in northern England exist on Alpha Centauri, would we be able to recognize them as the artifacts of intelligence? If Dawkins is correct and Darwinian evolutionary theory is a process without any particular purpose or ultimate goal, would intelligent life on an exoplanet even construct tools or features in the landscape and, if so, would we recognize them as such? If intelligent life exists on a waterworld, would it exist in a form closer to whales than humans? How would terrestrial archaeological science categorize intelligent life that produced no concomitant material culture?

Such questions bring us back to the *Lunar Reconnaissance Orbiter*. With NASA's LRO explorations of the Moon having a distinctly archaeological character, with its Lunar Crater Observation and Sensing Satellite (LCross) mission in search of polar water to facilitate a future human presence mission on the Moon (and announced as a confirmed fact following the impact of LCross into the Cabeus crater near the lunar south pole on 9 October 2009), and with discussions with Richard Branson's *Virgin Galactic* spacecraft for space tourism moving from fantasy to reality, the time is right for a comprehensive catalog of artifacts left behind on other lunar and planetary bodies by explorers from Earth, as well as those mobile artifacts that might never find a permanent resting matrix that would make them more familiar to traditional archaeology.

This book seeks to provide both current and future aerospace archaeologists with a unified basic catalog of artifacts that the human species has placed, lost, used and/or abandoned on celestial bodies in the solar system other than Earth. The book also explores issues of both archaeological method and theory in the aerospace environment, using aerospace sites on Earth as models for the potential research and management of cultural resources in the solar system.

To accomplish this, the book is divided into three parts, covering distinct but interconnected issues of lunar, planetary, and interstellar archaeology. In the first two parts, individual chapters cover the history behind each mission that left artifacts behind on the moons and planets of the solar system, along with the technical notes from the NSSDC and, in some cases, imagery of the artifacts, imagery of the location where the artifact was abandoned, if available, and discussions of the potential archaeological exploration of the artifact. We even take a short break from traditional archaeology at the start of Chapter Four to look at arguments for artifacts of alien intelligence in the solar system.

In Part Three, we explore the archaeology of mobile artifacts in the solar system and the wider galaxy. Specifically, in Chapter Eight, we take on the problem of the archaeological survey of artifacts that are not at rest and may never come to rest in any sense recognizable to traditional field archaeology.

PART I:
LUNAR ARCHAEOLOGY

La Voyage dans la lune (1902), a film by Georges Méliès. A rocket from Earth lands in the eye of the Man in the Moon.

1

Lunar Archaeology

1. Methodology

Archaeology, unlike history, cannot exist without the material residue of human triumph and failure, be it ruins of abandoned settlements or shipwrecks at the bottom of the sea. And while most people associate archaeology with the pyramids of ancient Egypt or the stone *moai* statues of Easter Island, the features and artifacts of prehistory or the beginnings of recorded history, archaeologists now believe that the crash sites of Soviet robot probes on the surface of the Moon and the unmanned spacecraft heading outwards from the solar system are just as important to understanding the behavior of *Homo sapiens*.

This human exploration of space contains within it a material culture as relevant to the course of human culture and human evolution as the Olduwan Industry tools developed in the East African rift valley and in Ethiopia more than two million years ago. In the case of sophisticated composite tools left behind or sent by humans to other locations in the solar system, they offer a wide new field of archaeological study. If we can study and isolate the processes by which humans adapt such technology to explore such extreme environments as space, we can gain insight into human behavior that will aid or even propel our movement as a species into the solar system and beyond. For example, eight Apollo missions left archaeological evidence behind on the lunar surface. These are discussed in detail in Chapter Two. Six of these resulted in a human presence on the Moon. As such, the Apollo expeditions comprise a crucial cultural resource database within the lunar archaeology of *Homo sapiens*.

The progress of aerospace technology and the projection of privately funded space vehicles carrying paying passengers into orbit have combined to motivate both theoretical discussions[1] and actual (if remote) studies of Apollo sites,[2] and how this database could be both preserved and utilized for studies within the field of aerospace archaeology.

The amount of artifactual material transported from Earth to the Moon is estimated at over 170,000 kilograms, or near 190 tons of material culture — the equivalent of sending twenty-five elephants to the Moon, or 150 mid-sized automobiles. It is therefore a substantial database to preserve and manage.

Cultural resource management of such aerospace sites in extreme environments as those of the Apollo program on the Moon will likely be founded on many of the same

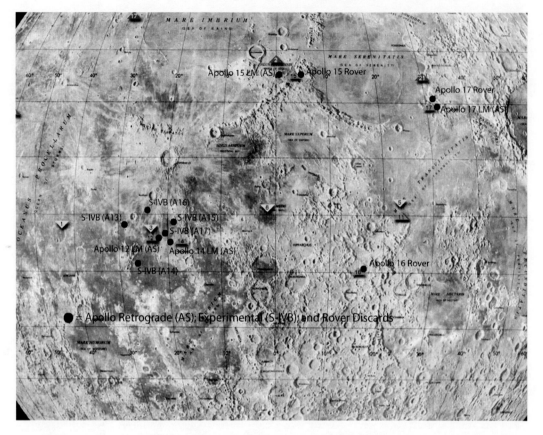

Figure 1.1. Locations of the Apollo landing sites, in relation to the locations of Apollo Retrograde (lunar module ascent stage); Experimental (S-IVB); and Lunar Rover discards. (Credit: Modified by author from National Space Science Data, Moon Landing Map.)

principles that currently guide the attempts at stabilization, preservation, and study of historic sites in Antarctica, where scientific exploration during the International Geophysical Year (IGY) of 1957–1958 led directly to the Antarctic Treaty of 1961, which in turn became "a model for subsequent international treaties about space."[3]

Under the treaty, nations such as New Zealand have established protection and study regimes for historic sites in Antarctica,[4] and archaeological techniques and technologies advanced for research in this extreme environment.[5] These techniques are episodic and directed toward particular sites during brief summer field seasons, as one might anticipate in any planning of a mission to a particular site of extraterrestrial archaeology.

The extreme environment in which the Apollo database is embedded is a temporary advantage in its preservation. It should preclude most cultural transformational processes for several decades until the expected advent of regular tourist or development travel to the Moon. The natural transformation processes of extreme temperatures and radiation can be partially ameliorated through a program of shielding the major artifact concentrations. But other natural processes, such as potential damage or destruction by meteorites, cannot be accounted for.

While the static base camps of the Apollo missions would comprise the main foci of cultural resource protection regimes, equally important will be the preservation of the Apollo wreck sites. These are artifacts that demonstrate, like the impact zones of the Saturn V S-IVB third-stage rockets, reuse of one form of technology for a distinct scientific experimental series, or, like the undiscovered wreckage of the *Apollo 10* descent stage and the undiscovered ascent stages of *Apollo 11* and *Apollo 16*, techno-cultural failure in the course of exploratory voyaging.

For example, the site where the Soviet *Luna 5* probe crash-landed onto the surface of the Moon with such force "that a German observatory claimed to have seen a 135 by 49 mile dust cloud where it impacted"[6] may one day provide excellent archaeological opportunities for the study of the secretive Luna series of unmanned probes launched in an era of intense superpower competition for priority on the Moon.

Until recently, we had no data on the condition of the crashed Apollo artifacts in their archaeological context. On Tuesday, 8 September 2009, the *Lunar Reconnaissance Orbiter* photographed the impact crater formed when the *Apollo 14* S-IVB second-stage booster rocket was deliberately crashed into the Moon on 4 February 1971. The booster rocket was thereby altered from its original purpose — to serve as a means of propelling the astronauts and their gear toward the Moon — to be reused as a source of energy to search the geology of the Moon using instruments placed on the surface by earlier Apollo missions.

In the imagery obtained by NASA researchers, the crater is about thirty-five meters in diameter, with bright lines of dislodged regolith extending for more than 1.5 kilometers from the impact zone. While this imagery cannot reveal any of the spacecraft wreck itself, it does provide direct evidence of the impact zone caused when a fifteen-ton artifact crashes into a planetary surface at more than 15,000 kilometers per hour.

In mid–September 2009, LRO settled into an orbit just fifty kilometers above the lunar surface. From this orbit, it made a close approach over the site of the *Apollo 17* landing. This expedition reached the Moon on 11 December 1972, and three days later the descent stage served as the launch pad for the ascent stage as it blasted off for a rendezvous with the command module *America*.

When LRO made its low-level pass over the site, it acquired imagery with two times better resolution than any previously acquired. Also critical to obtaining the level of surface detail was the high angle of the Sun, which helped to bring out distinct areas of brightness and shadow. In Figure 1.3, taken at fifty-centimeter resolution, the descent stage of the lunar module *Challenger* is visible in the center, surrounded by the suite of instrumentation left on the surface by the expedition.

Tracks to the east show where astronauts Jack Schmitt and Gene Cernan set up the Surface Electrical Properties experiment (SEP). Cernan then drove the lunar roving vehicle (LRV) in cross-shaped north-south and east-west tracks to mark positions for laying out

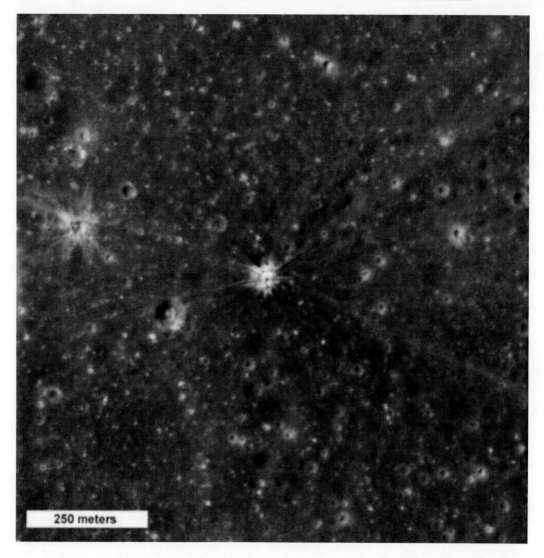

Figure 1.2. The crater in the center of the image shows the impact of the *Apollo 14* S-IVB upper stage rocket that was deliberately crashed into the surface of the Moon on February 4, 1971. Photograph taken from the *Lunar Reconnaissance Orbiter*. (Credit: NASA/Goddard Space Flight Center/Arizona State University.)

the SEP thirty-five-meter antennas. The dark spot just below the SEP experiment is where the astronauts left the rover, in a place from which its cameras could record the liftoff of the Lunar Module ascent stage.

LRO is providing so much high resolution imagery of the Apollo landing zones and associated artifact areas like the *Apollo 14* S-IVB impact zone that much of the framework for future archaeological field research on the Moon and elsewhere in the solar system will

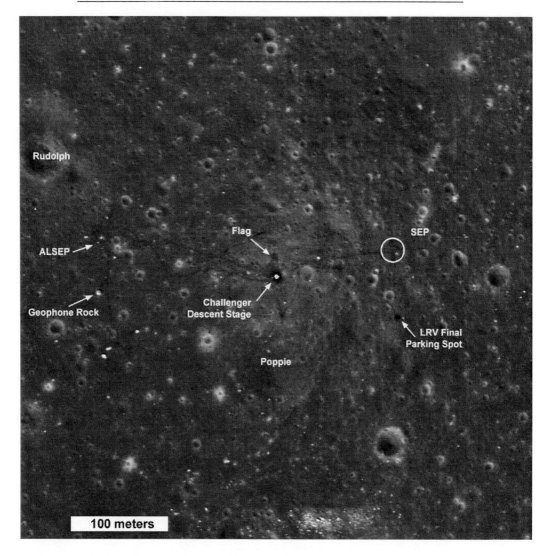

Figure 1.3. Region of Taurus Littrow valley around the *Apollo 17* landing site. This remarkable image, obtained at 50 cm resolution by a low-orbit pass over the site, combined with a favorable sun angle that brought out surface details, clearly shows the *Apollo 17* descent stage (center), the spot where the U.S. flag was planted, the astronaut walking paths as well as the tracks and final parking spot of the lunar roving vehicle. Photograph taken from the *Lunar Reconnaissance Orbiter*. (Credit: NASA/Goddard Space Flight Center/Arizona State University.)

already be accomplished before archaeologists visit these areas directly. And while it might seem rather extraordinary to consider the possibilities of direct archaeological field research on the Moon itself (as opposed to the archaeological remote-sensing research carried out by the LRO), we can take note of the fact that it has already taken place.

In fact, NASA has been conducting formational archaeology research on lunar sites

Figure 1.4. The *Apollo 12* lunar module (in the distance on the edge of Surveyor crater), with the *Surveyor 3* probe in the foreground. (Credit: http://history.nasa.gov/alsj/a12/AS12-48-7 090.)

at least since 1969.[7] On 20 November 1969, astronaut Charles Conrad, Jr., recovered pieces (the television camera, remote sampling arm, and pieces of tubing) from the unmanned *Surveyor 3* probe that had soft-landed in the Moon's Ocean of Storms on 19 April 1967. These artifacts were brought back to Earth so that the Johnson Space Center in Houston, Texas, and the Hughes Air and Space Corporation in El Segundo, California, could analyze the natural transformational processes operating on aerospace artifacts left on the Moon.

A study of the archaeological catalog left by the Apollo program on the lunar surface

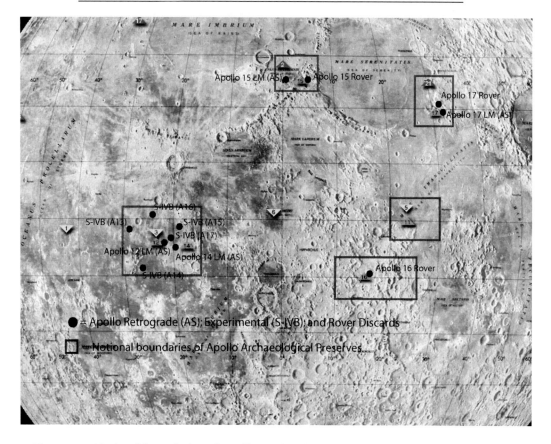

Figure 1.5. Notional boundaries of Apollo Archaeological Preserves. (Credit: Modified by author from National Space Science Data, Moon Landing Map.)

suggests that its deposits can be arranged into five cohesive geographic areas on the near side of the Moon. The areas can be thought of as notional archaeological preserves, areas of the Moon specially demarcated in order to place the entire database (minus the artifacts yet to be located) under a protective regime that will shield them both from environmental deterioration and from the effects of future exploration, visitation, and potential exploitation. The boundaries of the first of these notional archaeological parks would surround the landing site of *Apollo 11*, from 20° to 30° E and from 5°S to 5°N. This area would allow for the inclusion of the earlier unmanned *Surveyor 5* probe and perhaps enclose the undiscovered wreckage of the *Apollo 11* ascent stage as well.

If the first such lunar archaeological preserve is so designated for its obvious historical value and associations, the second would encompass by far the largest concentration of associated remains of the Apollo program. This second area, extending from 15° to 30° W and from 10°S to 3°N, would enclose the base camps of both the *Apollo 12* and *Apollo 14* missions, the wrecks of the discarded ascent stages of both missions, the deliberately crashed wreckage of the S-IVB third-stage rockets of the *Apollo 13, 14, 15, 16,* and *17* expeditions, and also the area around Surveyor crater and the *Surveyor 3* spacecraft and its associations with the *Apollo 12* mission. Such a preserve would offer an extraordinary database of aerospace archaeology and the history of science, exploration, and technology.

Next in importance would be the areas surrounding the missions of *Apollo 15* and *Apollo 17.* Both of these demarcated areas include not only the respective expedition base camps but, for the first time in the series (with *Apollo 15*), the additional technology of the lunar rover. Also associated within the *Apollo 15* preserve would be the remains of the unmanned Russian spacecraft *Luna 2.* The *Apollo 17* preserve likewise would include the remains of a Russian probe, in this case *Luna 21.* The *Apollo 15* site is also the highest latitude base camp of all of the Apollo missions. The final site is that of *Apollo 16,* which also has an associated lunar roving vehicle.

Ranking these areas according to cultural, archaeological, and historical value, and assuming the potential that each area might not receive complete protective quarantine, these preserves should be established in the following order:

1. *Apollo 11/Surveyor 5*
2. *Apollo 12/Surveyor 3/Apollo 14/S-IVB cluster*
3. *Apollo 15*
4. *Apollo 17*
5. *Apollo 16*

Shielding the Apollo base camps will require the development of a dome-like structure specifically engineered to address a combination of natural and cultural transformational processes. Such an "archaeodome" would first and foremost offer protection against the gradual natural decay of extreme temperatures and solar radiation. At the same time, connected to a nearby landing platform, the dome would allow for tourist visits while shaping the access pathways to the site. Tourist pathways across the dome — complete with handholds, interpretive panels, and emergency life support stations — would allow for both oblique and plan views of the archaeological sites while leaving sensitive areas like the original Apollo footprints and rover treads untouched. Such a concept, developed for the protection of the Apollo base camps and wreck sites on the Moon, could be adapted for similar cultural resource protection regimes for such sites as the Viking landers on Mars.

2. Theory

Prosaic questions of the survey, stabilization and preservation of archaeological sites on the Moon need not necessarily be examined in a theoretical, shall we say, vacuum. The archaeological study of both earthbound and planetary sites from the history of aerospace exploration leads neatly into cultural and biological considerations inherent in humanity's exploration of and expansion into space.

Hundreds of sites exist where operational spacecraft have been discarded, whether by mission requirements, accident, or obsolescence. Abandoned space *ports* testify to the base camps necessary to operate in the aerospace environment. The Apollo Lunar Module descent stages and the Saturn V third-stage S-IVBs on the Moon likewise testify to the extraordinary dual use of much of the Apollo technological catalog. When wrecks like the S-IVBs occur, or the Apollo base camp sites are abandoned, the artifact leaves history, where it was a part of people's thoughts and actions (what the archaeologist Michael Schiffer calls its *systemic context*), and enters Schiffer's *archaeological context*.[8]

In order to make credible use of the material record in the construction of screens through which to filter the words of the historical record, primary attention must be given to accounting for how what exists as the present day (archaeological) material record arrives in our time from the (systemic) past. This idea has no doubt long been an intuitive one on the part of archaeologists, but its explicit application as a primary mechanism in the analysis of material remains has come only recently. As Schiffer writes, "The past — manifest in artifacts — does not come to us unchanged."[9]

As mentioned in the preface, it was Ben Finney, who for much of his career had explored the technology and techniques used by Polynesians to settle the Pacific Ocean, who first suggested that it would not be premature to begin thinking about the archaeology of aerospace sites on the Moon and Mars. Finney was certainly clear-eyed about the improbability of anyone being able to conduct fieldwork any time soon, yet he was equally convinced that one day such work would be done. The path of this emerging field could be seen, by way of illustration, as early as the early and mid–1990s in the examinations made of aerospace base camps and other sites as recent as those remaining from the years of the Cold War.[10]

While the archaeologist O.G.S. Crawford "referred to obsolete aircraft as strictly archaeological"[11] and archaeologist James Deetz referred to "interplanetary space vehicles"[12] as a complex example of material culture, the first suggestion that aircraft wrecks might yield important anthropological data was made as early as 1983 by Richard A. Gould. Gould suggested that debates originating in the historical record could be evaluated through "the explanatory potential of archaeology ... [where] differing historical interpretations can be regarded as a source of alternate hypotheses, with archaeological evidence being used to test each alternative."[13]

Studies of the culture of Apollo must combine appropriate material recording and intensive historically particular documentation with anthropological approaches on the model of Gould's "trend analysis."[14] Gould suggests that there is "an urgent need to examine the relationship of specific kinds of behavior to the materials that are deposited at wreck sites," and goes on to suggest that such sites possess "signatures," and "distinctive patterns," "akin to what might appear as a particular configuration of sounds on sonar or other underwater listening apparatus to identify a particular submarine or class of submarine and what it might be doing."[15]

Any consideration of the nature of the mating of *Homo sapiens* to his machines throughout aerospace history inevitably leads to cultural and biological considerations inherent in humanity's exploration of and expansion into space, a move that "represents a continuation of our terrestrial behavior, not a radical departure from it."[16] "Our terrestrial behavior," of course, includes the triumphal (*Apollo 11, Apollo 12*), the precarious (*Apollo 13*), and the catastrophic (*Apollo 1, Challenger, Columbia*).

Though at first it may appear that Finney's notion of *Homo sapiens* as an explorer is ultimately too large and vague to test archaeologically, it contains several archaeological implications that can be applied to the Apollo sites on the Moon. Exploration is a uniquely human behavior and produces, as in the Apollo lunar archaeological preserves, a novel material component. As such it falls within the hard boundaries of credible archaeological analysis.

The testing of Finney's hypothesis should be directed at establishing links between the cultural responses to the need to explore read in the archaeological record and the suggestion that *Homo sapiens* has evolved as an inherently exploring species, one "that spread from [a] tropical homeland through developing technology to travel to and survive in a multitude of environments for which they were not biologically adapted."[17]

2

Artifacts of Manned Exploration of the Moon

Introduction

The archaeological evidence of manned missions to the Moon is exclusively American. Of the thirty-eight expeditions to the Moon that achieved impact on the surface, twenty-three were launched by the United States and, of these, eight were manned Apollo missions.

From 1969 to 1972, the Apollo missions left behind on the Moon twenty-three large-scale artifacts. These large-scale or "main body" artifacts fall into five categories: Lunar Module ascent stages (Fig. 2.3); Lunar Module descent stages (Fig. 2.4); Saturn V third-stage rockets (S-IVB) (Fig. 2.5); subsatellite science probes (Fig. 2.6); and lunar rovers (Fig. 2.7).

Around these main body archaeological assemblages, or collections of similar technologies, smaller artifacts include scientific instrument packages and their power generators, personal artifacts, and the only piece of artwork brought to the Moon and left there. Other evidence of human exploration include footprints and rover tread path left behind by astronauts and the vehicles they brought to the Moon to extend their exploring range beyond walking distance from the Lunar Module base camps.

These assemblages transitioned at different moments from their *systemic context* (operating as part of an active human enterprise) to enter the realm of archaeology, where they become relics embedded in the natural landscape. There they find, in Michael Schiffer's terms, their *archaeological context*. Most of the areas of the sites made this transition as soon as the humans vacated them. Others, like the ALSEP scientific instrument packages and their power generators, remained in systemic context until the generators were shut down by commands sent from Earth several years later. Taken together, the several sites of manned exploration of the Moon can be thought of in archaeological terms as a culture. In this case, they are the culture of Apollo. This chapter explores the historical archaeology of these assemblages in order to create a descriptive catalog of the culture of Apollo.

Figure 2.1. A lunar ranging site, in association with the footprints of bipedal *Homo sapiens* from Earth. (Credit: NASA.)

The Archaeological Catalog

1) *APOLLO 10*[1]

History

The *Apollo 10* expedition lifted off from Cape Canaveral in the afternoon of 18 May 1969, closely orbited the Moon in a test of the full *Apollo* spacecraft, and returned to Earth almost exactly eight days later, on 26 May. The objective of the mission was to

SATURN V LAUNCH VEHICLE

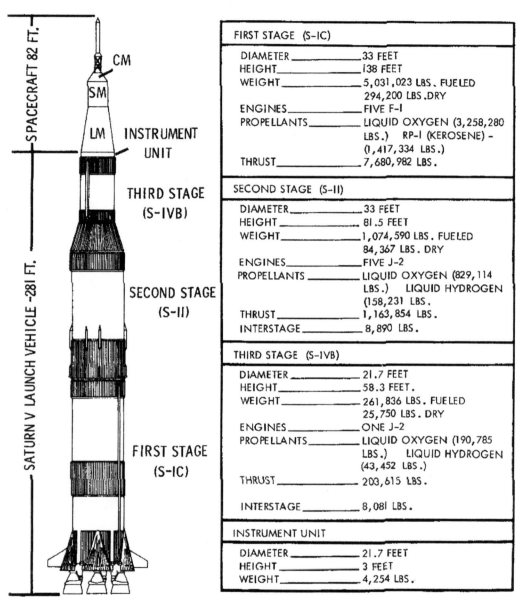

FIRST STAGE (S-IC)	
DIAMETER	33 FEET
HEIGHT	138 FEET
WEIGHT	5,031,023 LBS. FUELED 294,200 LBS .DRY
ENGINES	FIVE F-I
PROPELLANTS	LIQUID OXYGEN (3,258,280 LBS.) RP-I (KEROSENE) - (1,417,334 LBS.)
THRUST	7,680,982 LBS.

SECOND STAGE (S-II)	
DIAMETER	33 FEET
HEIGHT	81.5 FEET
WEIGHT	1,074,590 LBS. FUELED 84,367 LBS. DRY
ENGINES	FIVE J-2
PROPELLANTS	LIQUID OXYGEN (829,114 LBS.) LIQUID HYDROGEN (158,231 LBS.
THRUST	1,163,854 LBS.
INTERSTAGE	8,890 LBS.

THIRD STAGE (S-IVB)	
DIAMETER	21.7 FEET
HEIGHT	58.3 FEET.
WEIGHT	261,836 LBS. FUELED 25,750 LBS. DRY
ENGINES	ONE J-2
PROPELLANTS	LIQUID OXYGEN (190,785 LBS.) LIQUID HYDROGEN (43,452 LBS.)
THRUST	203,615 LBS.
INTERSTAGE	8,081 LBS.

INSTRUMENT UNIT	
DIAMETER	21.7 FEET
HEIGHT	3 FEET
WEIGHT	4,254 LBS.

NOTE: WEIGHTS AND MEASURES GIVEN ABOVE ARE FOR THE NOMINAL VEHICLE CONFIGURATION FOR APOLLO 10. THE FIGURES MAY VARY SLIGHTLY DUE TO CHANGES BEFORE LAUNCH TO MEET CHANGING CONDITIONS.

Figure 2.2. The stages of the *Apollo* spacecraft. (Credit: *Apollo 10* Press Kit, p. 49a.)

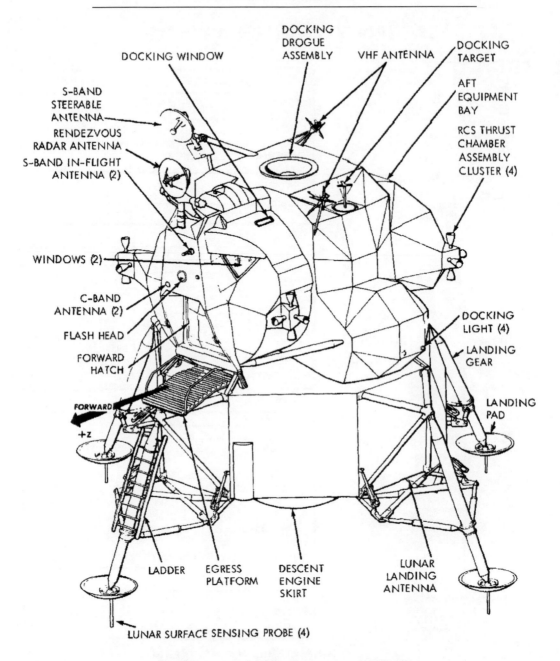

DOCKING
DROGUE
ASSEMBLY

DOCKING WINDOW

VHF ANTENNA

DOCKING
TARGET

S-BAND
STEERABLE
ANTENNA

AFT
EQUIPMENT
BAY

RENDEZVOUS
RADAR ANTENNA

RCS THRUST
CHAMBER
ASSEMBLY
CLUSTER (4)

S-BAND IN-FLIGHT
ANTENNA (2)

WINDOWS (2)

C-BAND
ANTENNA (2)

DOCKING
LIGHT (4)

FLASH HEAD

LANDING
GEAR

FORWARD
HATCH

LANDING
PAD

FORWARD

+z

LADDER

EGRESS
PLATFORM

DESCENT
ENGINE
SKIRT

LUNAR
LANDING
ANTENNA

LUNAR SURFACE SENSING PROBE (4)

APOLLO LUNAR MODULE

Figure 2.3. The lunar module, showing the ascent or upper stage attached to the descent stage. (Credit: *Apollo 10* Press Kit, p. 42a.)

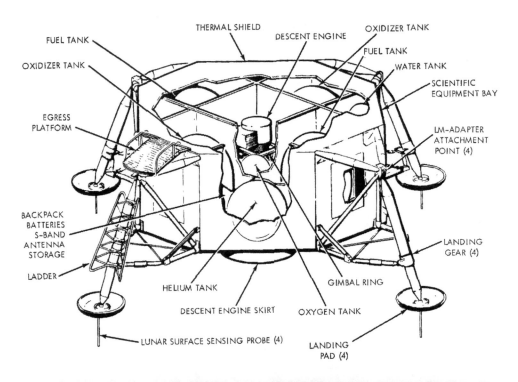

FUEL TANK
OXIDIZER TANK
EGRESS PLATFORM
BACKPACK BATTERIES S-BAND ANTENNA STORAGE
LADDER
THERMAL SHIELD
DESCENT ENGINE
OXIDIZER TANK
FUEL TANK
WATER TANK
SCIENTIFIC EQUIPMENT BAY
LM-ADAPTER ATTACHMENT POINT (4)
LANDING GEAR (4)
HELIUM TANK
DESCENT ENGINE SKIRT
GIMBAL RING
OXYGEN TANK
LUNAR SURFACE SENSING PROBE (4)
LANDING PAD (4)

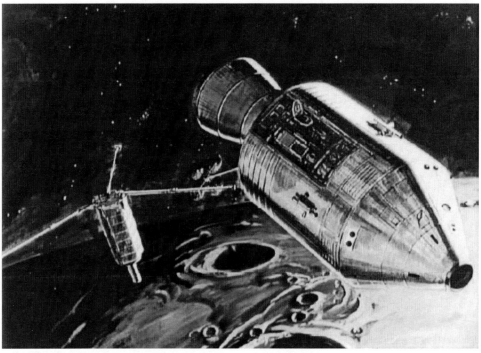

Top: Figure 2.4. The Lunar Module descent stage. (Credit: *Apollo 10* Press Kit, p. 43a.)
Bottom: Figure 2.6. Artist's drawing of the *Apollo 16* subsatellite science probe. (Credit: http:// nssdc.gsf.nasa.gov/nmc/masterCatalog.do?sc=1972-031D.)

Figure 2.5. Saturn V third stage S-IVB rocket consisted of the entire area below the enclosed lunar module. (Credit: *Apollo 10* Press Kit, p. 19a.)

Figure 2.7. The lunar roving vehicle during the *Apollo 17* expedition. (Credit: http://his tory.nasa.gov/alsj/a17/AS17-4=140-21367.jpg.)

evaluate the complete complement of manned *Apollo* technologies and their associated Earth-based support systems prior to an actual landing on the Moon planned for the *Apollo 11* mission later that summer. All operations of the later *Apollo 11* mission were simulated with the exception of the actual landing on the Moon. As in all Apollo missions, the expedition consisted of a three-man crew, led by mission commander Thomas P. Stafford, Command Module pilot John W. Young, and Lunar Module pilot Eugene A. Cernan. The technology that reached the Moon included the Command and Service Module and the Lunar Module.

After a three-day cruise to the Moon, the Lunar Module was separated from the Command Module and flown to within 14 km of the lunar surface. Returning toward the Command Module, the descent stage of the Lunar Module was discarded and jettisoned into lunar orbit. The two-person LM crew returned to the Command Module, and then the ascent stage of the Lunar Module was discarded and jettisoned into solar orbit. The crew returned to Earth on board the Command Module. The crew capsule re-entered Earth's atmosphere and splashed down 643 kilometers east of American Samoa where both crew and capsule were recovered by the USS *Princeton*.

Archaeology

The *Apollo 10* Lunar Module descent stage is the first object of manned exploration humans left behind on the Moon. It was jettisoned into lunar orbit after the LM made its closest inspection of the lunar surface. Immediately after its separation, the ascent

Descent Orbit Insertion   **Lunar Module Staging**   **Apollo Docking**

LM
Ascent Engine Firing to Depletion   **Lunar Landmark Tracking**

Figure 2.8. The *Apollo 10* lunar module descent and rendezvous operation, showing the discard of the descent stage (upper middle panel) onto the surface of the Moon. (Credit: *Apollo 10 Press Kit*, p. 7.)

stage of the LM made a quick maneuver to avoid hitting the descent stage. NASA mission records do not record what happened to the descent stage after separation from the ascent stage.[2] When official records speak of jettisoning operations, it is with regards to the jettison of the ascent stage after rendezvous with the Command Service Module.[3]

The discarded descent stage would have continued in orbit around the equator of the Moon until the orbit decayed and the artifact impacted into the surface, transitioning as it did so from systemic to archaeological context. The wreck site, as well as the degree of damage done to the descent stage during impact, is unknown. All known archaeological sites created by the Apollo program exist on the near side of the Moon. The possibility exists that the wreck of the *Apollo 10* LM descent stage — along with the wrecks of the *Apollo 11* and *Apollo 16* ascent stages and the *Apollo 16* subsatellite — comprise the only evidence of manned exploration to have been discarded on the far side of the Moon.

2) APOLLO 11[4]

History

The *Apollo 11* expedition left Earth on the morning of 16 July 1969, with the purpose of landing the first humans on the Moon and returning them safely. The crew consisted of Commander Neil A. Armstrong, Command Module pilot Michael Collins, and Lunar Module pilot Edwin E. (Buzz) Aldrin, Jr.

At the launch point in the coastal estuaries of eastern Florida, roads and parking areas overflowed with an estimated one million eyewitnesses, including the author. One did not see so much as feel the launch of the Saturn V rocket, as the 7.6 million pounds of its main engines shook the ground for several miles around.

Two days later, during the afternoon of 19 July, the spacecraft — now consisting of the Command Service Module attached to the Lunar Module — enters lunar orbit and passes to the far side of the Moon. Each orbit requires about two hours.

On 20 July, Aldrin and Armstrong entered the Lunar Module, separated the lander from the CSM, and descended toward the surface of the Moon. In the late afternoon of 20 July, the Lunar Module was set down on the southwestern edge of the Sea of Tranquility, about twelve kilometers from its target point. Armstrong's radio message to Mission Control, "The Eagle has landed," marked the first time humans established a manned base camp on another planetary body. A few hours later, Armstrong crawled backwards through the Lunar Module hatch, descended the three-meter-tall ladder, and stepped out onto the surface of the Moon. Armstrong, soon joined by Aldrin, began a rapid series of both scientific recording and sampling and the emplacement and photography of symbols such as flags and memorial plaques. Less than three hours later, with their exploratory and symbolic work accomplished, the two humans climbed back on board the Lunar Module.

Sleeping overnight in the module, the explorers left the Moon the following afternoon after less than a day on the surface. The ascent engine of the ascent stage of the Lunar Module was fired and, using the platform of the descent stage as a launch pad, the spacecraft lifted off and the first human base camp on the Moon was abandoned.

Archaeology

More than 5,000 pounds of spacecraft and other exploratory gear, flags, and plaques were left behind at the landing site/base camp, along with hundreds of footprints in the soft, dusty soil. These artifacts include the descent stage/launch pad, video and still cameras, scientific sampling tools, discarded life support systems, an American flag, and several remotely operated scientific instruments, including a laser beam reflector, seismic detector, and a gnomon, a device to verify colors of objects photographed.

The base camp is located just north of the lunar equator, at 0° 40' 26.69" N, 23° 28' 22.69" E. What is unknown is the location of the *Apollo 11* Lunar Module ascent stage. Two hours after the Lunar Module ascent stage re-docked with the Command Service Module, the ascent stage was jettisoned. As with the *Apollo 10* descent stage jettisoned and lost two months earlier, the location of the *Apollo 11* ascent stage was not recorded.

3) APOLLO 12[5]

History

Four months after *Apollo 11*, on 14 November 1969, the second mission to land humans to explore the lunar surface lifted off from Earth. The *Apollo 12* expedition consisted of mission commander Charles P. "Pete" Conrad, Lunar Module pilot Alan L. Bean, and Command and Service Module pilot Richard F. Gordon. On the morning of 19 November 1969, Bean and Conrad landed in Oceanus Procellarum (the Ocean of Storms) on the Moon. The Lunar Module touched down on the rim of a crater that was named after an unmanned *Surveyor 3* probe that had landed on the Moon two and a half years earlier.

Near the Lunar Module base camp area, Bean and Conrad emplaced an Apollo lunar surface experiments package (ALSEP) and a solar wind collector. The ALSEP instruments were placed on the surface of the Moon and connected by cables to a central power unit. The power unit used a small amount of Plutonium-238 to create heat and convert this heat into electricity.

During a long (1.3 kilometers) walk away from the Lunar Module on 20 November, the astronauts reached the *Surveyor 3* probe inside the crater and removed several components of it. These components, weighing some ten kilograms, were returned to Earth for study. This research — an analysis of the transformation processes at work on an artifact during its years in the lunar environment — can be appropriately considered the first example of extraterrestrial archaeology.

After more than thirty-one hours on the lunar surface, the two astronauts lifted off from the Moon in the Lunar Module ascent stage and rendezvoused with the Command Service Module. The ascent stage was jettisoned and deliberately crashed back into the lunar surface to create an artificial quake recorded by the ALSEP's seismometer. The expedition returned to Earth on 24 November 1969.

Archaeology

In terms of material culture, *Apollo 12* both conducted archaeological research in the form of retrieving components of the *Surveyor 3* probe and also created distinct archaeological assemblages in the form of the Lunar Module descent stage base camp and its associated scientific experiments and footprints, and the wreck of the Lunar Module ascent stage. The descent stage launch pad/base camp with the associated ALSEP experiment package is located south of the lunar equator at 2.99° S, 23.34° W. The wreck of the ascent stage is located slightly south and east of the base camp, at 3.94° S, 21.2° W. The ALSEP instruments, powered up on 20 November 1969, were powered down along with other ALSEP instrument assemblages, on 30 September 1977, making them the last of the *Apollo 12* artifacts to make the transition from systemic to archaeological context.

The surviving Command Module was placed on display at the Virginia Air and Space Center in Hampton, Virginia, while the television camera recovered from the *Surveyor 3* probe was placed on display at the Smithsonian Air and Space Museum in Washington, D.C. For the purposes of archaeological research and cultural resource protection, the entire area around Surveyor crater, to include the *Apollo 12* base camp, the human foot tracks leading to and from the *Surveyor 3*, the Surveyor probe itself, and the wreck site of the ascent stage, should be considered as a single heritage unit.

4) APOLLO 13[6]

History

The *Apollo 13* mission, from 11 to 17 April 1970, was intended to explore the Fra Mauro region of the Moon. The expedition was aborted when one of the oxygen tanks on board the service module exploded en route to the Moon. The cause of the explosion was later determined to be a short caused by damaged wires. With nearly half the Service Module's oxygen supply gone, the astronauts, led by Captain James A. Lovell, Jr., and including Command Module pilot John L. Swigert, Jr., and Lunar Module pilot Fred W. Haise, Jr., transferred to the Lunar Module. They used its supplies for survival until the whole Command Service Module–Lunar Module assembly could orbit the Moon and make a return voyage to Earth.

Archaeology

The only evidence of the *Apollo 13* mission that survives on the Moon is the wreck of the Saturn V third-stage S-IVB (S-IVB-508), which lies at 2.75° S, 27.86° W, just west of the base camp of the *Apollo 12* mission. After separation from the Command Service Module, the S-IVB was placed on a lunar impact trajectory and impacted the Moon on 14 April 1970.

Possible remains of the Lunar Module exist on Earth, in the Pacific Ocean off the coast of New Zealand where they would have fallen if they survived re-entry in Earth's atmosphere. The Command Module was eventually placed on display at the Kansas Cosmosphere and Space Center in Hutchinson, Kansas.

5. *APOLLO 14*[7]

History

The *Apollo 14* expedition left Earth on 31 January 1971, on a mission to land on the Moon near the Fra Maura crater. The expedition was led by commander Alan B. Shepard, Jr., and included Lunar Module pilot Edgar D. Mitchell and Command Module pilot Stuart A. Roosa. The Saturn V third-stage S-IVB was powered into a lunar impact trajectory during the flight to the Moon and crashed into the lunar surface on 4 February.

Shepard and Mitchell landed on the Moon in the Lunar Module, 24 km from Fra Mauro, on 5 February 1971, and emplaced a series of scientific experiments, including an Apollo lunar surface experiments package (ALSEP); took photographs; and collected more than forty-two kilograms of geological samples from the lunar environment. Before concluding the second of their two walks on the Moon, Shepard teed up two golf balls and hit them away into space using a 6-iron attached to the end of a scientific sampling device.

The Lunar Module ascent stage left the Moon on 6 February and the astronauts returned to Earth on board the Command Module on 9 February.

Archaeology

The *Apollo 14* S-IVB Saturn V third-stage was deliberately crashed into the lunar surface to trigger a Moon quake that could be recorded by the *Apollo 12* ALSEP. The impact point, 8.09° S, 26.02° W, places the wreckage in a cluster of S-IVB discards surrounding the *Apollo 12* and *Apollo 14* base camps. After being jettisoned by the crew, the *Apollo 14* Lunar Module ascent stage crashed into the Moon on 7 February 1971, at 3.42° S, 19.67° W, a spot roughly midway between the *Apollo 12* and *Apollo 14* base camps.

The base camp itself, with the Lunar Module descent stage and the associated walking area of the astronauts, is located at 3° 38' 43.08" S, 17° 28' 16.90" W. The ALSEP station, which recorded the impact of the Lunar Module ascent stage, was turned on on 5 February 1971. It was powered down by commands from Earth and entered its archaeological context along with the other ALSEP stations on 30 September 1977. The Command Module was placed on display at the Astronaut Hall of Fame in Titusville, Florida.

6) APOLLO 15 [8]

History

The *Apollo 15* expedition left Earth on 26 July 1971 on a mission to explore the Hadley Rille/Apennines region of the Moon, the northernmost landing site in the Apollo series of lunar explorations. The mission was led by commander David R. Scott and included Lunar Module pilot James B. Irwin and Command Module pilot Alfred M. Worden.

The Saturn V third-stage S-IVB separated from the Command Service Module when the spacecraft reached orbit around Earth and was then sent on a collision course with the Moon.

Scott and Irwin landed on the Moon on 30 July 1971 at the foot of the Apennine mountain range. During the course of their time on the surface, they deployed a lunar roving vehicle from its storage "garage" on board the descent stage of the Lunar Module. This was the first time such a human-driven, wheeled vehicle had been used on the Moon. With the rover, the astronauts were able to journey nearly twenty-eight kilometers over the lunar surface while collecting over seventy-seven kilograms of geological samples, taking photographs, and setting up an ALSEP instrument package.

The Lunar Module descent stage, the rover, and the array of scientific instruments were left behind when the Lunar Module ascent stage left the Moon on 2 August. The mission concluded when the astronauts returned to Earth on board the Command Module on 7 August.

Archaeology

The *Apollo 15* Saturn V rocket's S-IVB third-stage was crashed into the lunar surface at 1.51° S, 17.48° W, a position north-northwest of the *Apollo 12* and *14* base camps and where the ALSEPs emplaced there could record its impact. *Apollo 15*'s ALSEP was activated on 31 July 1971 and entered its archaeological context when it and the other ALSEP stations were powered down on 30 September 1977.

The *Apollo 15* expedition was the first manned lunar mission to employ a lunar roving vehicle. This four-wheeled machine allowed the astronauts to extend their range up to five kilometers away from the Lunar Module base camp site. The rover and the *Apollo 15* Lunar Module descent stage base camp area are located at 26° 7' 55.99" N, 3° 38' 1.90" E. It is also here on the lunar surface that a small work of art — a stylized astronaut — was left behind with a plaque dedicated to the Americans and Russians who had died in the development of the nations' respective space exploration programs.

When the *Apollo 15* Lunar Module ascent stage was jettisoned, it crashed into the Moon at 26.36 N, 0.25 E, within 100 kilometers of the expedition's base camp. Another archaeological element of the *Apollo 15* mission was a so-called "subsatellite" that was released into orbit around the Moon from the expedition Service Module. When its orbit decayed, the cylindrical satellite with its three booms crashed at an unrecorded location on the lunar surface.

7) APOLLO 16[9]

History

The *Apollo 16* expedition left Earth on 16 April 1972, on a mission to explore the Descartes region of the Moon. The expedition was led by commander John W. Young and included Charles M. Duke, Jr., as Lunar Module pilot and Thomas K. Mattingly II as Command Module pilot.

The Saturn V third-stage S-IVB separated from the Command Service Module after the spacecraft reached Earth orbit. The S-IVB was then sent on to an impact on the Moon, where it crashed on 19 April at 1.3 N, 23.8 W, continuing the cluster of S-IVB wreckage around the landing sites/base camps of the *Apollo 12* and *14* missions.

Young and Duke landed on the Moon in the Lunar Module on 21 April. During the course of three excursions away from the Lunar Module base camp, they drove a total of twenty-seven kilometers with the lunar roving vehicle. Another ALSEP scientific instrument was emplaced on the Moon, and another sampling of lunar rocks and soil was collected for return to Earth.

The LM took off from the Moon on 24 April and the astronauts returned to Earth on 27 April.

Archaeology

The *Apollo 16* Saturn V rocket's S-IVB third-stage was crashed into the lunar surface at 1.3° N, 23.9° W, just north of the lunar equator and within the general cluster of S-IVB wrecks from *Apollo 13* through *17*. The *Apollo 16* base camp with its lunar roving vehicle and ALSEP station is located at 8° 58' 22.84" S, 15° 30' 0.68" E, southwest of the original *Apollo 11* landing site.

A fault in *Apollo 16*'s Lunar Module ascent stage meant that the planned crash into the lunar surface had to be abandoned. Like the expedition's subsatellite, both machines were placed in orbit around the Moon. It is estimated that the ascent stage remained in orbit for a year before it fell from orbit to an unknown location on the lunar surface. The expedition's subsatellite experienced mechanical problems as well, and its planned lunar orbit of one year was shortened to one month before it too crashed into an unrecorded location on the lunar surface. The expedition's ALSEP station was the final piece of the expedition to transition from systemic to archaeological context. Activated on 21 April 1972, it was powered down with the other ALSEP stations on 30 September 1977.

8) APOLLO 17[10]

History

The *Apollo 17* expedition left Earth on 7 December 1972 on a mission to explore the Taurus-Littrow region of the Moon. The expedition was led by commander Eugene

A. Cernan with Lunar Module pilot Harrison H. Schmitt and Command Module pilot Ronald E. Evans. The mission was both the final Apollo mission and the last time humans reached and walked on the surface of the Moon.

The Saturn V third-stage S-IVB separated from the Command Service Module soon after the spacecraft entered orbit around Earth and sent on course to the Moon. Cernan and Schmitt landed on the Moon in the Lunar Module on 11 December 1972 on the southeastern rim of Mare Serenitatis (the Sea of Serenity). There they deployed the lunar roving vehicle from its storage area on board the Lunar Module descent stage. Over the next seventy-five hours, they explored the area around the base camp, extending the range by driving the rover a total of thirty kilometers. The astronauts collected over 110 kilograms of lunar samples and emplaced an ALSEP instrument package.

The Lunar Module ascent stage lifted off from the Moon on 14 December and the astronauts returned to Earth on board the Command Module on 19 December.

Archaeology

The *Apollo 17* Saturn V third-stage S-IVB rocket crashed into the lunar surface on 10 December at 4.21 S, 12.31 W, completing a cluster of S-IVB wreckage from *Apollo 13, 14, 15, 16,* and *17* arrayed around the descent stage base camps of *Apollo 12* and *14.*

The *Apollo 17* Lunar Module descent stage/base camp, with its associated lunar roving vehicle and ALSEP instrument array, is located at 20° 11' 26.88" N, 30° 46' 18.05" E. After being jettisoned from the Command Module, the ascent stage of the expedition's Lunar Module crashed into the lunar surface at 19.96° N 30.50° E.

The final element of the expedition to transition from systemic to archaeological context was the ALSEP array. Activated on 12 December 1972, it was closed down with the other ALSEP stations on 30 September 1977. The only artifact to return to Earth, the *Apollo 17* Command Module, was placed on display at the Johnson Space Center in Houston, Texas.

Conclusions

The Apollo program left six lunar module descent stages fixed at base camps on the Moon, another descent stage at an undiscovered site, and another six ascent stages deliberately discarded and impacted on the lunar surface after they had delivered their crews back to the mission's command module. These spacecraft, dead and discarded, have all found Schiffer's archaeological context.

Of the scientific instruments packages (ALSEP) left behind on the Moon and powered by small amounts of Plutonium-238, these were the last Apollo artifacts to leave their systemic context. When, nearly five years after the last human walked on the Moon, all of the ALSEP stations were powered down on 30 September 1977, they too entered their archaeological context along with the rest of the Apollo archaeological database.

The goals of aerospace archaeologists with regard to the culture of Apollo from this moment forward should be twofold. First, a protective regime should be adopted to preserve this database as the vital cultural and behavioral catalog of scientific exploration that it is. Second, the database should be seen as a primary tool in the examination of *Homo sapiens* as an exploratory, migratory species.

3

Artifacts of Unmanned Exploration of the Moon

Introduction

As the constant nearby presence in the evening sky, as the engine of the tides, the moon is the one object in the heavens that is both indisputably a part of Earth and is also making the voyage through space and time with Earth. As my colleague (and the first archaeologist to map culture features on the Moon) Beth O'Leary writes, "The Moon features in stories created by cultures from Australia to the Arctic. Every culture from prehistoric times can rightfully claim the Moon as a part of its cultural heritage."[1] The Moon is both the first and last place *Homo sapiens* set foot outside the cocoon of their home planet, and very likely will be the next such place visited and perhaps permanently occupied.

The archaeological evidence of unmanned missions to the Moon begins with the hard impact of the Soviet Union's *Luna 2* spacecraft on the surface on 14 September 1959. Since that moment, thirty-seven more unmanned expeditions to the Moon have achieved impact on the surface. Twenty of these missions were undertaken by the United States and another fourteen by the Soviet Union. In the past twenty years, the European Union, Japan, China, and India have all launched probes toward and ultimately into the Moon.

These missions led to the first hard, scientific knowledge of the composition and age of the Moon. Its surface consists of a heavily cratered regolith, with highland crags and smooth lowland *maria*. It has no significant atmosphere or magnetic field. This knowledge has led to various theories on the formation of the Moon, including the idea that Earth may have suffered a direct impact of a Mars-sized object some 4.5 billion years ago. This impact would have sent material into space that eventually coalesced into the Moon. Since that time, as these unmanned probes discovered, the Moon has been something of an intergalactic pin cushion, absorbing thousands of impacts by meteorites large and small.

In this chapter, the missions of each nation are arranged chronologically, followed by the goals, landing sites, materials used and materials abandoned in each mission.

Figure 3.1. The *Surveyor 3* spacecraft, which landed on 20 April 1967. In the background is the *Apollo 12* lunar module, which in November 1969 landed about 180 meters from *Surveyor*. Parts of the earlier space probe were removed during the *Apollo 12* mission and returned to Earth for analysis. The mission marked the first extraterrestrial archaeological research. (Credit: NASA.)

The Archaeological Catalog

1) *LUNA 2* [2]

History

The history of unmanned spacecraft from the former Soviet Union that were targeted at the Moon rests exclusively with the Luna (from the Russian word for moon) Program.

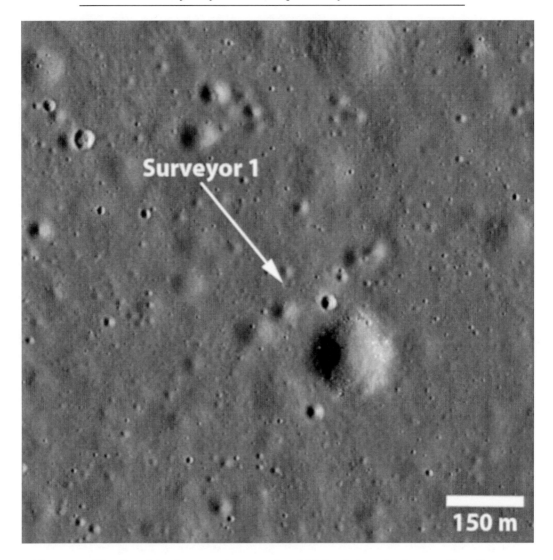

Figure 3.2. The site of the *Surveyor 1* spacecraft, which landed on the Oceanus Procellarum of the Moon on 2 June 1966. *Surveyor 1* was the first American spacecraft to land on the surface of our nearest neighbor in the solar system. This image of the 3.3m-tall artifact was taken on 1 October 2009 by the Lunar Reconnaissance Orbiter. (Credit: NASA/Goddard Space Flight Center/Arizona State University.)

At least two dozen missions were attempted between 1959 and 1976, but because of the secrecy that surrounded the Soviet space program, unless such a mission was deemed a success its history was not revealed to the public.

Fifteen of the Luna probes were successful in either orbiting or soft-landing on the Moon. Others made it to the Moon but flew past it, or crash-landed onto the surface. *Luna 1,* for example, missed the Moon by nearly 6,000 kilometers and became to first artifact of human intelligence to be captured by the gravitational pull of the Sun and begin a heliocentric orbit at a point between the orbits of Earth and Mars.

The *Luna 2* was a spherical spacecraft that carried five antennas and other instruments including scintillation and Geiger counters for measuring ionizing radiation, a magnetometer, and micrometeorite detectors. The probe also carried pennants testifying to its origin in the Soviet Union. It was launched from the Cosmodrome at Baikonur and carried into space on board a rocket on 12 September 1959. The spacecraft had a mass of 390.2 kilograms, but no propulsive capacity of its own. The mission determined that the Moon had neither a significant magnetic field nor radiation belts.

Archaeology

On 14 September 1959, thirty-eight hours after launch, the *Luna 2* became the first unmanned spacecraft to land on the Moon. It crash-landed to the east of Mare Serenitatis near the Aristides, Archimedes, and Autolycus craters, at a point thought to be around 29.1° N, near three craters in the North Mare Imbrium. The third stage of *Luna 2*'s rocket impacted the Moon thirty minutes later, presumably near the impact site of the probe itself.

Both *Luna 2* and its third-stage rocket carried symbolic pennants indicating its origin in the Soviet Union. The pennants carried on board the probe were made of stainless steel and embossed with the coat of arms of the nation along with the month and year (September 1959) of the mission. On the third-stage rocket, aluminum strips were embossed with the same symbols and messages.

2) *RANGER 4*[3]

History

Launched on 23 April 1962, *Ranger 4* was designed to transmit pictures of the lunar surface to Earth stations during a period of ten minutes of flight prior to impacting on the Moon, to rough-land a seismometer capsule on the Moon, to collect gamma-ray data in flight, to study radar reflectivity of the lunar surface, and to continue testing of the Ranger program for development of lunar and interplanetary spacecraft.

The first series of Ranger probes (Block 1: *Ranger 1* and *2*) was designed to test technologies for reaching and studying the Moon. Block 2 would then to make the journey to gather close-up images of the Moon by flying straight at it and returning photography right up until the moment of impact. *Rangers 6* through *9* (Block 3) flew to the Moon in 1964 and 1965; each successfully returned data to Earth before crashing into the lunar surface. Of the nine Ranger probes eventually launched into space, five impacted on the surface of the Moon.

Perhaps as important as its technical and scientific objectives, the Ranger series of probes was designed and constructed at the same moment that American scientists convinced the National Aeronautics and Space Agency that any spacecraft designed to impact upon the surface of the Moon must be sterilized before it left Earth. Only in this way could potential signs of extraterrestrial life be detected on the Moon free from any biological contamination from Earth.[4]

Ranger 4 was virtually identical to *Ranger 3*, in the so-called "Block 2" series of unmanned Ranger spacecraft that were launched toward the Moon in 1962. *Rangers 3* and *5* both missed their lunar target and, like *Luna 2*, flew past the Moon and into heliocentric orbit.

The spacecraft was 3.1 meters tall and equipped with a large high-gain dish antenna attached to the base. Two wing-like solar panels (5.2 meters across) were attached to the base. These held 8,680 solar cells to charge the spacecraft's batteries. At its top, the probe carried a lunar capsule that was covered with balsa wood in an attempt to limit damage from the impact with the Moon. The capsule was designed to release from the main spacecraft just short of the Moon, at which point the capsule would descend more slowly to the surface. Inside the capsule was a seismometer immersed in shock-absorbing oil, which would drain from the capsule when it landed. Once on the Moon, the seismometer would begin transmitting data to Earth.

Technical Notes

The telemetry system aboard the spacecraft consisted of two 960 MHz transmitters, one at three watts power output and the other at fifty mW power output, the high-gain antenna, and an omni-directional antenna. White paint, gold and chrome plating, and a silvered plastic sheet encasing the retrorocket furnished thermal control. The experimental apparatus included (1) a vidicon television camera, which employed a scan mechanism that yielded one complete frame in ten seconds; (2) a gamma-ray spectrometer mounted on a 1.8 meters boom; (3) a radar altimeter; and (4) a seismometer to be rough-landed on the lunar surface. The seismometer was immersed in shock-absorbing oil inside the lunar capsule along with an amplifier, a fifty-milliwatt transmitter, voltage control, a turnstile antenna, and six silver-cadmium batteries capable of operating the lunar capsule transmitter for thirty days.

Archaeology

An onboard computer failure caused failure of the deployment of the solar panels and navigation systems; the spacecraft impacted on the far side of the Moon without returning any scientific data. The impact point was 229.3° E by 15.5° S and the mass of the artifact was 331 kilograms. With the spacecraft's failure to deploy its solar panels, it is unlikely that the capsule, meant to separate from the main spacecraft prior to impact and then transmit data, ever did so.

3) RANGER 6[5]

History

Ranger 6 was the first of the so-called Block 3 variants of the Ranger unmanned lunar probes. It was sterilized to avoid any contamination of the Moon. The balsa-encased capsule carried on the Block 2 series was replaced by a unit containing a series of high-resolution television cameras. Launched on 30 January 1964, the probe was designed to reach the Moon and transmit high-resolution video images of the lunar surface just before the spacecraft impacted onto the lunar surface. No other scientific recording equipment was carried on the expedition. The video mission failed when none of the half-dozen onboard cameras returned any data to Earth, a failure later attributed to a short-circuit that had occurred earlier in the mission.

Technical Notes

The spacecraft carried six television vidicon cameras, two wide-angle (channel F, cameras A and B) and four narrow-angle (channel P), to accomplish these objectives. The cameras were arranged in two separate chains, or channels, each self-contained with separate power supplies, timers, and transmitters so as to afford the greatest reliability and probability of obtaining high-quality video pictures.

The spacecraft consisted of a hexagonal aluminum frame base 1.5 meters across on which was mounted the propulsion and power units, topped by a truncated conical tower which held the TV cameras. Two solar panel wings, each 73.9 centimeters wide by 153.7 centimeters long, extended from opposite edges of the base with a full span of 4.6 meters, and a pointable high-gain dish antenna was hinge-mounted at one of the corners of the base away from the solar panels. A cylindrical quasi-omnidirectional antenna was seated on top of the conical tower.

Power was supplied by solar cells contained in the two solar panels, giving a total array area of 2.3 square meters and producing 200 watts. Two 1200-watt batteries rated at 26.5 Volts with a capacity for nine hours of operation provided power to each of the separate communication/TV camera chains. Two 1000-watt-hr batteries stored power for spacecraft operations. Communications were through the quasi-omnidirectional low-gain antenna and the parabolic high-gain antenna.

Archaeology

After a flight lasting 65.5 hours, the spacecraft impacted into the Moon on 2 February 1964, on the eastern edge of Mare Tranquillitatis (Sea of Tranquility), in the same general area where the first Apollo mission to land on the Moon would touchdown five years later. The mass of the spacecraft was 381 kilograms and the place of impact was 9.4°N and 21.5°E.

4) RANGER 7[6]

History

Ranger 7, like the other Block 3 spacecraft in the Ranger series, was a flying television camera, designed to return images of the Moon that would be used by the designers of the Apollo program in their preparations for landing humans on the Moon. Launched on 28 July 1964, the probe reached the Moon after a flight of 68.6 hours. For the final fifteen minutes of the mission, before impact, *Ranger 7* returned over 4,300 images of the Moon, the first spacecraft ever to do so.

Technical Notes

The spacecraft carried six television vidicon cameras, two wide-angle (channel F, cameras A and B) and four narrow-angle (channel P), to accomplish these objectives. The cameras were arranged in two separate chains, or channels, each self-contained with separate power supplies, timers, and transmitters so as to afford the greatest reliability and probability of obtaining high-quality video pictures. The spacecraft consisted of a hexagonal aluminum frame base 1.5 meters across on which was mounted the propulsion and power units, topped by a truncated conical tower which held the TV cameras. Two solar panel wings, each 73.9 centimeters wide by 153.7 centimeters long, extended from opposite edges of the base with a full span of 4.6 meters, and a pointable high-gain dish antenna was hinge-mounted at one of the corners of the base away from the solar panels. A cylindrical quasi-omnidirectional antenna was seated on top of the conical tower. The overall height of the spacecraft was 3.6 meters.

Power was supplied by solar cells contained in the two solar panels, giving a total array area of 2.3 square meters and producing 200 watts. Two 1200-watt-hr batteries rated at 26.5 Volts with a capacity for nine hours of operation provided power to each of the separate communication/TV camera chains. Two 1000-watt-hr batteries stored power for spacecraft operations. Communications were through the quasi-omnidirectional low-gain antenna and the parabolic high-gain antenna.

Archaeology

Ranger 7 impacted on the Moon on 31 July 1964, in an area between Mare Nubium and Oceanus Procellarum (subsequently named Mare Cognitum) at approximately 10.35° S, 339.42° E. The spacecraft had a mass of 365.7 kilograms. This area is in an important cluster of artifacts that includes the impact sites of *Rangers 7* and *9* and the Soviet *Luna 5*, and the landing sites of *Surveyors 2* and *3*, and *Apollo 12* and *Apollo 14*.

5) RANGER 8[7]

History

Launched on 17 February 1965, *Ranger 8* was another flying television camera in the Ranger series designed reach the Moon and then to transmit high-resolution photographs of the lunar surface in the final moments of the mission up to moment of impact. *Ranger 8* transmitted over 7,100 images of the Moon in the final twenty minutes of its flight, with the final image, taken just before impact, having a resolution of 1.5 meters.

Technical Notes

The spacecraft carried six television vidicon cameras, two wide-angle (channel F, cameras A and B) and four narrow-angle (channel P). The cameras were arranged in two separate chains, or channels, each self-contained with separate power supplies, timers, and transmitters so as to afford the greatest reliability and probability of obtaining high-quality video pictures.

The spacecraft consisted of a hexagonal aluminum frame base 1.5 meters across on which was mounted the propulsion and power units, topped by a truncated conical tower which held the TV cameras. Two solar panel wings, each 73.9 centimeters wide by 153.7 centimeters long, extended from opposite edges of the base with a full span of 4.6 meters, and a pointable high-gain dish antenna was hinge-mounted at one of the corners of the base away from the solar panels. A cylindrical quasi-omnidirectional antenna was seated on top of the conical tower. Power was supplied by solar cells contained in the two solar panels, giving a total array area of 2.3 square meters and producing 200 watts. Two 1200-watt-hr batteries rated at 26.5 Volts with a capacity for nine hours of operation provided power to each of the separate communication/TV camera chains. Two 1000-watt-hr batteries stored power for spacecraft operations. Communications were through the quasi-omnidirectional low-gain antenna and the parabolic high-gain antenna.

Archaeology

After a flight of 64.9 hours, *Ranger 8* impacted into the Moon in the Sea of Tranquility (Mare Tranquillitatis) on 20 February 1965. The mass of the spacecraft was 367 kilograms and the impact point was 2.67° N, 24.65° E. *Ranger 8* is embedded in the Moon not far from the landing sites of the later *Surveyor 5* and *Apollo 11* archaeological sites. The site was later photographed on 20 November 1966, by *Lunar Orbiter 2.*

6) *RANGER 9*[8]

History

The final probe in the unmanned Ranger series, *Ranger 9* was launched on 21 March 1965, and reached the Moon three days later. Like *Rangers 6–8*, it carried a series of television cameras designed to transmit high-resolution photographs of the lunar surface during the final minutes of flight just prior to final impact. Like *Rangers 7* and *8*, *Ranger 9* was a success. After the cameras were warmed up for one minute, the spacecraft transmitted over 5,800 photographs back to Earth during the last nineteen minutes of its flight, with the final image taken before impact having a resolution of 0.3 meters.

Technical Notes

The spacecraft carried six television vidicon cameras, two wide-angle (channel F, cameras A and B) and four narrow-angle (channel P), to accomplish these objectives. The cameras were arranged in two separate chains, or channels, each self-contained with separate power supplies, timers, and transmitters so as to afford the greatest reliability and probability of obtaining high-quality video pictures.

The spacecraft consisted of a hexagonal aluminum frame base 1.5 meters across on which was mounted the propulsion and power units, topped by a truncated conical tower which held the TV cameras. Two solar panel wings, each 73.9 centimeters wide by 153.7 centimeters long, extended from opposite edges of the base with a full span of 4.6 m, and a pointable high gain dish antenna was hinge mounted at one of the corners of the base away from the solar panels. A cylindrical quasi-omnidirectional antenna was seated on top of the conical tower.

Power was supplied by solar cells contained in the two solar panels, giving a total array area of 2.3 square meters and producing 200 watts. Two 1200-watt-hr batteries rated at 26.5 volts with a capacity for nine hours of operation provided power to each of the separate communication/TV camera chains. Two 1000-watt-hr batteries stored power for spacecraft operations. Communications were through the quasi-omnidirectional low-gain antenna and the parabolic high-gain antenna.

Archaeology

After a flight of 64.5 hours, *Ranger 9* impacted the Moon on 24 March 1965, at a point 12.83° S, 357.63° E. The spacecraft's mass was 367 kilograms. The impact point is in the ancient impact crater called Alphonsus, which is situated in the lunar highlands of the Mare Nubium, approximately equidistant from the impact site of the earlier *Ranger 7* and the landing site of the later *Apollo 16*. The impact site is thought to be a short distance to the northeast of a pyramid-shaped central peak in the crater called Alphonsus Alpha.

7) LUNA 5 [9]

History

Intended to continue Russian investigations of a potential soft landing on the Moon, *Luna 5* was launched on 9 May 1965 from the Baikonur Cosmodrome. The mission sought to soft-land a camera system on the Moon. The spacecraft carried both an imaging system and a radiation detector. Problems with a gyroscope and a planned firing of the main engine caused Soviet mission control to lose control of the spacecraft. It headed toward a rendezvous with the Moon but far away from its original destination.

Archaeology

Luna 5 impacted the lunar surface with a mass of 1474 kilograms. According to NASA, a contemporary Soviet new release placed the crash site in the Sea of Clouds (Mare Nubium), not far from the enormous Tycho crater on the near side of the Moon, at approximately 31° S, 8° W. Subsequent research showed the impact point to be much farther north and west at 8° N, 23° W. An observatory in Germany reported a dust cloud in the Mare Nubium area of some 80 × 220 km, indicating the massive force of the impact.

8) *Luna 7*[10]

History

Luna 7 was launched from Baikonur Cosmodrome on 4 October 1965, on a mission to soft-land on the surface of the Moon. The expedition successfully approached the Moon on 7 October, when a retro-rocket fired too early and Soviet mission control could not regain control of the spacecraft.

Archaeology

Luna 7 crashed into the Moon with a mass of 1,504 kilograms on 7 October 1965. The impact location was at 9°N, 40°W, west of the Kepler Crater and close to the intended landing spot. This is near the Ocean of Storms (Oceanus Procellarum), the western edge of the near side of the Moon.

9) *Luna 8*[11]

History

Luna 8 was launched from Baikonur Cosmodrome on 3 December 1965, on a mission to soft-land on the surface of the Moon. The expedition successfully approached the Moon three days later, when a retro-rocket fired too late and Soviet mission control could not regain control of the spacecraft. Just before the final descent toward the surface, a command was sent from Earth to inflate a series of airbags that would cushion the impact of the lander. It is thought that one of the bags was accidentally pierced, which caused the spacecraft to spin out of control.

Archaeology

Luna 8 impacted the lunar surface with a mass of 1,550 kilograms on 6 December 1965. The impact point is located in the Ocean of Storms (Oceanus Procellarum), at 9.8°N, 63.2°W, west of the Kepler Crater in the same region of the impact site of the earlier *Luna 7*.

10) *Luna 9*[12]

History

Luna 9 was launched on 31 January 1966, from the Baikonur Cosmodrome, on a mission to land an experimental research station and camera on the lunar surface. On 3 February 1966, the spacecraft became the first tool fashioned by *Homo sapiens* on Earth to make a planned, soft landing on the Moon. This probe weighed about 100 kilograms, and was designed with four flower-like petals that opened to stabilize the experimental station on the Moon. Antennas opened to permit transmission of data and, a few hours later, *Luna 9* became the first lunar probe to return photographs from the surface of the Moon back to Earth. The apparent firm surface revealed in the images allowed space agencies in both Russia and the U.S. to feel confident that manned vehicles sent to the Moon would not sink into a deep layer of dust, as some theorists had speculated.

When astronomers at the Jodrell Bank Observatory of the University of Manchester in England realized that the photographic data was being transmitted to Earth in the same manner as that used by newspapers to send and receive photographs, the British newspaper *Daily Express* hurried a receiver to the observatory so that the images could be intercepted and they were soon published worldwide.

Technical Notes

The spacecraft comprised two parts, which had a total mass of 1538 kilograms and stood 2.7 meters tall. The *Luna 9* automatic lunar station that achieved the soft landing was a spherical body with a diameter of fifty-eight centimeters and a mass of ninety-nine kilograms. The station consisted of a hermetically sealed container, pressurized to 1.2 atmospheres, which held the radio system, programming device, batteries, thermal control system and scientific apparatus. Four antennas that automatically opened after landing were mounted on the outside of the compartment. An airbag amortization system to cushion the landing was also mounted outside the station. The entire compartment was mounted above a flight stage which held the main KTDU-5A retrorocket, four outrigger vernier rockets, a toroidal aluminum alloy fuel tank, a ninety-centimeter diameter spherical oxidizer tank, fuel-pumping system, the nitrogen tank for airbag inflation, and guidance and landing sensor equipment. This equipment included gyroscopes, electro-optical apparatus, the soft-landing radar system, and small orientation engines. Compartments on either side of the main body with a total mass of 300 kilograms contained guidance radar and the three nitrogen jets and gas bottles of the attitude control system for the cruise stage, designed to be jettisoned once the descent was underway. The total propellant load (amine-based fuel and nitric acid oxidizer) was about 800 kilograms. The scientific equipment comprised a lightweight (1.5 kilograms) panoramic television camera and an SBM-10 radiation detector. A mirror on an eight-centimeter turret was mounted on the top of the lander above the camera to allow 360-degree coverage. The scientific container was designed to separate from the flight stage immediately before touchdown. The thermal control system maintained the interior temperature between 19 and 30 degrees Celsius. All operations were battery powered.

Archaeology

The *Luna 9* probe landed on the Moon on 3 February 1966 in the Ocean of Storms (Oceanus Procellarum). The impact point was at 7.13° N, 60.36°W, west of the Reiner and Marius craters and further west than the previous impact points of the *Luna 7* and *8* probes. *Luna 9* continued to send data to Earth for eight hours and five minutes over three days before its batteries ceased to function. Twenty-seven images were returned to Earth.

At the moment the batteries on the lunar station ceased, the probe itself entered its archaeological context. The probe survives in this context today as the first artifact sent from Earth to survive a landing on another celestial body.

11) *SURVEYOR 1*[13]

History

The Surveyor program sent seven robot spacecraft towards the Moon between 1966 and 1968 to study the feasibility of soft landings on the lunar surface; allow NASA to evaluate their engineering designs for the Apollo program in light of actual conditions on the Moon; and add to the growing scientific knowledge of the lunar surface. All seven probes reached the Moon, but control over *Surveyors 2* and *4* was lost during their respective flights and they crash-landed into the lunar surface. The other five probes all soft-landed and carried out data-gathering operations.

Surveyor 1 was launched on 30 May 1966 atop an Atlas Centaur rocket from Launch Complex 36-A of the Eastern Test Range at Cape Canaveral, Florida. It had a mass of 995.2 kilograms at launch. When the probe was 75.3 kilometers above the Moon, a retrorocket was fired that slowed the spacecraft from 2,612 meters per second to 110 meters per second. When the craft was 5.5 kilometers above the Moon the engines were turned off and the *Surveyor 1* dropped freely toward the surface. The spacecraft landed on the Moon on 2 June 1966, in the Ocean of Storms (Oceanus Procellarum). At the time of landing, it was moving at approximately three meters per second and had a mass of 294.3 kilograms. The landing marked the first time an American spacecraft successfully reached another celestial body.

The primary mission life of the spacecraft lasted for about eleven days, during which time it returned 11,240 photographs back to Earth. After that, NASA continued to "talk" to the spacecraft until 7 January 1967.

Technical Notes

The basic *Surveyor* spacecraft structure consisted of a tripod of thin-walled aluminum tubing and interconnecting braces providing mounting surfaces and attachments for the power, communications, propulsion, flight control, and payload systems. A central mast extended about one meter above the apex of the tripod. Three hinged landing legs were attached to the lower corners of the structure. The legs held shock absorbers; crushable, honeycomb aluminum blocks; and the deployment locking mechanism and they terminated in footpads with crushable bottoms. The three footpads extended out 4.3 meters from the center of *Surveyor*. The spacecraft was about three meters tall. The legs folded to fit into a nose shroud for launch.

A 0.855 square meter array of 792 solar cells was mounted on a positioner on top of the mast and generated up to eighty-five watts of power which was stored in rechargeable silver-zinc batteries. Communications were achieved via a movable, large planar-array, high-gain antenna mounted near the top of the central mast to transmit television images; two omnidirectional conical antennas mounted on the ends of folding booms for uplink and downlink, two receivers and two transmitters. Thermal control was achieved by a combination of white paint, high IR-emittance thermal finish, and polished aluminum underside. Two thermally controlled compartments — equipped with superinsulating blankets, conductive heat paths, thermal switches and small electric heaters — were mounted on the spacecraft structure. One compartment, held between 5 and 50 degrees Celsius, housed communications and power supply electronics. The other, held between -20 and 50 degrees Celsius, housed the command and signal processing components. The TV survey camera was mounted near the top of the tripod, and strain gauges, temperature sensors, and other engineering instruments are incorporated throughout the spacecraft. One photometric target was mounted near the end of a landing leg and one on a short boom extending from the bottom of the structure. Other payload packages, which differed from mission to mission, were mounted on various parts of the structure depending on their function.

A Sun sensor, Canopus tracker and rate gyros on three axes provided attitude knowledge. Propulsion and attitude control were provided by cold-gas (nitrogen) attitude-control jets during cruise phases; three rocket engines during powered phases, including the landing; and the solid-propellant retrorocket engine during terminal descent. The retrorocket was a spherical steel case mounted in the bottom center of the spacecraft. The fuel was stored in spherical tanks mounted to the tripod structure. For the landing sequence, an altitude-marking radar initiated the firing of the main retrorocket for primary braking. After firing was complete, the retrorocket and radar were jettisoned and the doppler and altimeter radars were activated. These provided information to the autopilot which controlled the vernier propulsion system to touchdown.

No instrumentation was carried specifically for scientific experiments, but considerable scientific information was obtained. *Surveyor 1* carried two television cameras — one mounted on the bottom of the frame for approach photography, which was not used, and the survey television camera. Over 100 engineering sensors were on board.

Archaeology

Surveyor 1 lies at 2.45° S, 43.22 W. On the evening of 13 July 1966, with its battery power running low, the mission of *Surveyor 1* was terminated. The final communications with the probe were made on 7 January 1967. On that day, the spacecraft entered its archaeological context and remains there today. Like the rest of the series, the probe was not constructed to allow it to return to Earth so it remains on the Moon, where its 3.3-meter height was observed casting a long shadow by the *Lunar Reconnaissance Orbiter* on 1 October 2009.

12) *Lunar Orbiter 1*[14]

History

The Lunar Orbiter program sent five spacecraft to the Moon to orbit the celestial body and gather photographic data to allow for the mapping of the lunar surface. This was required in order to study and select appropriate landing sites for the later Surveyor and Apollo missions.

Lunar Orbiter 1 was launched on 10 August 1966 atop an Atlas-Agena D rocket and reached the Moon ninety-two hours later, where it began its orbital mission. Over the course of eleven days, 18–29 August 1966, the probe returned forty-two high-resolution and 187 medium-resolution images of the lunar surface, as well as the first ever images of Earth seen from the Moon. The imagery of the lunar surface covered some five million square kilometers.

Technical Notes

The main bus of the Lunar Orbiter had the general shape of a truncated cone, 1.65 meters tall and 1.5 meters in diameter at the base. The spacecraft was comprised of three decks supported by trusses and an arch. The equipment deck at the base of the craft held the battery, transponder, flight programmer, inertial reference unit (IRU), Canopus star tracker, command decoder, multiplex encoder, traveling wave tube amplifier (TWTA), and the photographic system. Four solar panels were mounted to extend out from this deck with a total span across of 3.72 meters.

Also extending out from the base of the spacecraft were a high-gain antenna on a 1.32 meter boom and a low-gain antenna on a 2.08 meter boom. Above the equipment deck, the middle deck held the velocity control engine, propellant, oxidizer and pressurization tanks, Sun sensors, and micrometeoroid detectors. The third deck consisted of a heat shield to protect the spacecraft from the firing of the velocity control engine. The nozzle of the engine protruded through the center of the shield. Mounted on the perimeter of the top deck were four attitude control thrusters.

Power of 375 watts was provided by the four solar arrays containing solar cells which directly ran the spacecraft and also charged the twelve-amp-hr nickel-cadmium battery. Propulsion for major maneuvers was provided by the gimbaled velocity control engine, a hypergolic 100-pound-thrust Marquardt rocket motor. Three-axis stabilization and attitude control were provided by four one-lb nitrogen gas jets. Navigational knowledge was provided by five Sun sensors, Canopus star sensor, and the IRU equipped with internal gyros. Communications were via a ten-watt transmitter and the directional one-meter-diameter high-gain antenna for transmission of photographs and a 0.5-watt transmitter and omnidirectional low-gain antenna for other communications. Thermal control was maintained by a multilayer aluminized mylar and dacron thermal blanket which enshrouded the main bus, special paint, insulation, and small heaters.

Archaeology

Following the completion of its photographic mission and after orbiting the Moon 577 times, *Lunar Orbiter 1* began to lose fuel it needed to maintain its orbit. The probe was directed to impact the lunar surface at 7° N, 161° E, on the far side of the Moon, on 29 October 1966. This was done essentially to remove the spacecraft from lunar orbit so as not to pose any potential hazards to the upcoming manned Apollo missions. The same directive applied to the subsequent four Lunar Orbiter spacecraft, all of which were deliberately crashed in the Moon. With a total cost of the entire project at $163 million, they were almost certainly the world's most expensive disposable cameras.

13) *Surveyor 2*[15]

History

Like the other unmanned probes in the same series, *Surveyor 2* was designed to reach and land on the Moon and then return photographic data for determining characteristics of the lunar terrain for manned Apollo lunar landing missions. This included a planned "bounce" on the lunar surface where the spacecraft would photograph the terrain under itself, as well as studying the load-bearing nature of the surface. The spacecraft was launched atop an Atlas-Centaur rocket on 20 September 1966, from Cape Canaveral. The failure of a mid-course correction during the flight to the Moon caused NASA to lose control of the spacecraft on 22 September 1966.

Archaeology

The intended target area on the Moon was within Sinus Medii (the "Bay of the Center"), a small mare located at the intersection of the Moon's prime meridian and its equator, a place where Earth always appears overhead. Because of the mid-course failure, the spacecraft impacted the Moon with a mass of 292.0 kilograms on 23 September 1966. The point of impact was near the large Copernicus crater in the eastern Oceanus Procellarum (Ocean of Storms), which is located at 9.7° N, 20.0° W.

14) *Lunar Orbiter 2*[16]

History

Launched on 6 November 1966, *Lunar Orbiter 2* was designed primarily to photograph smooth areas of the lunar surface for selection and verification of safe landing sites for the Surveyor and Apollo missions. Reaching the Moon four days later, the spacecraft went into orbit 196 kilometers above the lunar surface. Five days later, the orbit was lowered to less than fifty km above the surface. For one week, 18–25 November 1966, the spacecraft acquired a total of 609 high-resolution and 208 medium-resolution photographic frames, which included the famous "Picture of the Century," an oblique photograph of the 100-kilometer diameter Copernicus crater.

The photographic downloads took place on 7 December 1966. After this, NASA changed the orbit of the probe to study lunar gravity, and after this tracked the spacecraft until the following October.

Technical Notes

The main bus of the Lunar Orbiter had the general shape of a truncated cone, 1.65 meters tall and 1.5 meters in diameter at the base. The spacecraft was comprised of three decks supported by trusses and an arch. The equipment deck at the base of the craft held the battery, transponder, flight programmer, inertial reference unit (IRU), Canopus star tracker, command decoder, multiplex encoder, traveling wave tube amplifier (TWTA), and the photographic system. Four solar panels were mounted to extend out from this deck with a total span across of 3.72 meters.

Also extending out from the base of the spacecraft were a high-gain antenna on a 1.32-meter boom and a low-gain antenna on a 2.08-meter boom. Above the equipment deck, the middle deck held the velocity control engine, propellant, oxidizer and pressurization tanks, Sun sensors, and micrometeoroid detectors. The third deck consisted of a heat shield to protect the spacecraft from the firing of the velocity control engine. The nozzle of the engine protruded through the center of the shield. Mounted on the perimeter of the top deck were four attitude-control thrusters.

Power of 375 watts was provided by the four solar arrays containing 10,856 solar cells which directly ran the spacecraft and also charged the twelve-amp-hr nickel-cadmium battery. The batteries were used during brief periods of occultation when no solar power was available. Propulsion for major maneuvers was provided by the gimbaled velocity control engine, a hypergolic 100-pound-thrust Marquardt rocket motor. Three-axis stabilization and attitude control were provided by four one-pound nitrogen gas jets. Navigational knowledge was provided by five Sun sensors, Canopus star sensor, and the IRU equipped with internal gyros. Communications were via a ten-watt transmitter and the directional one-meter-diameter high-gain antenna for transmission of photographs and a 0.5-watt transmitter and omnidirectional low-gain antenna for other communications. Thermal control was maintained by a multilayer aluminized mylar and dacron thermal blanket which enshrouded the main bus, special paint, insulation, and small heaters.

Archaeology

Lunar Orbiter 2 impacted the lunar surface on command at 3° N, 119.1° E on 11 October 1967, with a mass of 385.6 kilograms. During its life as a systemic artifact, on 20 November 1966, the orbiter photographed the impact point of the earlier *Ranger 8* spacecraft, which had impacted into the Moon in the Sea of Tranquility (Mare Tranquilitatis) on 20 February 1965.[17] This is the first instance of a spacecraft imaging an archaeological site on the Moon.

15) LUNA 13[18]

History

Luna 13 was launched towards the Moon from a platform orbiting Earth, and made a soft landing on the Moon on 24 December 1966. The landing spot was in the Oceanus Procellarum (Ocean of Storms) at a point 18.81° N, 297.95° W. The 1,700-kilogram lander was designed within a spherical container, and once on the lunar surface this container opened like the petals of a flower, antennas were extended, and data gathering begun. On Christmas Day and the day following, the lander transmitted panoramic images of the surrounding lunar environment.

Technical Notes

The spacecraft was equipped with a mechanical soil-measuring penetrometer, a dynamograph, and a radiation densitometer for obtaining data on the mechanical and physical properties and the cosmic-ray reflectivity of the lunar surface.

Archaeology

Contact with the lander was lost a few days after it had transmitted a series of panoramic photographs to Earth. Once the batteries of the probe had failed, the spacecraft entered its archaeological context.

16) LUNAR ORBITER 3[19]

History

Launched atop an Atlas-Agena D rocket from Cape Canaveral on 5 February 1967, Lunar Orbiter 3 continued the work of its series predecessors in gathering photographic data for upcoming unmanned Surveyor and manned Apollo missions to the Moon. It reached the Moon three days later and assumed about 210 kilometers above the lunar surface. This was subsequently lowered to fifty-five kilometers above the Moon. For eight days, 15–23 February 1967, the orbiter gathered data which was then transmitted to Earth on 7 March 1967. A problem with the film advance mechanism caused about a quarter of the data to be left unread. A total of 149 medium-resolution and 477 high-resolution frames were returned to Earth, with resolution down to one meter.

Technical Notes

The probe was designed to gather photographic data and it was also equipped to collect selenodetic, radiation intensity, and micrometeoroid impact data. The main bus of the lunar orbiter had the general shape of a truncated cone, 1.65 meters tall and 1.5 meters in diameter at the base. The spacecraft was comprised of three decks supported by trusses and an arch. The equipment deck at the base of the craft held the battery, transponder, flight programmer, inertial reference unit (IRU), Canopus star tracker, command decoder, multiplex encoder, traveling wave tube amplifier (TWTA), and the photographic system. Four solar panels were mounted to extend out from this deck with a total span across of 3.72 meters. Also extending out from the base of the spacecraft were a high-gain antenna on a 1.32-meter boom and a low-gain antenna on a 2.08-meter boom. Above the equipment deck, the middle deck held the velocity control engine, propellant, oxidizer and pressurization tanks, Sun sensors, and micrometeoroid detectors. The third deck consisted of a heat shield to protect the spacecraft from the firing of the velocity-control engine. The nozzle of the engine protruded through the center of the shield. Mounted on the perimeter of the top deck were four attitude-control thrusters.

Power of 375 watts was provided by the four solar arrays containing 10,856 solar cells which would directly run the spacecraft and also charge the twelve-amp-hr nickel-cadmium battery. The batteries were used during brief periods of occultation when no solar power was available. Propulsion for major maneuvers was provided by the gimbaled velocity control engine, a hypergolic 100-pound-thrust Marquardt rocket motor. Three-axis stabilization and attitude control were provided by four one-pound nitrogen gas jets. Navigational knowledge was provided by five Sun sensors, Canopus star sensor, and the IRU equipped with internal gyros. Communications were via a ten-watt transmitter and the directional one-meter-diameter high-gain antenna for transmission of photographs and a 0.5-watts transmitter and omnidirectional low-gain antenna for other communications. Thermal control was maintained by a multilayer aluminized mylar and dacron thermal blanket which enshrouded the main bus, special paint, insulation, and small heaters.

Archaeology

NASA tracked *Lunar Orbiter 3* for several months after the conclusion of its mission, until it impacted the lunar surface on command at 14.3° N, 97.7 ° W, on 9 October 1967, with a mass of 385.6 kilograms. During its mission, like the earlier *Lunar Orbiter 2*, this orbiting spacecraft located and photographed a previous spacecraft on the surface. This was the landing site of *Surveyor 1*, which had soft-landed on the Moon the previous June, and which had been in its archaeological context since 7 January 1967. This was the first time that imagery had been obtained of an archaeological object on the Moon that had not crash-landed there.

17) SURVEYOR 3 [20]

History

Launched atop at Atlas-Centaur rocket from Complex 36B at Cape Canaveral's Eastern Test Range on 17 April 1967, *Surveyor 2* was the second spacecraft of the Surveyor series to achieve a lunar soft landing. The second of seven robotic lunar soft-landing flights, the Surveyors were to support the upcoming, manned Apollo landings by continuing NASA's development of soft landings on the Moon; studying the current Apollo designs with regards to the data gathered on the prevailing conditions of the lunar surface; and continuing NASA's science program on the Moon.

Surveyor 3 arrived at the Moon on 20 April 1967 and at an altitude of 76 kilometers above the surface the descent speed of the spacecraft was slowed from 2,626 meters per second to 137 meters per second. The descent engines failed to cut off after the probe landed on the Moon, and it subsequently lifted off twice more (moving about twenty meters on the first bounce and eleven on the second) before settling and sliding into the inner slope of a 200-meter crater in the Oceanus Procellarum (Ocean of Storms) about 370 kilometers south of Copernicus crater.

Within an hour of landing, the spacecraft was returning images of the lunar surface. Within days, the extending sampler arm was gathering samples of the lunar surface for testing. The sampler was operated for more than eighteen hours, digging trenches in the soil down to eighteen centimeter, while the onboard television camera returned over 6,300 images.

Technical Notes

Surveyor 3 consisted of a tripod of thin-walled aluminum tubing and interconnecting braces providing mounting surfaces and attachments for the power, communications, propulsion, flight control, and payload systems. A central mast extended about one meter above the apex of the tripod. Three hinged landing legs were attached to the lower corners of the structure. The legs held shock absorbers; crushable, honeycomb aluminum blocks; and the deployment locking mechanism, and they terminated in footpads with crushable bottoms. The three footpads extended out 4.3 meters from the center of *Surveyor*. The spacecraft was about three meters tall. The legs folded to fit into a nose shroud for launch.

A 0.855-square-meter array of 792 solar cells was mounted on a positioner on top of the mast and generated up to 85 watts of power which was stored in rechargeable silver-zinc batteries. Communications were achieved via a movable, large-planar-array high-gain antenna mounted near the top of the central mast to transmit television images, two omnidirectional conical antennas mounted on the ends of folding booms for uplink and downlink, two receivers and two transmitters. Thermal control was achieved by a combination of white paint, high IR-emittance thermal finish, polished aluminum underside. Two thermally controlled compartments, equipped with superinsulating blankets, conductive heat paths, thermal switches and small electric heaters, were mounted on the spacecraft structure. One compartment, held at 5–50 degrees Celsius, housed communications and power supply electronics. The other, held between -20 and 50 degrees Celsius, housed the command and signal-processing components.

The TV survey camera was mounted near the top of the tripod and strain gauges, temperature sensors, and other engineering instruments are incorporated throughout the spacecraft. One photometric target was mounted near the end of a landing leg and one on a short boom extending from the bottom of the structure. Other payload packages, which differed from mission to mission, were mounted on various parts of the structure depending on their function.

A Sun sensor, Canopus tracker and rate gyros on three axes provided attitude knowledge. Propulsion and attitude control were provided by cold-gas (nitrogen) attitude control jets during cruise phases, three vernier rocket engines during powered phases, including the landing, and the solid-propellant retrorocket engine during terminal descent. The retrorocket was a spherical steel case mounted in the bottom center of the spacecraft. The fuel was stored in spherical tanks mounted to the tripod structure. For the landing sequence, an altitude-marking radar initiated the firing of the main retrorocket for primary braking. After firing was complete, the retrorocket and radar were jettisoned and the doppler and altimeter radars were activated. These provided information to the autopilot which controlled the vernier propulsion system to touchdown.

Surveyor 3 was similar in design to *Surveyors 1* and *2* but had several changes in the payload. It carried a survey television camera, soil mechanics experiments, and devices to measure temperature and radar reflectivity as on the earlier missions, but the TV camera had an extended glare hood. A surface sampler, consisting of a scoop twelve centimeters long by five centimeters wide that was mounted on a 1.5-meter pantograph arm, replaced the approach television camera. Two flat auxiliary mirrors were attached to the frame to provide the camera with a view of the ground beneath the engines and one of the footpads. *Surveyor 3* had a mass of 1026 kilograms at launch and 296 kilograms at landing.

Archaeology

Surveyor 3 landed on the Moon on 20 April 1967, with a mass of 296.0 kilograms, at a position of 14.3° N, 97.7° W. The spacecraft ceased transmitting data to Earth on 4 May 1967, and at that moment entered its archaeological context. The probe is particularly important in the history of space archaeology since it was visited two and a half years later by astronauts of the *Apollo 12* mission. On 19 November 1969, astronauts Pete Conrad and Alan Bean landed near the crater where the probe lay resting at an angle, and walked to it during their second moonwalk.

During their visit to the *Surveyor 3* site, they took a series of photographs of the artifact and removed ten kilograms of components of it — including the television camera — for return to Earth on board their Lunar Module ascent stage. This event can be rightly considered the first field archaeology beyond the limits of Earth. Conrad's and Bean's fieldwork led to subsequent studies of the component parts on Earth that gave insight in the wear of materials in the environment of the Moon, as well as the startling discovery of a strain of bacteria, *Streptococcus mitis*, contaminating part of the television camera. If true, the discovery would indicate the hardiness of bacteria even in the vacuum and extreme temperatures prevailing on the lunar surface.

18) LUNAR ORBITER 4 [21]

History

Lunar Orbiter 4 was launched atop an Atlas-Agena D rocket from Cape Canaveral, Florida, on 4 May 1967. Because the earlier Lunar Orbiter probes had fulfilled the immediate objective of providing lunar surface data for upcoming Apollo missions, *Lunar Orbiter 4* had a more generalized science mission. This involved a more general search for sites of scientific opportunity on the Moon that might become possible on future orbital and lander missions.

After arrival at the Moon, the spacecraft was placed in a polar orbit for its data gathering operations. When the orbiter began to experience problems with the thermal door that protected the camera, a command was sent to the spacecraft to keep the door open. Subsequent fogging of the camera lens was fixed by altering the spacecraft's attitude. Continuing problems caused the shutdown of the photography mission on 26 May 1967. Nevertheless, a total of 419 high-resolution and 127 medium-resolution frames were acquired covering 99 percent of the Moon's near side at resolutions from 58 meters to 134 meters. The orbit of the spacecraft was then lowered to gather orbiter data for the upcoming mission of *Lunar Orbiter 5*.

Technical Notes

The main bus of the Lunar Orbiter had the general shape of a truncated cone, 1.65 meters tall and 1.5 meters in diameter at the base. The spacecraft was comprised of three decks supported by trusses and an arch. The equipment deck at the base of the craft held the battery, transponder, flight programmer, inertial reference unit (IRU), Canopus star tracker, command decoder, multiplex encoder, traveling wave tube amplifier (TWTA), and the photographic system. Four solar panels were mounted to extend out from this deck with a total span across of 3.72 meters. Also extending out from the base of the spacecraft were a high-gain antenna on a 1.32-meter boom and a low-gain antenna on a 2.08-meter boom. Above the equipment deck, the middle deck held the velocity control engine, propellant, oxidizer and pressurization tanks, Sun sensors, and micrometeoroid detectors. The third deck consisted of a heat shield to protect the spacecraft from the firing of the velocity control engine. The nozzle of the engine protruded through the center of the shield. Mounted on the perimeter of the top deck were four attitude control thrusters.

Power of 375 watts was provided by the four solar arrays containing 10,856 solar cells which directly ran the spacecraft and also charged the twelve-amp-hr nickel-cadmium battery. The batteries were used during brief periods of occultation when no solar power was available. Propulsion for major maneuvers was provided by the gimbaled velocity-control engine, a hypergolic 100-pound-thrust Marquardt rocket motor. Three-axis stabilization and attitude control were provided by four one-pound nitrogen gas jets. Navigational knowledge was provided by five Sun sensors, Canopus star sensor, and the

IRU equipped with internal gyros. Communications were via a ten-watt transmitter and the directional one-meter-diameter high-gain antenna for transmission of photographs and a 0.5-watt transmitter and omnidirectional low-gain antenna for other communications. Thermal control was maintained by a multilayer aluminized mylar and dacron thermal blanket which enshrouded the main bus, special paint, insulation, and small heaters.

Archaeology

The *Lunar Orbiter 4* was tracked for several months until its orbit began to decay and it impacted the lunar surface on or about 31 October 1967, with a mass of 385.6 kilograms. The impact site is thought to be between 22°W and 30° W.

19) SURVEYOR 4[22]

History

Surveyor 4 was launched atop an Atlan-Centaur rocket from Cape Canaveral, Florida, on 14 July 1967. Like its earlier missions, this surveyor was designed to achieve a soft landing on the Moon and to return photography of the lunar surface for determining characteristics of the lunar terrain for Apollo lunar landing missions. The spacecraft reached the Moon three days later, but radio signals from the spacecraft were lost as it descended to the surface, with approximately two and a half minutes remaining before touchdown. Contact with the spacecraft was never reestablished, and the mission was deemed a failure.

Technical Notes

Equipment on board included a television camera and auxiliary mirrors, a soil-mechanics surface sampler, strain gauges on the spacecraft landing legs, and numerous engineering sensors.

Archaeology

Surveyor 4 was aiming for a point in the Sinus Medii (Central Bay) region of the Moon, at a point 0.4° N, 1.33° W. NASA concluded that the lander might have exploded when contact was lost, so if or where it might have impacted the Moon is not known.

20) LUNAR ORBITER 5[23]

History

Lunar Orbiter 5 was launched atop an Atlas-Agena D rocket from Cape Canaveral, Florida, on 1 August 1967. It was designed to take additional Apollo and Surveyor landing site photography and to take broad survey images of the unphotographed parts of the Moon's far side. The spacecraft achieved a near polar orbit of the Moon on 5 August 1967, at an altitude of 195 kilometers above the surface. This was lowered to 100 kilometers on

7 August and then again to ninety-nine kilometers on 9 August. Before the photographic portion of the mission ended on 18 August 1967, the orbiter had collected a total of 633 high-resolution and 211 medium-resolution frames at resolution down to two meters. The five Lunar Orbiter missions succeeded in providing researchers back on Earth with photographic coverage of 99 percent of the Moon's surface.

Technical Notes

In addition to its primary mission, *Lunar Orbiter 5* was also equipped to collect selenodetic, radiation intensity, and micrometeoroid impact data and was used to evaluate the Manned Space Flight Network tracking stations and Apollo Orbit Determination Program.

The main bus of the lunar orbiter had the general shape of a truncated cone, 1.65 meters tall and 1.5 meters in diameter at the base. The spacecraft was comprised of three decks supported by trusses and an arch. The equipment deck at the base of the craft held the battery, transponder, flight programmer, inertial reference unit (IRU), Canopus star tracker, command decoder, multiplex encoder, traveling wave tube amplifier (TWTA), and the photographic system. Four solar panels were mounted to extend out from this deck with a total span across of 3.72 meters. Also extending out from the base of the spacecraft were a high-gain antenna on a 1.32-meter boom and a low-gain antenna on a 2.08-meter boom. Above the equipment deck, the middle deck held the velocity-control engine, propellant, oxidizer and pressurization tanks, Sun sensors, and micrometeoroid detectors. The third deck consisted of a heat shield to protect the spacecraft from the firing of the velocity control engine. The nozzle of the engine protruded through the center of the shield. Mounted on the perimeter of the top deck were four attitude-control thrusters.

Power of 375 watts was provided by the four solar arrays containing 10,856 solar cells which would directly run the spacecraft and also charge the twelve-amp-hr nickel-cadmium battery. The batteries were used during brief periods of occultation when no solar power was available. Propulsion for major maneuvers was provided by the gimbaled velocity-control engine, a hypergolic 100-pound-thrust Marquardt rocket motor. Three-axis stabilization and attitude control were provided by four one-pound nitrogen gas jets. Navigational knowledge was provided by five Sun sensors, Canopus star sensor, and the IRU equipped with internal gyros. Communications were via a ten-watt transmitter and the directional one-meter-diameter high-gain antenna for transmission of photographs and a 0.5-watt transmitter and omnidirectional low-gain antenna for other communications. Thermal control was maintained by a multilayer aluminized mylar and dacron thermal blanket which enshrouded the main bus, special paint, insulation, and small heaters.

Archaeology

NASA continued to track *Lunar Orbiter 5* until it impacted the lunar surface on command on 31 January 1968, with a mass of 385.6 kilograms. The impact site is located at 2.79° S, 83° W.

21) SURVEYOR 5[24]

History

Surveyor 5 was launched atop an Atlas-Centaur rocket from the Eastern Test Range complex 36B at Cape Canaveral, Florida, on 8 September 1967. It was the third spacecraft in the Surveyor series to achieve a successful lunar soft landing. The specific objectives for this mission were to perform a soft landing on the Moon in the Mare Tranquillitatis (Sea of Tranquility) and to obtain post-landing television pictures of the lunar surface. A problem with a helium valve during the flight caused NASA to alter the spacecraft's descent, and it landed twenty-nine kilometer from its original destination. The touchdown, on the inside edge of a small crater at an angle of about twenty degrees, caused the probe to slide slightly and create a small trench.

During its first day of operation, *Surveyor 5* returned over 18,000 images to Earth. An experiment to fire the probes descent rockets for a minute to study the effects of the engine firing on the surface was conducted on 13 September. Transmitting data over four lunar days, from landing until 17 December 1967, and shutting down during the lunar nights, the probe returned over 19,000 images to Earth.

Technical Notes

In addition to the primary research mission, secondary objectives included conducting a vernier engine erosion experiment, determining the relative abundances of the chemical elements in the lunar soil by operation of the alpha-scattering instrument, obtaining touchdown dynamics data, and obtaining thermal and radar reflectivity data.

The basic Surveyor spacecraft structure consisted of a tripod of thin-walled aluminum tubing and interconnecting braces providing mounting surfaces and attachments for the power, communications, propulsion, flight control, and payload systems. A central mast extended about one meter above the apex of the tripod. Three hinged landing legs were attached to the lower corners of the structure. The legs held shock absorbers; crushable, honeycomb aluminum blocks; and the deployment locking mechanism, and they terminated in footpads with crushable bottoms. The three footpads extended out 4.3 meters from the center of the Surveyor. The spacecraft was about 3 meters tall. The legs folded to fit into a nose shroud for launch.

A 0.855-square-meter array of 792 solar cells was mounted on a positioner on top of the mast and generated up to 85 watts of power which was stored in rechargeable silver-zinc batteries. Communications were achieved via a movable large-planar-array high-gain antenna mounted near the top of the central mast to transmit television images, two omnidirectional conical antennas mounted on the ends of folding booms for uplink and downlink, two receivers and two transmitters. Thermal control was achieved by a combination of white paint, high IR-emittance thermal finish, and polished aluminum underside. Two thermally controlled compartments — equipped with superinsulating blankets, conductive heat paths, thermal switches and small electric heaters — were mounted on the spacecraft structure. One compartment, held at 5–50 degrees Celsius, housed communications and power supply electronics. The other, held between -20 and 50 degrees Celsius, housed the command and signal processing components. The TV survey camera was mounted near the top of the tripod and strain gauges, temperature sensors, and other engineering instruments are incorporated throughout the spacecraft. One photometric target was mounted near the end of a landing leg and one on a short boom extending from the bottom of the structure. Other payload packages, which differed from mission to mission, were mounted on various parts of the structure depending on their function.

A Sun sensor, Canopus tracker and rate gyros on three axes provided attitude knowledge. Propulsion and attitude control were provided by cold-gas (nitrogen) attitude control jets during cruise phases, three vernier rocket engines during powered phases, including the landing, and the solid-propellant retrorocket engine during terminal descent. The retrorocket was a spherical steel case mounted in the bottom center of the spacecraft. The fuel was stored in spherical tanks mounted to the tripod structure. For the landing sequence, an altitude-marking radar initiated the firing of the main retrorocket for primary braking. After firing was complete, the retrorocket and radar were jettisoned and the doppler and altimeter radars were activated. These provided information to the autopilot which controlled the vernier propulsion system to touchdown.

The instrumentation for *Surveyor 5* was similar to that of the previous Surveyors and included the survey television camera and numerous engineering sensors. An alpha-scattering instrument was installed in place of the surface sampler, and a small bar magnet attached to one footpad was included to detect the presence of magnetic material in the lunar soil. Convex auxiliary mirrors were attached to the frame to allow viewing of the surface below the spacecraft. *Surveyor 5* had a mass of 1006 kilograms at launch and 303 kilograms at landing.

Archaeology

The *Surveyor 5* probe touched down on the lunar surface with a mass of 303.0 kilograms. The probe landed on 11 September 1967 at 1.41° N, 23.18° E, in the southwestern sector of the Mare Tranquilitatis. Upon completion of its systemic mission, it entered its archaeological context on 17 December 1967, when it made its final data transmissions to Earth. Of the unmanned probes sent to the Moon, it is the closest to the *Apollo 11* site of the first manned mission to the Moon.

22) SURVEYOR 6 [25]

History

Surveyor 6 was launched atop an Atlas-Centaur rocket from the Eastern Test Range complex 36B Cape Canaveral, Florida, on 7 November 1967, and became the fourth of the Surveyor series to successfully soft-land on the Moon three days later. In addition to the overall goals of the whole Surveyor series in pioneering soft landings and the technologies required to undertake them for the upcoming Apollo missions, the specific primary objectives for this mission were to perform a soft landing on the Moon in the Sinus Medii (Bay of the Center) region and obtain post-landing television pictures of the lunar surface. The secondary objectives were to determine the relative abundance of the chemical elements in the lunar soil by operation of the alpha-scattering instrument, obtain touchdown dynamics data, obtain thermal and radar reflectivity data, and conduct a vernier-engine erosion experiment. On 17 November, the vernier engines were fired for 2.5 seconds, lifting the spacecraft off the lunar surface and setting it down again about 2.4 meters to the west of its original touchdown spot, again in a controlled, soft landing. This brief experiment was the first powered takeoff from the lunar surface. It also allowed comparative and stereoscopic images to be taken of the lunar surface from the resulting different angles.

Technical Notes

The basic Surveyor spacecraft structure consisted of a tripod of thin-walled aluminum tubing and interconnecting braces providing mounting surfaces and attachments for the power, communications, propulsion, flight control, and payload systems. A central mast extended about one meter above the apex of the tripod. Three hinged landing legs were attached to the lower corners of the structure. The legs held shock absorbers: crushable, honeycomb aluminum blocks; and the deployment locking mechanism, and they terminated in footpads with crushable bottoms. The three footpads extended out 4.3 meters from the center of the Surveyor. The spacecraft was about three meters tall. The legs folded to fit into a nose shroud for launch.

A 0.855-square-meter array of 792 solar cells was mounted on a positioner on top of the mast and generated up to 85 watts of power which was stored in rechargeable silver-zinc batteries. Communications were achieved via a movable large-planar-array high-gain antenna mounted near the top of the central mast to transmit television images, two omnidirectional conical antennas mounted on the ends of folding booms for uplink and downlink, two receivers and two transmitters. Thermal control was achieved by a combination of white paint, high IR-emittance thermal finish, polished aluminum underside. Two thermally controlled compartments — equipped with superinsulating blankets, conductive heat paths, thermal switches and small electric heaters — were mounted on the spacecraft structure. One compartment, held at 5 — 50 degrees Celsius, housed communications and power supply electronics. The other, held between -20 and 50 degrees Celsius, housed the command and signal processing components. The TV survey camera was mounted near the top of the tripod and strain gauges, temperature sensors, and other engineering instruments are incorporated throughout the spacecraft. One photometric target was mounted near the end of a landing leg and one on a short boom extending from the bottom of the structure. Other payload packages, which differed from mission to mission, were mounted on various parts of the structure depending on their function.

A Sun sensor, Canopus tracker and rate gyros on three axes provided attitude knowledge. Propulsion and attitude control were provided by cold-gas (nitrogen) attitude control jets during cruise phases, three vernier rocket engines during powered phases, including the landing, and the solid-propellant retrorocket engine during terminal descent. The retrorocket was a spherical steel case mounted in the bottom center of the spacecraft. The fuel was stored in spherical tanks mounted to the tripod structure. For the landing sequence, an altitude-marking radar initiated the firing of the main retrorocket for primary braking. After firing was complete, the retrorocket and radar were jettisoned and the doppler and altimeter radars were activated. These provided information to the autopilot which controlled the vernier propulsion system to touchdown.

With a payload virtually identical to that of *Surveyor 5*, this spacecraft carried a television survey camera, a small bar magnet attached to one footpad to detect magnetic material, an alpha-scattering instrument to study surface composition, and convex auxiliary mirrors mounted on the frame to view the surface under the spacecraft, as well as the necessary engineering equipment. The main differences were that *Surveyor 6* had polarizing filters on the TV camera, a different type of glare hood, and had three auxiliary mirrors instead of two.

Archaeology

Surveyor 6 had a mass of 1006 kilograms at launch and 299.6 kilograms on landing. Its touchdown spot in a flat, heavily cratered mare region of the Sinus Medii, was at 0.49° N, 358.60° E, in the center of the Moon's visible hemisphere. The lift-off test of the *Surveyor 6* creates special problems for cultural resource managers, as the entire area of that test, including the original touchdown spot and the lift-off blast zone and the new touchdown spot 2.5 meters west, will have to be demarcated and explained for future visitors.

23) SURVEYOR 7[26]

History

Surveyor 7 was the fifth and final spacecraft of the Surveyor series to achieve a lunar soft landing. It was launched atop an Atlas-Centaur rocket from complex 36A of the Eastern Test Range at Cape Canaveral, Florida, on 7 January 1968. As with the other probed in the series, the primary objectives were to support the coming crewed Apollo landings by developing and validating the technology for landing softly on the Moon; providing data on the compatibility of the Apollo design with conditions encountered on the lunar surface; and adding to the scientific knowledge of the Moon.

The *Surveyor 7* mission also had an extensive series of scientific objectives, and for these carried a more elaborate suite of scientific instruments that the previous Surveyors. Among the scientific objectives were to perform a lunar soft landing in a highland area well removed from the maria to provide a type of terrain photography and lunar sample significantly different from those of other Surveyor missions; obtain post-landing TV pictures; determine the relative abundances of chemical elements; manipulate the lunar material; obtain touchdown dynamics data; and obtain thermal and radar reflectivity data.

The spacecraft successfully landed on the Moon on 10 January 1968, about 46 km north of the northern rim of the large Tycho crater, which is located in the southern lunar highlands and has a series of prominent rays extending from it that are visible from Earth. *Surveyor 7* thus became the only *Surveyor* craft to land in the lunar highland region.

Data-gathering operations commenced once the spacecraft had landed. During its first lunar day, it nearly 21,000 images of the surface, as well as, after the lunar sunset, images of Earth and the stars. The lunar surface sampler arm operated for more than thirty-six hours, trenching the soil near the spacecraft and moving four rocks. *Surveyor 7* performed chemical measurements of the surface near the Tycho crater that revealed its composition to be different from the lunar maria, having less iron components. Laser beams sent from Earth were also detected by the probe.

Technical Notes

The basic *Surveyor* spacecraft structure consisted of a tripod of thin-walled aluminum tubing and interconnecting braces providing mounting surfaces and attachments for the power, communications, propulsion, flight control, and payload systems. A central mast extended about one meter above the apex of the tripod. Three hinged landing legs were attached to the lower corners of the structure. The legs held shock absorbers; crushable, honeycomb aluminum blocks; and the deployment locking mechanism, and they terminated in footpads with crushable bottoms. The three footpads extended out 4.3 meters from the center of the *Surveyor*. The spacecraft was about 3 meters tall. The legs folded to fit into a nose shroud for launch.

A 0.855-square-meter array of 792 solar cells was mounted on a positioner on top of the mast and generated up to 85 watts of power which was stored in rechargeable silver-zinc batteries. Communications were achieved via a movable large-planar-array high-gain antenna mounted near the top of the central mast to transmit television images, two omnidirectional conical antennas mounted on the ends of folding booms for uplink and downlink, two receivers and two transmitters. Thermal control was achieved by a combination of white paint, high IR-emittance thermal finish, and polished aluminum underside. Two thermally controlled compartments, equipped with superinsulating blankets, conductive heat paths, thermal switches and small electric heaters, were mounted on the spacecraft structure. One compartment, held at 5–50 degrees Celsius, housed communications and power supply electronics. The other, held between -20 and 50 degrees Celsius, housed the command and signal processing components. The TV survey camera was mounted near the top of the tripod and strain gauges, temperature sensors, and other engineering instruments were incorporated throughout the spacecraft. One photometric target was mounted near the end of a landing leg and one on a short boom extending from the bottom of the structure. Other payload packages, which differed from mission to mission, were mounted on various parts of the structure, depending on their function.

A Sun sensor, Canopus tracker and rate gyros on three axes provided attitude knowledge. Propulsion and attitude control were provided by cold-gas (nitrogen) attitude control jets during cruise phases, three vernier rocket engines during powered phases, including the landing, and the solid-propellant retrorocket engine during terminal descent. The retrorocket was a spherical steel case mounted in the bottom center of the spacecraft. The fuel was stored in spherical tanks mounted to the tripod structure. For the landing sequence, an altitude-marking radar initiated the firing of the main retrorocket for primary braking. After firing was complete, the retrorocket and radar were jettisoned and the doppler and altimeter radars were activated. These provided information to the autopilot which controlled the vernier propulsion system to touchdown.

Surveyor 7 was similar in design to *Surveyor 6,* but the payload was the most extensive flown during the Surveyor program. It carried a television camera with polarizing filters, an alpha-scattering instrument, a surface sampler similar to that flown on *Surveyor 3,* bar magnets on two footpads, two horseshoe magnets on the surface scoop, and auxiliary mirrors. Of the auxiliary mirrors, three were used to observe areas below the spacecraft, one to provide stereoscopic views of the surface sampler area, and seven to show lunar material deposited on the spacecraft. It also carried over 100 items to monitor engineering aspects of spacecraft performance.

Archaeology

Surveyor 7 touched down with a mass of 305.7 kilograms at 40.86° S, 348.53° E on an ejecta blanket about north of the rim of Tycho crater in the lunar highlands. It ceased systemic operations on 21 February 1968 and entered its archaeological context. Its landing area makes it one of the most remote of the unmanned probes sent to the Moon, well away from the equatorial cluster of both unmanned and manned landing or impact sites, and the farthest south that a spacecraft has been soft-landed on the Moon.

24) *LUNA 15* [27]

History

Luna 15 was launched atop a Proton rocket from Baikonur Cosmodrome in the former Soviet Union on 13 July 1969. The spacecraft was placed in an intermediate earth orbit after launch and was then sent toward the Moon. The spacecraft was capable of studying circumlunar space, the lunar gravitational field, and the chemical composition of lunar rocks.

After completing eighty-six communications sessions and fifty-two orbits of the Moon at various inclinations and altitudes, the spacecraft began its descent to the lunar surface, where it was planned to collect rocks from the surface and return them to Earth, presumably ahead of the simultaneous American *Apollo 11* mission. The mission of *Luna 15* coincided with the arrival of the manned *Apollo 11* mission at the Moon, and the astronauts of the Apollo mission were already on the Moon as the Soviet probe began its descent on 21 July 1969. When the unmanned Soviet probe was about three kilometers above the lunar surface, transmissions to Earth ceased and all contact with the probe was lost.

Archaeology

It is thought that the spacecraft impacted the lunar surface, perhaps into the side of a mountain, with a mass of 2,718 kilograms, on 21 July 1969, a few hours before the *Apollo 11* astronauts lifted off for their return flight to Earth. The coordinates of the impact site are 17° N, 60° E in the Mare Crisium (the Sea of Crises), just east of the Sea of Tranquility where *Apollo 11* had its base camp.

25) *LUNA 16* [28]

History

Luna 16 was launched atop a Proton rocket from Baikonur Cosmodrome on 12 September 1970. It became the first robotic probe to land on the Moon and return a sample to Earth and represented the first lunar sample return mission by the Soviet Union and the third overall, following the *Apollo 11* and *12* missions. The probe arrived at the Moon on 17 September 1970, and following a series of orbits descended to the surface on 20 September. Like the American Lunar Module, *Luna 16* carried both a descent and an ascent stage, with the former acting as a launch pad for the eventual return of the ascent stage with its soil sample.

The spacecraft soft-landed on the lunar surface in Mare Fecunditatis (the Sea of Fertility) as planned, approximately 100 kilometers from Webb crater in the eastern part of the Moon near the equator. This was the first landing made in the dark on the Moon. The drill was deployed and penetrated to a depth of 35 cm before encountering hard rock or large fragments of rock. The column of regolith in the drill tube was then transferred to the soil sample container. After twenty-six hours and twenty-five minutes on the lunar surface, the ascent stage, with the hermetically sealed soil sample container, lifted off from the Moon carrying 101 grams of collected lunar surface soil, leaving the bulk of the probe behind. The capsule with the soil sample landed approximately eighty kilometers southeast of the city of Dzhezkazgan in Kazakhstan on 24 September 1970.

Technical Notes

The spacecraft consisted of two attached stages, an ascent stage mounted on top of a descent stage. The descent stage was a cylindrical body with four protruding landing legs, fuel tanks, a landing radar, and a dual descent engine complex. A main descent engine was used to slow the craft until it reached a cutoff point which was determined by the onboard computer based on altitude and velocity. After cutoff a bank of lower thrust jets was used for the final landing. The descent stage also acted as a launch pad for the ascent stage. The ascent stage was a smaller cylinder with a rounded top. It carried a cylindrical, hermetically sealed soil sample container inside a re-entry capsule. The space-craft descent stage was equipped with a television camera, radiation and temperature monitors, telecommunications equipment, and an extendable arm with a drilling rig for the collection of a lunar soil sample.

Archaeology

Luna 16 marked the first time a robotic tool from Earth had been sent to another celestial body and succeeded in returning a sample of that body to Earth. In 1993, a tiny sample of this lunar material was auctioned off for more than $440,000 U.S., providing a benchmark of sorts for discussions of the value of private tourist and exploitation missions to the Moon.[29]

The *Luna 16* descent stage remained behind after the lift-off of the ascent stage carrying the collected lunar soil. The descent stage continued to transmit lunar temperature and radiation data. Once the probe ceased its transmission, it entered its archaeological context. This historic site, along with the proximity of five other and later Luna missions nearby, would seem to argue for the creation of the Luna-specific cultural protection area in this sector of the Moon.

26) *LUNA 17 / LUNOKHOD 1*[30]

History

The *Luna 17* spacecraft was launched atop a Proton rocket from Baikonur Cosmod-rome on 10 November 1970. Upon reaching an Earth parking orbit, the probe was sent to the Moon where it arrived and entered lunar orbit on 15 November. The probe successfully soft-landed on the Moon on 17 November 1970, in the Mare Imbrium (Sea of Showers).

The spacecraft was similar to the *Luna 16* probe, except that the return capsule was replaced by a robotic eight-wheeled lunar roving vehicle called *Lunokhod 1* (Russian for "Moonwalker"). Upon touchdown, two sets of dual ramps were lowered on either side of the *Luna 17* descent stage, and the rover maneuvered onto the lunar surface. During its mission, the probe transmitted more than 20,000 TV pictures and more than 200 TV panoramas back to Earth, and conducted more than 500 lunar soil tests.

Technical Notes

The spacecraft had dual ramps by which the payload, *Lunokhod 1*, descended to the lunar surface. *Lunokhod 1* was a lunar roving vehicle formed of a tub-like compartment with a large convex lid on eight independently powered wheels. *Lunokhod* was equipped with a cone-shaped antenna, a highly directional helical antenna, four television cameras, and special extendable devices to impact the lunar soil for soil density and mechanical property tests. An X-ray spectrometer, an X-ray telescope, cosmic-ray detectors, and a laser device were also included. The vehicle was powered by a solar cell array mounted on the underside of the lid.

Archaeology

The spacecraft and its rover soft-landed in the Mare Imbrium with a mass of 5,600 kilometers. Its landing position was at 38°17' N, 35° W, making it the farthest north that a spacecraft has landed on the Moon. The *Lunokhod 1* vehicle was intended to operate through three lunar days but actually operated for eleven lunar days, returning more than 20,000 images to Earth. Over 322 Earth days, the vehicle traveled more than 10.5 kilometers across the lunar surface before communications with it were finally terminated on 4 October 1971, and the vehicle and its descent stage entered their archaeological context.

The final archaeological context of the *Lunokhod 1* roving vehicle is uncertain within a few kilometers, as attempts to locate it by lunar laser ranging technology have thus far been unsuccessful.[31] The two associated sites (the descent stage landing site and the eventual stopping point of the rover) mark the first time a remote-controlled robot had landed on another celestial body. As such, they take on a special cultural significance as the model for similar such missions to Mars and other planets that by the twenty-first century had become the norm.

27) LUNA 18 [32]

History

Luna 18 was launched atop a Proton rocket from the Baikonur Cosmodrome on 2 September 1971. The spacecraft was placed in an earth parking orbit after it was launched and was then sent towards the Moon, where it arrived and entered into lunar orbit on 7 September. The spacecraft completed eighty-five communications sessions and fifty-four lunar orbits before it was sent towards the lunar surface by use of braking rockets. The goal of the mission was similar to that of *Luna 16*: to return lunar soil samples to Earth. Signals from the probe ceased at the moment of impact, suggesting a crash-landing and mission failure.

Archaeology

On 11 September 1971, *Luna 18* impacted the Moon with a mass of 5,600 kilograms at 3° 34' N, 56° 30' E, in rugged mountainous terrain near the edge of the Mare Fecunditatis (Sea of Fertility). Signals ceased at the moment of impact, indicating that the probe had entered its archaeological context the moment it reached the lunar surface. If in fact the probe managed to land without being destroyed, it would comprise a complete example of the successful *Luna 16* probe that was the first composite robotic tool from Earth to return a soil sample from another celestial body.

28) LUNA 20 [33]

History

Luna 20 was launched atop a Proton rocket from the Baikonur Cosmodrome on 14 February 1972. The spacecraft was placed in an intermediate earth parking orbit and from this orbit was sent towards the Moon, which it reached, and entered lunar orbit on 18 February. Three days later, the probe successfully soft-landed on 21 February 1972. Once on the surface, the descent stage panoramic television system began operation. Within a few hours after landing, samples of lunar material were gathered by means of an extendable drilling apparatus, transferred to the capsule atop the ascent stage, and launched from the lunar surface on 22 February.

Archaeology

The *Luna 20* had soft-landed with a mass of 5,600 kilograms on the Moon in a mountainous area known as the Apollonius highlands near Mare Fecunditatis (Sea of Fertility), about 120 kilometers from where *Luna 16* had impacted. The ascent stage, carrying thirty grams of collected lunar samples in a sealed capsule, was returned to Earth where it landed in the Soviet Union on 25 February 1972. The capsule was recovered the following day after parachuting down to an island in the Karkingir River in Kazakhstan.

29) *LUNA 21/LUNOKHOD 2*[34]

History

The *Luna 21/Lunokhod 2* combination lunar lander/lunar rover was launched atop a Proton rocket from Baikonur Cosmodrome on 8 January 1973. Four days later, the spacecraft entered lunar orbit, which was gradually lowered to sixteen kilometer above the surface. A braking rocket was fired, and the probe began a freefall to the surface. This was broken at 750 meters above the Moon by the main thruster, and then by secondary thrusters when the probe was just twenty-two meters above the surface. At one and a half meters, the engines were cut off and the probe settled onto the Moon on 15 January 1973. There it deployed the second Soviet lunar rover, *Lunokhod 2*. The primary objectives of the mission were to collect images of the lunar surface, examine ambient light levels to determine the feasibility of astronomical observations from the Moon, perform laser-ranging experiments from Earth, observe solar X-rays, measure local magnetic fields, and study mechanical properties of the lunar surface material.

Once on the surface, the *Lunokhod 2* rover began to photograph the surrounding area before leaving the descent stage via a landing ramp in order to look back to image the probe and its landing site. The rover recharged its batteries for two days before taking more photographs of the lander and the starting out on its journey across the Moon. The rover, an improved version of its predecessor, ran during the lunar day, and then slept during the lunar night while its instruments were kept heated by a polonium-210 radioisotope heater. By the end of its operational life, the rover had driven more than thirty-five kilometers across the lunar surface and returned over 80,000 television pictures and eighty-six panoramic images.

Technical Notes

The *Lunokhod 2* rover stood 135 centimeters high and had a mass of 840 kilograms. It was about 170 centimeters long and 160 centimeters wide and had eight wheels, each with an independent suspension, motor and brake. The rover had two speeds, around one kilometer per hour and around two kilometers per hour. *Lunokhod 2* was equipped with three TV cameras, one mounted high on the rover for navigation, which could return high-resolution images at different rates. These images were used by a five-man team of controllers on Earth who sent driving commands to the rover in real time. Power was supplied by a solar panel on the inside of a round hinged lid which covered the instrument bay, which would charge the batteries when opened. A polonium-210 isotopic heat source was used to keep the rover warm during the lunar nights. There were four panoramic cameras mounted on the rover. Scientific instruments included a soil-mechanics tester, solar X-ray experiment, an astrophotometer to measure visible and UV light levels, a magnetometer deployed in front of the rover on the end of a two-and-a-half-meter boom, a radiometer, a photodetector for laser-detection experiments, and a French-supplied laser corner-reflector.

Archaeology

The *Luna 21/Lunokhod 2* lander/rover together weighed 1,814 kilograms. The landing occurred in the LeMonnier crater at 25.85° N, 30.45° E. The lander carried a bas relief of Lenin and the Soviet coat-of-arms. The *Lunokhod 2* rover traveled over thirty-five kilometers over the lunar surface before controllers on Earth inadvertently drove it into a crater, where its became covered in dust after the rover's cover swept along the crater wall. When the lid was opened, the dust-covered radiator could not cool the rover, and it soon overheated and failed.[35]

The rover's retroreflector array, like those positioned on the Moon by several Apollo missions, can be recorded by lunar laser-ranging experiments from Earth, so its position on the eastern edge of the Mare Serentatis (Sea of Tranquility) is known within a few centimeters.

The *Luna 21/Lunokhod 2* lander/rover also holds a unique place in the ongoing discussions concerning the control, ownership, and protection of cultural resources on the Moon. The builder of the spacecraft, the Russian aerospace company Lavochkin Research and Production Association, sold both the lander and the rover at auction in New York in 1993 for $68,500. The purchaser, a computer gaming designer and son of a former astronaut, therefore claims to be the only human to own an artifact on a celestial body other than Earth.[36]

A third Lunokhod rover was planned to be sent to the Moon but this mission was eventually canceled. Both the rover and its associated lander are now on display as museum exhibits in Moscow.

30) *LUNA 23* [37]

History

Luna 23 was launched atop a Proton rocker from Baikonur Cosmodrome on 28 October 1974, on a mission intended to return a lunar sample to Earth.

Archaeology

The spacecraft impacted onto the lunar surface with a mass of 5,600 kilograms on 6 November 1974. The landing area is thought to be in the area of the Mare Crisium (Sea of Crises). The probe was damaged during landing and the sample collecting apparatus could not operate. No samples were returned to Earth and the spacecraft, after transmitting data to Earth for three more days, entered its archaeological context on 9 November 1974.

31) *LUNA 24* [38]

History

The *Luna 24* spacecraft was launched atop a Proton rocket from Baikonur Cosmodrome on 9 August 1967. The last of the Luna series of spacecraft, the mission of the *Luna 24* probe was the third Soviet mission to retrieve lunar ground samples. The probe landed in the area known as Mare Crisium (Sea of Crisis) at 12.75° N, 62.2° E, on 18 August 1976. Deploying a sampler arm and drill, the probe successfully collected 170.1 grams of lunar samples and deposited them into a collection capsule, which was then launched from the Moon on 19 August. The capsule returned to Earth on 22 August where it landed in western Siberia.

Archaeology

The *Luna 24* probe impacted on the Moon on 18 August 1976, with a mass of 4,800 kilograms. A part of this mass was removed when the collection capsule was launched on a return voyage to Earth on 19 August. The Soviet Union continued to communicate with the remainder of the probe, so it is not known when the *Luna 24* entered its archaeological context. The spacecraft was the last probe of any nation to make a soft landing on the Moon.

32) *HITEN* (MUSES-A) [39]

History

Hiten (a Japanese word meaning "flying angel") was launched atop an M-3SII rocket from the Uchinoura Space Center in Japan on 24 January 1990. The mission was sponsored by the Institute of Space and Aeronautical Science at the University of Tokyo in Japan. The spacecraft was the first composite tool from Earth to be sent to the Moon by a country other than the United States or the Soviet Union, and the first since the Soviet Union's *Luna 24* in 1976.

The Earth-orbiting satellite was designed primarily to test and verify technologies for future lunar and planetary expeditions. The spacecraft carried a small satellite named *Hagoromo* which was released in the vicinity of the Moon, since the main spacecraft passed by the Moon ten times during its mission. The primary objectives of the mission were to (1) test trajectory control utilizing gravity assist double lunar swingbys, (2) insert a sub-satellite into lunar orbit, (3) conduct optical navigation experiments on a spin-stabilized spacecraft, (4) test fault tolerant onboard computer and packet telemetry, (5) conduct cis-lunar aerobraking experiments, and (6) detect and measure mass and velocity of micro-meteorite particles. This mission included Japan's first-ever lunar flyby, lunar orbiter, and lunar surface impact, making Japan only the third nation to achieve each of these goals.

Technical Notes

Hiten was a cylindrically shaped spacecraft, 1.4 meters in diameter and 0.8 meters high. The small polyhedral-shaped *Hagoromo* lunar orbiter was mounted on top of the spacecraft. The fully fueled mass of *Hiten* was 197 kilograms, this included forty-two kilograms of hydrazine fuel and the twelve kilograms *Hagoromo* orbiter.

The *Hagoromo* orbiter was a twelve-kilogram, twenty-six-faced polyhedron, thirty-six centimeters between opposite faces. A solid propellant (KM-L) retrorocket with a mass of four kilograms was mounted inside the spacecraft for lunar orbit insertion. Sixteen of the surfaces were covered with 1000 sheets of indium-phosphorus solar cells which could generate about ten watts of power. Solar cells on the cylindrical surface of the spacecraft supplied the power requirement of 110 watts, backed up by a small onboard battery.

Archaeology

The *Hagoromo* probe was released from *Hiten* during its first approach of the Moon on 18 March 1990. However, the transmitter on board *Hagoromo* had failed about a month earlier, so it is unknown if the probe ever entered lunar orbit or impacted the surface thereafter. The *Hiten* spacecraft itself continued to collect scientific data until it was placed in lunar orbit on 15 February 1993. The last bit of fuel of the spacecraft was used to crash it into the lunar surface on 10 April 1993, and the point 55.6° E, 34.3° S.

33) LUNAR PROSPECTOR[40]

History

The *Lunar Prospector* was part of a program by NASA to develop more inexpensive, tightly focused, and rapidly fielded science robes. It was launched atop an Athena 2 rocket from Cape on 7 January 1998. The probe was designed for a low polar orbit investigation of the Moon, including mapping of surface composition and possible deposits of polar ice, measurements of magnetic and gravity fields, and study of lunar outgassing events.

Technical Notes

The spacecraft carried six experiments: a Gamma Ray Spectrometer (GRS), a Neutron Spectrometer (NS), a Magnetometer (MAG), an Electron Reflectometer (ER), an Alpha Particle Spectrometer (APS), and a Doppler Gravity Experiment (DGE). The instruments were omnidirectional and required no sequencing. The normal observation sequence was to record and downlink data continuously.

The spacecraft was a graphite-epoxy drum, 1.37 meters in diameter and 1.28 meters high with three radial 2.5-meter instrument booms. A 1.1-meter extension boom at the end of one of the 2.5 meter booms held the magnetometer. Total initial mass (fully fueled) was 296 kilograms. It was spin-stabilized (nominal spin rate of twelve rpm) with its spin axis normal to the ecliptic plane. The spacecraft was controlled by six hydrazine-mono-propellant, twenty-two-Newton thrusters, two aft, two forward, and two tangential. Three fuel tanks mounted inside the drum held 138 kilograms of hydrazine pressurized by helium. The power system consisted of body mounted solar cells which produced an average of 186 watts and a 4.8-amp-hr rechargeable NiCd battery. There was no onboard computer, since all control was from the ground, commanding a single onboard command and data-handling unit. Data was downlinked directly and also stored on a solid-state recorder and downlinked after fifty-three minutes to ensure all data collected during communications blackout periods was received.

Archaeology

After a mission that lasted for 570 days, the *Lunar Prospector* was deliberately targeted to impact in a permanently shadowed area of the Shoemaker Crater near the lunar South Pole. The impact took place on 31 July 1999, with a mass of 158 kilograms, and, as with the L-Cross mission of 2009, the 1999 *Lunar Prospector* impact targeted the South Polar Region in a search for water on the Moon. Scientists hoped that ice deposits would be found when the collision cast a plume up into space, but no such plume of vapor could be recorded from Earth.

34) SMART-1[41]

History

The Small Missions for Advanced Research in Technology 1 (*SMART-1*) mission was launched atop an Ariane 5 rocket from French Guiana on 27 September 2003. The probe was designed in Sweden for the European Space Agency. The primary technology being tested was a solar-powered ion drive Hall thruster, which operated for nearly 5,000 hours through 843 starts and stops. The probe also carried an experimental deep-space telecommunications system and an instrument payload to monitor the ion drive and study the Moon. The primary scientific objective for the mission was to return data on the geology, morphology, topography, mineralogy, geochemistry, and exospheric environment of the

Moon in order to answer questions about planetary formation accretional processes, origin of the Earth-Moon system, the lunar near-far-side dichotomy, long-term volcanic and tectonic activity, thermal and dynamical processes involved in lunar evolution, and water ice and external processes on the surface.

Technical Notes

SMART-1 was a box-shaped spacecraft roughly a meter on a side with two large solar panel wings spanning fourteen meters extending from opposite sides. The launch mass, including fuel, was 366.5 kilograms; the mass at the time it reached the Moon was thought to be about 305 kilograms. A solar-electric propulsion system used xenon gas as a propellant by ionizing the xenon and accelerating and discharging the plasma from the spacecraft at high speed. Electrons were also released into the flow to maintain a neutral charge on the spacecraft. A thrust of seventy milliNewtons was produced. Eighty-two kilograms of supercritical xenon propellant was carried aboard *SMART-1* in a tank mounted in the center of the structure, above the thruster. The spacecraft was three-axis stabilized using four skewed reaction wheels and eight hydrazine thrusters mounted on the corners of the spacecraft bus. Attitude data was provided by a star tracker, sun sensor, and angular rate sensors.

The science instruments included a pan-chromatic camera (AMIE) for lunar imaging, Langmuir probes mounted on booms to measure the plasma environment, and radio-science experiments (RSIS). Science instruments which were being tested as part of the technology verification were a miniaturized visible/near-infrared spectrometer for lunar crustal studies, a miniature X-ray spectrometer for astronomy and lunar chemistry, and an X-ray spectrometer to study the Sun. The Electric Propulsion Diagnostic package (EPDP) was a multi-sensor suite designed specifically to monitor the ion propulsion system. The RSIS was also used to monitor the ion propulsion system.

Archaeology

After a mission lasting nearly three years, the *SMART-1* spacecraft was deliberately crashed into the Moon at about two kilometers per second on 3 September 2006, with a mass of about 287 kilograms. The impact site is in the mid-southern region of the near side of the Moon in Lacus Excellentiae (Lake of Excellence) at 34.4° S, 46.2° W.

35) CHANG'E 1[42]

History

Chang'e is the Chinese goddess of the Moon. In 2007, the People's Republic of China launched its first lunar probe named in honor of this goddess. The spacecraft was launched atop a Long March 3A rocket from the Xichang Satellite Launch Center in Sichuan Province in China, on 24 October 2007. The primary technical objectives of the mission were to develop and launch China's first lunar orbiter, validate the technology necessary to fly lunar missions, build a basic engineering system for lunar exploration, start scientific exploration of the Moon, and gain experience for subsequent missions. The primary science objectives were to obtain three-dimensional stereo images of the lunar surface, analyze the distribution and abundance of elements on the surface, survey the thickness of lunar soil, evaluate helium-3 resources and other characteristics, and explore the environment between the Moon and Earth.

The probe entered lunar orbit on 5 November 2007, and the original mission of one year was extended into 2009.

Technical Notes

The orbiter was based on the DFH-3 Comsat bus with a mass of 2,350 kilograms, approximately half of which is propellant and 130 kilograms of which is the scientific payload. It was basically a 2.0 × 1.7 × 2.2 meter box with two solar panel wings extending from opposite sides. The science payload comprised eight instruments: a stereo camera system to map the lunar surface in visible wavelengths, an interferometer spectrometer imager to obtain multispectral images of the Moon, a laser altimeter to measure the topography, a gamma ray and an X-ray spectrometer to study the overall composition and radioactive components of the Moon, a microwave radiometer to map the thickness of the lunar regolith, and a high-energy particle detector and solar wind monitors to collect data on the space environment of the near-lunar region.

Archaeology

On 1 March 2009, *Chang'e 1* was deliberately crashed into the Moon with a mass of 2,350 kilograms. The impact site is 1.5° S, 52.36° E.[43] This first Chinese mission to the Moon was intended to pave the way for a soft landing in 2011, followed by a lunar roving vehicle in 2012.

36) CHANDRAYAAN-1 LUNAR ORBITER[44]

History

Chandrayaan-1 (Sanskrit for "moon traveller") was launched atop a PSLV-XL rocket from the Satish Dhawan Space Centre, Sriharikota, India on 22 October 2008. The spacecraft was an Indian Space Research Organization (ISRO) mission designed to orbit the Moon over a two-year period with the objectives of upgrading and testing India's technological capabilities in space and returning scientific information on the lunar surface. The probe entered lunar orbit on 8 November 2008, after which a Moon Impact Probe separated from the main orbiter and crashed into the lunar South Pole after a controlled descent.

Technical Notes

The spacecraft bus was roughly a one-and-a-half meter cube with a dry weight of 523 kilograms (the launch mass of the system, including its Lunar Apogee Motor, LAM, was 1380 kilograms). It was based on the Kalpansat meteorological satellite. Power was provided by a solar array which generated 750 watts and charged a bank of lithium ion batteries. A bipropellant propulsion system was used to transfer *Chandrayaan-1* into lunar orbit and maintain attitude. The spacecraft was three-axis stabilized using attitude-control thrusters and reaction wheels. Navigational data was provided by star sensors, accelerometers, and an inertial reference unit.

Archaeology

The thirty-five-kilogram Moon Impact Probe (MIP) was designed to be released from the orbiter and crash in a controlled manner into the lunar surface. The MIP carried a video camera, a radar altimeter, and a mass spectrometer. The side panels of the box-like probe were painted with the Indian flag, and when the probe impacted the Shackleton Crater on 14 November 2008, India became the fourth nation to contribute to the archaeological remains on the Moon — soon followed by China and *Chang'e 1*. The MIP entered its archaeological context the moment it impacted the Shackleton crater.

Contact with the *Chandrayaan-1* probe itself was lost on 29 August 2009, after it had transmitted over 70,000 images to Earth. It is expected that the probe will orbit the Moon for another three years before its orbit decays and it impacts the surface. On 25 September 2009, the Indian Space Research Organization announced that data from both the MIP and the *Chandrayaan-1* supported the hypothesis that water was locked up in ice at the lunar poles.[45]

37) Lunar Crater Observation and Sensing Satellite (*LCROSS*)[46]

History

The *LCROSS* mission was launched atop an Atlas V401 rocket from Cape Canaveral, Florida, on 18 June 2009. It was designed to search for water on the Moon by directing the double impact of both the Shepherding Spacecraft (S-S/C) and a 2,000-kilogram Centaur upper stage into a crater near the lunar South Pole. The plan was to send the Centaur into the Moon at 2.5 kilometers per hour while the orbiter observed the impact as it followed in its path and impacted itself a few moments later. The mission precisely targeted a shadowed area near the lunar South Pole, as it was hypothesized that the resulting ejecta plume would produce evidence of water ice.

Technical Notes

The S-S/C is built on an EELV Secondary Payload Adaptor (ESPA) 158-centimeter-diameter ring with a dry mass of 534 kilograms and 300 kilograms of hydrazine propellant. Peak power for the system of 372 watts is supplied by a 600-watt solar array charging a 40A-h Li-Ion battery. Propulsion is through two eight-thruster pods supplied by a mono-propellant fuel tank mounted inside the ring. Communications were via an

S-band transponder and two omnidirectional and two medium-gain horn antennas. Outer radiator panels, heat pipes, and multilayer insulation were used for thermal control. The S-S/C was equipped with two visible cameras, three infrared cameras, three spectrometers, and a photometer for observations.

Archaeology

The Centaur upper stage impacted the Cabeus crater, about 100 kilometers from the lunar South Pole, with a mass of 2,305 kilograms at 0731 EST on 9 October 2009. The resulting crater was believed to be about twenty meters across and four meters deep. The main body of the Shepherding Spacecraft (S-S/C), descending through the plume of material created by the Centaur impact, followed six minutes later. On 13 November 2009, NASA announced that the *LCROSS* impact had in fact uncovered evidence for the water at the lunar South Pole.[47]

Conclusions

In the short summers of the Norwegian Arctic archipelago of Svalbard, in recent years, there has been something called the Arctic Mars Analog Svalbard Expedition (AMASE), a research project designed to study the instruments and techniques of space exploration in the extreme, Mars-like environment of Svalbard.[48] The volcanic and geologic histories, the layered sedimentary deposits, the survival of life forms in a harsh environment, and the challenges of adapting technologies to explore rugged terrain all are considered similar to what teams of explorers will encounter upon arrival on Mars.

In another, archaeological sense, however, Svalbard is the only place on Earth that is analogous to the Moon. From this perspective, the historic mining operations ruins at sites like Pyramiden and Grumant in Svalbard are the most extensive Soviet-era archaeological sites outside the boundaries of the former Soviet Union with the possible exception of the numerous unmanned spacecraft left behind on the Moon by Soviet Russian lunar exploration activities.

It would make for an interesting archaeological comparison to study how the superpower competition between the Soviet Union and the United States can be read in these two extreme, related areas. In Svalbard, the secretive mining operations had nonetheless to interact with Norwegian sovereignty over the archipelago — and after 1949 with Norway as a member of the North Atlantic Treaty Organization, with its focus on the collective defense of democracy and individual liberty in the North Atlantic area. Svalbard was therefore the northernmost frontier of the Cold War.

On the Moon, on the High Frontier, the Soviet Union was engaged in direct cultural and technological competition with its primary Cold War adversary and fellow contestant in the "space race." Some of the important Soviet sites on the Moon, like the precise location of the first soft landing on the Moon by *Luna 9*, or the location of the first rover, the Soviet *Lunokhod 1*, are unknown. As lunar researcher and author of the *International*

Atlas of Lunar Exploration Philip Stooke points out: "If in the future it is decided to confer special designations or protection on these sites, finding them is essential."[49]

These sites possess unique archaeological characters: not only as tools sent to another celestial body by *Homo sapiens*, but as artifacts of a bygone system of human behavior. It is important to find these sites and place them under a cultural protection regime. This will offer a measure of protection from the effects of future lunar exploration, and allow their study as comparative archaeological materials to those that lie in ruins at the much more accessible Soviet mining villages of Svalbard.

PART II:
PLANETARY ARCHAEOLOGY

The wreck of a Soviet four-engine TB-3 aircraft, specially modified for Arctic flying, surveyed on Rudolf Island in Franz Josef Land in the Russian Arctic in 2006. (Credit: Author.)

4

Planetary Archaeology

1. Artifacts of Intelligence

The postulation of artifacts of intelligence in the solar system has a long and fascinating history. It is one that touches on science, astronomy, theology, and popular culture. This is as it should be, as the discipline of archaeology touches on these among many other elements of culture. From Percival Lowell's theory of non-natural canals on Mars, to the monolith and the Star Gate of *2001: A Space Odyssey* and the continual use of archaeological themes in *Star Trek* (where Jean-Luc Picard, captain of the *Enterprise* in *Star Trek: The Next Generation*, received his university training in archaeology and where the search for "new life and new civilizations" always appears preoccupied with the archaeological rather than the biological), archaeology has provided a wealth of ideas for both real as well as fictional attempts to explore space.

These attempts to introduce the idea of artifacts of intelligence in the solar system and the universe at large has also led to a tendency to wish extraterrestrial artifacts into existence, to see artifacts in shapes and shadows, and even to invent global (if not intergalactic) conspiracies to cover up evidence of presumed fellow travelers in the cosmos. When I started my graduate work in archaeology in the pre–Internet era, such speculations colored any attempt even to discuss the possibility of archaeological research in space. It was considered a mad fantasy and delegated to the outermost fringes of fringe archaeology along with the works of Erich von Daniken's *Chariots of the Gods.*

Works like those of von Daniken became extremely popular because they went to perhaps the core dilemma of human life on Earth: are we alone in a vast, lifeless universe or have other forms of intelligent life evolved under similar conditions elsewhere in a Darwinian universe? Darwin presents numerous intellectual challenges to *Homo sapiens's* view of itself and life in general, not the least that we are a unique evolutionary adaptation to a unique set of environmental challenges. If so, the very real possibility exists that we are in fact alone in a pointless universe. Or, as one of my students remarked during a discussion of evolutionary theory, "Darwin is really depressing!"

It is one of the enduring and endearing traits of *Homo sapiens* to seek out ways to escape the inevitable depressions that come with such stark self-awareness. Extraterrestrial archaeology, along with suggestions that alien visitors have influenced human culture on

85

earth, has long provided such an avenue to those not inclined to either the warm consolations of faith or the cold comforts of Darwinian evolutionary theory. Books like David Hatcher Childress' immensely entertaining *Extraterrestrial Archaeology* used perceived anomalies or geometric shapes and patterns in low-resolution space-agency photography to argue that the solar system was filled with artifacts of intelligent societies. Detailed photogrammetric studies were made by Mark Carlotto, Richard C. Hoagland and others of the eerily suggestive humanoid face in the Cydonia region of Mars originally photographed in 1976 by the *Viking 1* spacecraft, to suggest that the remains of an advanced civilization perhaps millions of years old lay in ruins on the surface of the planet.

I am anything but immune to such speculations: so much so that while doing my doctoral reading in archaeology I tried to find ways to introduce such corollaries into my dissertation. In this I found an ally in the great Isaac Asimov, whose brilliant *Extraterrestrial Civilizations* (1979) became a constant companion. In it, he modified Drake's equation in such a way as to suggest the possibility of hundreds of millions of civilizations in ruins throughout the universe. The idea of hundreds of millions of civilizations — with its implied total of billions of individual archaeological sites making up those civilizations — was enough to stagger the imagination of any archaeologist. Accordingly, I slipped Asimov's "chain of reasoning" into my dissertation on aerospace archaeology in 1996, and then again in an article on the subject in *Archaeology* in 2004.

By this point, the internet had arrived in full force and was providing a wild garden of hard data via national space agency sites — for example, the discovery of earth-like planets in the galaxy — combined with an almost equally great number of interpretative and speculative sites that sought to use this data to demonstrate a conclusive argument for intelligent life in the universe.

Almost inevitably, the *Archaeology* article — which deliberately tossed in the potential for extraterrestrial archaeology along with more conventional historical archaeology at sites of aerospace exploration — drew me into this web. In 2006, a clever marketing campaign for a PlayStation 2 game called *Shadow of the Colossus* created a video that purported to show a team of Arctic archaeologists landing in a remote area by helicopter and using an augur to uncover a massive life form covered in a kind of faux Aztec body armor. The video was shot in a herky-jerky way, purposefully designed so that one could not get a long, still view of either the archaeologists or the massive life form that they had under apparent study. Even the language of the archaeologists was in doubt — so the location of both the apparent alien and the nationality of the researchers were kept hidden. The only wide shot lasted for about two seconds and showed a truly massive organism, face covered by a kind of helmet, lying partially buried under snow and ice. You can find the video today on YouTube (along with priceless comments directed at the gullible such as "It's a viral commercial, you fools...").

As it happened, this same summer, as the fictional alien was making the viral rounds of the internet, I made two voyages to the North Pole on board the Russian icebreaker *Yamal*. During the second voyage, as we returned from the pole, we landed by helicopter on Rudolf Island in the Franz Josef Land archipelago. There, on the northernmost land north of Europe, we located and surveyed the wreck of an enormous aircraft used by the Soviet Union in 1937 for polar exploration. It was a fascinating find that followed up research on the island by my Norwegian colleague Susan Barr from the early 1990s. The archaeology of this site — the northernmost aerospace artifact ever surveyed — allowed us a glimpse into the kinds of themes such expeditions in extreme environments could reveal. In the case of the Rudolf Island aircraft, this was especially important since we learned that it had ended in failure, which in the former Soviet Union meant that the history of the expedition was buried as deeply as an embarrassed government could bury it.

This fairly benign aerospace archaeology — albeit in a very extreme environment — was taken up as a central element of an argument for the presence of artifacts of extraterrestrial intelligence here on earth. In a series of articles called "Stargates, Ancient Rituals, and Those Invited Through the Portal" and posted on the internet news site Raiders News Update, author Thomas Horn speculated that it was the disbelievers that were being conned, in this case by a specially created hoax that was in fact part of a larger cosmic conspiracy involving, you guessed it, me.

> Recently a story we avoided at Raiders News Update but that flourished elsewhere on the web told of a giant Leviathan-type creature discovered in the polar ice of Franz Josef Land. The colossal being was described as having horns *"immense in dimension"* that protruded from its head *"with incredible length. The body is covered with a combination of coarse fur and what can best be described as 'body armor' (like an American armadillo)—protects its enormous joints and head..."*
>
> The story included video and audio reports. Steve Quayle did some investigative work and after talking to the helicopter pilot in the Leviathan Video, determined it was a fake. Evidently Sony had hired a team to create a docudrama for a new playstation game called "Shadow of the Colossus."
>
> Or *is* that what happened? Further research suggests this *could be* another classic MIB bait-and-switch scenario designed to throw people off the trail of legitimate recovery efforts at or near the Franz Josef site. During RNU's own investigate research we uncovered several interesting and potentially telling pieces of the puzzle not the least of which involves P.J. Capelotti — senior lecturer in anthropology and American studies at Penn State University Abington College in Abington — conducting extensive archaeological studies of several polar expedition sites including Franz Josef Land (where the hoax was perpetuated). Capelotti followed his polar studies with a thesis on the need to establish international laws and/or treaties *preserving alien artifacts.* Among other things, Capelotti pointed out that:

> The late biochemist and science fiction writer Isaac Asimov once speculated that the galaxy may contain 325 million planets with traces of civilizations in ruins. Perhaps our astronomers and their SETI stations are hearing only static through their radio telescopes because they are, in effect, listening for a message from the extraterrestrial equivalent of the ancient Maya or the Sumerians — dead civilizations that can speak to us now only through archaeology. Constructing a catalog of visual signatures of advanced civilizations will someday be within the province of aerospace archaeology. And with a potential cultural resource database of 325

million planets with civilizations in ruins, there sure is a lot of fieldwork to do "out there."

Did Capelotti's team discover something in Franz Josef Land and/or elsewhere needing international protection … something that corresponds to artificial remains elsewhere in the galaxy that also needs international protection … something big enough, let's say, to hire Sony to concoct a cover-up? As extraordinary as that sounds, history proves repeatedly that governments have participated in similar scenarios on more than one occasion.[1]

I wish I could say that I had gained access to a "stargate," or uncovered an alien life form in Franz Josef Land. We did locate, study, and eventually identify the wreck of the Soviet TB-3 bomber that had been originally photographed fifteen years earlier by my polar ethnologist colleague Susan Barr. (And, as is any researcher's responsibility, published the results just as fast as possible. The conspiracist's usual notion that an academic in the modern world of publish or perish would deliberately choose not to publish is probably a more far-fetched idea than finding an alien creature in the Arctic!) The reality of my archaeological research in the Arctic, which has proceeded in fits and starts since 1993, was somewhat different, but no less fascinating.

2. "Prehistoric" Aviation

I clung by my fingernails to the side of a high narrow ridge, near the crest of a rocky Arctic island called Danskøya. Loose scree scudded down the steep slope each time I grappled my way upwards. Danskøya (Norwegian for Dane's Island) is only 1,100 windswept kilometers from the North Pole; the nearest telephone was 160 kilometers away; the nearest town, more than 300. Oslo, the capital of Norway and farther north than northern Labrador, was well over 1,600 kilometers to my south. Few archaeologists conduct research this far north — there is little land and few possibilities for cultural research beyond Danskøya, and no one had ever done aviation archaeology at this latitude.

I was suddenly struck by an irony. Too nearsighted to be the astronaut of my boyhood dreams, here I was exploring the closest thing our planet has to the cold surface of Mars. The fact that within ten years NASA would be using Svalbard as an analog for the exploration of the Martian surface only served to intensify the intersection between this extreme environment and the archaeological remains of human attempts to leave Earth and explore new frontiers.

Scrambling to the top of the ridge, I gained the view I had worked for half of my life to see. Here was the desolate shoreline of Virgo Harbor where, in 1906, the American journalist and explorer Walter Wellman had established a base camp from which he hoped to explore the polar basin and the pole itself from the air. From this small and historic arctic harbor on the northeast corner of Danskøya, Wellman launched three airship expeditions in search of the geographic North Pole, two of which actually succeeded in leaving

Figure 4.2. A polar base of the past: Walter Wellman's polar airship base and hangar in the Norwegian Arctic, 1909. (Credit: The Aerial Age.)

the ground. Wellman abandoned his camp in the incomparable month of September 1909, the month that both Robert Peary and Frederick Cook claimed to have reached the Pole — Cook in 1908 and Peary a year later. It was also the same month in which the claims of Cook and Peary would cause the Norwegian explorer Roald Amundsen to abandon his own search for the North Pole and turn toward the south, putting him on a collision course with the British Antarctic explorer Robert Falcon Scott and leading ultimately to the death of Scott and his entire polar party.

Now, in the short Arctic summer of 1993, the ruins of Wellman's hangar, collapsed on the stony shoreline like some prehistoric beast, awaited an archaeological survey. Clouds of kittiwakes buzzed past the ridge, shrieking in laughter at the remains of the human folly below. To me the sight was anything but foolish. It was instead majestic, even magnificent, an archaeological tribute to a biocultural human imperative to explore. I would have taken a picture of it if my camera wasn't at the bottom of the harbor, where I had dropped it on my first day on the island. (As it sank beneath the surface I envied the quadruple redundancy enjoyed by NASA astronauts.)

In the months and years that followed my summer in Svalbard, I would often be asked why it had been necessary to journey 8,000 kilometers from my home base in Philadelphia in order to study aeronautical artifacts in such a bleak place. Couldn't one get all the details about Wellman's expeditions from books, or from visits to an air museum? (Or, as one acerbic critic wrote in response to the very idea of aerospace archaeology, "Go ask your grandfather.") Even while still doing field research on the uninhabited Danskøya, several cruising yachts carrying Arctic tourists visited Virgo Harbor; as I gave them a brief guided tour and description of the place it was the one question I could be certain would be asked each time. *What is an archaeologist doing in a place like this?*

Like many a seemingly simple question, the answer was anything but simple. I knew in general terms, of course, that archaeological theory had long accepted very recently discarded artifacts as worthy subjects for archaeological analysis. But there was something even more basic about the polar airship base camp and its associated materials that placed them in a new and unique classification never before seen in the history of human culture. It was this new classification that was proving so elusive, and it was years before the problem began to sort itself.

It was true that many details of such expeditions as Wellman's polar airships could be dug out of books and other primary documents. But, in Wellman's case, for example, he had left behind no plans, no diary and, in the United States, at least, preciously few photographs. There was more than enough to get the general outlines of what he had tried to achieve, but the fine details of the Arctic landscape and the new technologies he tried to use there were always missing.

Ordinarily, in such a case, an archaeologist could plan a visit to a museum or other collection to examine the "type specimen" of a species or a machine, the prototype or preserved model against which to compare all other finds from the field. But there was no museum where one could visit to look at a preserved Arctic airship or its unique propulsion systems, instruments, or supplies.

It is true that museums can perform amazing jobs of interpreting such "building-friendly" artifacts as historic First World War biplanes or Mars rovers; but the dinosaurs of aerospace history — Zeppelins, transoceanic flying boats, Saturn V rockets, turn-of-the-century polar dirigibles, or the four-engine TB-3 we surveyed at Rudolf Island — these are immense curatorial problems and as such are rarely preserved much less put on permanent display. Balloons and airships in particular, because most of their form is simply empty space, do not make ideal candidates for a museum collection. It is more often the case that a museum visitor will see a scale model of such behemoths rather than the behemoth itself.

So, for someone interested in the fine details of how a massive polar airship was put together in 1906, for example, the only place to see such an artifact is in the "open-air museum" of the shoreline of Virgo Harbor on Danskøya in the Norwegian Arctic — just as the only place to see any surviving remnants of a U.S. Navy *Akron*-class airship is under the sea, where both of them sank in the 1930s. Only three hangars were ever designed specifically to house polar airships, and all three were built in the Svalbard archipelago; the ruins of two of them lay on the shoreline at Virgo Harbor.

In the early 1930s, the Russian geophysicist Yevgeny Fedorov was conducting research on Rudolf Island, not far from where we surveyed the giant Soviet aircraft. Even in Fedorov's time, he could see that Rudolf Island was a museum of relics from the history of polar exploration. His chapter is even entitled: "Summer in a Museum." As the snow melted that summer, frame buildings and assorted other remains began to appear. Fedorov identified the main ruins at Teplitz Bay as those of the 1903–1905 expedition of the American Anthony Fiala, who spent two winters in Franz Josef Land in a desultory attempt to reach the North Pole. Clearing a path into Fiala's expedition hut, Fedorov writes that he

> found the most amazing things there — even a small printing press on which the expedition journal was printed instead of our more simple wall newspaper. There were also many small US flags. We chopped one package containing several dozen flags out of the snow, and there were many more such packages. Apparently Fiala had prepared to discover many unknown lands....
>
> Many expeditions left traces here. In effect it was a museum telling about the race to the Pole at the turn of the century. That museum should be put in order.[2]

The ruins at Virgo Harbor on Danskøya are a similar type of museum. They mark a kind of "prehistoric" space age, when explorers operated largely free from either government funding or government control, and piloted vehicles that did not have to take into account any other aircraft, spacecraft or, for that matter, telephone poles! Yet no one had ever mapped these aeronautical base camps on Danskøya. Right up until a few months prior to my journey to the Arctic, the "common knowledge" was that there was not much to see. It was a visit by the archaeologist John Bockstoce to Virgo Harbor that provided me with a remarkable series of photographs of the site, which showed that, far from being a barren ground, Virgo Harbor was a rich vein of archaeological materials.

But the question kept coming: were not these materials too recent to be considered archaeological? The ruins at Virgo Harbor, if it was even thought of in an archaeological manner, were considered too new, too radical a departure from archaeology's traditional focus on stone tools and primitive society. Fedorov's idea — which was extremely radical for 1933!— that a polar museum could easily be founded on the turn-of-the-century remains at Teplitz Bay, less than thirty years after they had been deposited there, would not become a common thought in archaeological theory for another half-century.

Part of this feeling stemmed from the long-standing dismissal of aviation archaeology by academic professionals as the province of amateur groups seeking Amelia Earhart's lost *Electra* in the Pacific, or any one of several other famous wrecks. The immense value of some salvaged and restored aircraft, moreover, had turned much of what was considered aviation archaeology into a cannibalistic race by treasure salvagers to locate individual parts and even entire airframes in order to complete the work of various historic aircraft restoration projects.

Consequently, and until recently, little work had been done, on even a basic level, toward using this part of the archaeological record as a tool to elucidate particular events and general trends in aeronautical history. Neither had it been applied to the far more complex process of offering general propositions about human behaviors, behaviors for which it is especially suited to comment upon, like the human urge to explore, to fly, and to seek out all those "new worlds and new civilizations" that aeronautical technology opened up to us. Such research, one could argue, only grows in importance the more dependent we become upon technology, to the point of becoming a spacefaring species that of necessity would be required to live a kind of ambulatory, cocoon existence if we are to directly explore other celestial geographies.

So, in addition to the technological details of historic expeditions that sought to reach a very human conceit and construction like the North Pole, the archaeological remains at Virgo Harbor might also provide some direct connection with early polar explorers and their world. If one could reach back into Walter Wellman and his world, it might then be possible to reach forward from Wellman's world to our own. The site on Danskøya, despite being disturbed over the course of the twentieth century by small knots of chill tourists, tracks of reindeer and polar bear, by ice and snow and rock slides, could, one had to believe, provide such connections.

Then of course there was that nagging theoretical question that wouldn't go away. What exactly was the basic principle about the polar airship base camp in particular and aerospace remains in general that placed them in a new and unique classification never before seen in the history of archaeology? The location of such remains in extreme environments was a central element of the dilemma, but matching the location to the principle continued to be elusive.

And that location presented serious problems. Virgo Harbor is a very remote place and it is anything but simple to spend more than a few hours there. It is cold, of course, with near-constant fogs and drizzle, and one must account for free-roaming polar bears for which the area is home and all life forms within it a potential source of food. The fact that you can read a book, speak French, or carry a camera does not make you any less desirable as dinner to a polar bear. My friend and polar guide Magnus Forsberg goes so far as to call them the Great White Monsters, never to be toyed or trifled with. In addition, the area of Northwest Spitsbergen holds innumerable historic ruins, along with a magnificent natural landscape and proximity to the polar ice cap that is a magnet for visitors. For all of these reasons and more, almost all tourist visits to Virgo Harbor last less than an hour.

But the human brain needs at the very least several weeks in order to process connections on a much-disturbed archaeological site. As a professor once remarked to a group of us students, the best way to train to be an archaeologist was to do jigsaw puzzles. In this I am inclined to agree. The ability to stare at the same cluster of objects for minutes, hours, or days on end until a connection is made is at the very heart of archaeological research.

But until 1993 no aviation historian or archaeologist had ever set foot on Danskøya to stare at the thousands of artifacts there, to learn what they might reveal about Wellman, about aerospace exploration in its infancy, or about what it might say about human exploration now and in the future. One expected no dramatic frozen bodies to be found, like those strewn over the high Arctic by explorers from Willem Barents to Sir John Franklin, but there was hope of finding some traces of pioneering aerospace technologies or, at the very least, the airship hangars themselves, which could be plainly discerned from the photographs sent to me by John Bockstoce. One could then use these remains to open an archaeological door to the history of polar aeronautics at the turn of the century, and then walk through that door to a new theoretical understanding of human exploration.

3. "Daring in His Conceptions"

Between 1896 and 1930, no less than eight attempts were made to fly from Svalbard to the North Pole in balloons and airships. A Swedish engineer attempted the flight in a free-floating balloon named *Örnen* (*The Eagle*) in 1896 and again in 1897; Wellman tried in his airship called *America* in the summers of 1906, '07, and '09; the Norwegian explorer Roald Amundsen achieved the pole in the dirigible *Norge* in 1926; and the Italian airship designer and pilot Umberto Nobile reached the pole two years later in the airship *Italia*. Three of these aeronautical expeditions crashed on their way to the pole, Nobile's crashed on the way back. Amundsen succeeded in reaching the pole and returning safely, while three of the expeditions never got off the ground.

One of the crashes belongs to the enigmatic Swede, Salomon August Andrée. Two of the crashes and one of the never-got-off-the-grounds belong to Wellman. The spectacular failures of the Andrée and Wellman expeditions created on a remote shoreline in the Arctic an as yet unwritten catalog of archaeological remains relating to the first attempts at scientific aerial exploration in the Arctic. The catalog remains unwritten because history does not deal kindly with failures and, as manifest failures, Andrée and Wellman have been largely forgotten by history.

Wellman had earlier launched two sledging expeditions in search of the North Pole, one from Svalbard in 1894 and one from Franz Josef Land in 1899. The 1894 voyage reached 81° N extremely rapidly, but there Wellman's ship was caught in the ice and sunk, creating the world's northernmost shipwreck — a dubious record Wellman held for ten years when Fiala's expedition ship was lost in a storm at the even farther north Tepliz Bay.

In 1899, Wellman reached another degree further north before breaking his leg off the east coast of Rudolf Island. Subsequent to this expedition, Wellman grew more determined than ever both to reach the pole and to wrestle the technology of exploration out of the sails and sledges of the nineteenth century and, like a true-life Jules Verne character, thrust it into the promising new century of air and space.

His early failures convinced Wellman that the only true route to the Pole lay through the air. In 1897, Andrée had sought the Pole by floating from Danskøya in a balloon controlled only by drag-ropes. Andrée vanished with his two companions and their remains were not discovered for more than three decades. (Virgo Harbor is in fact named after Andrée's supply ship.)

Wellman proposed instead that a dirigible airship — that is, a powered airship capable of being steered and of fighting headwinds — could reach the Pole from Andrée's launch point at Virgo Harbor in about twenty-four hours. After a flight in 1907 that covered about thirty kilometers and another that went about 100 kilometers in 1909, Wellman abandoned his northern base camp in September 1909, never to return again.

As daring turn-of-the-century polar airship flights, Wellman's expeditions were colossal failures (as one newspaper opined, "[Wellman] has always been daring in his conceptions, but rather backward in his performances"). Nevertheless, they blazed a technological trail that other explorers, notably Amundsen and Nobile, soon followed. As Wellman himself enjoyed pointing out, when the pole was finally and unquestionably attained by Amundsen's airship *Norge* in 1926, it was done with the aeronautical methods of Wellman, not the sledging tortures of Peary. Wellman lived to see the day when the *Norge* lifted off from a hangar just south of Danskøya, reached the Pole, and continued on across the top of the world to Alaska.

Our survey of Wellman's base camp located the wrecks of the two different airships Wellman used on his polar flights. (The fuel tank for his 1909 dirigible looks much like a solid rocket booster for the space shuttle.) Original ballast bags lay underneath the collapsed hangar, still filled with rocks, as if awaiting the return of the airship from the pole. A wooden funnel behind the hangar still channeled icy water from a spring toward the ruins of Wellman's hut, as if the old aeronaut himself would somehow appear and take a drink after ninety years' absence.

The details of these and other artifacts found on the site are beginning to reveal much of Wellman's world, details unavailable in the written record. As they do, they open up whole new avenues of questions. One day, by combining all the small artifactual details recorded on dozens of sites from the history of polar aviation and exploration, we should be able to say something about the seemingly biological need for the human species to explore. This aerospace archaeology can and must address this central hypothesis. If we can study and isolate the processes by which humans adapt technology to explore such extreme environments as the Arctic, we may gain insights that will aid or even propel our movement as a species into the solar system and beyond.

4. Aerospace Artifacts as the Subject of Archaeological Study

Questions of the veracity of accounts of polar aeronautical expeditions concern much more than what might appear as mere quibbling over seeming historical trivia or something one can easily answer by asking Grandpa. On a grand scale, the twentieth century stands as the first in which the human species rose above Earth to study both its own habitat and its capability to visit and potentially inhabit other worlds. Questions of where, how, and why humankind first sought to use air and space technology for scientific and geographic exploration have a direct bearing on behavioral questions of why we have become, as Ben Finney writes, the "most inquisitive, exploring animal."

In addition, the worldwide development and application of aeronautical technology in the twentieth century has created an enormous and largely unexplored resource base of aviation sites and wrecks that could be employed to examine the implications of Finney's hypothesis. Increasingly, however, and perhaps inevitably, such resources are under pressure from expeditions organized, mounted, and patronized under the title of "aviation archaeology."

But is there such a thing? If so, what is it? And does it have any relation to systematic archaeological investigation like those carried out in search of Olduwan industry tools in the Rift Valley of East Africa or those probing the geographic limits of the Movius Line? Such questions as these were just beginning to be asked when I began my doctoral reading in archaeology, as salvage operations of historic aircraft were meeting with either great success or, in some cases, catastrophic failure.

Aside from the professional job accomplished in recovering Salomon August Andrée's base camp on White Island in 1930, aerospace archaeology in Arctic regions until now has been dominated by amateur efforts of various levels of skill and intention, wherein the principle object has been an antiquarian desire to remove principle objects, either for restoration or sale or both.

Such work has been accomplished with complete success in western Greenland, where the Stinson monoplane *Greater Rockford* that crashed in 1928 was recovered in 1968; with partial success in southern Greenland, where part of a flight of Lockheed P-38 Lightnings and a Boeing B-17 lost in 1942 were removed from under 80m of ice in the 1980s; and with disastrous results in northwest Greenland, when an attempt to refurbish and fly off the ice cap a Boeing B-29 crashed in 1947 led to the complete destruction of the craft by fire in 1995 and its subsequent abandonment by those who sought to retrieve it.

All things considered, such mini-epics seem the very model of productive adventuring and pluck and, with the exception of the B-29 incineration, rather harmless entertainment. However, to those who would study such wreck sites for what they can tell us about the progression of earthbound humans into the third dimensions of air and space, or the ways in which our technological society wages war, such salvage adventures often dredge up unintended consequences, none of them very obvious at the time.

More often than not, it seems, salvers destroy the very thing they seek. In 1986, salvers discovered a Handley Page Hampden bomber in 600 feet of water near Vancouver, the sole intact survivor of 160 produced in Canada during World War II. Items that could have provided material evidence of bomber training in the war were recovered without their positions being recorded and, in any case, the aircraft was itself torn to pieces during the salvage.

More recently, in a failed attempt to retrieve a Curtiss F9C-2 Sparrowhawk from the wreck of the Navy airship *Macon*, salvers wrenched apart sections of the airship instead. A B-24 Liberator was plucked from the bottom of the Mediterranean in 1995 after half a century undersea — with the remains of three crew members still on board. The recovery was undertaken before even a rudimentary recording of the aircraft's position and condition or the human remains inside had been undertaken, much less completed.

This state of affairs is in part to be expected. Let us be generous and give aeronautical artifact hunters the benefit of the doubt that they actually do care about understanding why wreck sites occur, or why they exist in the states they do, and what they might tell us. While not forgiving their chronic ignorance of archaeological method, to be fair to these mostly well-meaning souls it must be said that no organized body of theory or set of standardized methods exists to guide them.

Professional restoration teams have done spectacular work in reconstructing aircraft salvaged from wreck and other sites. Such sites have been documented frequently in the past, usually by local hobbyist groups or governmental cultural resource evaluation teams, and include the occasional survey find (like the aircraft engine surveyed in Antarctica by Spude and Spude in 1993), and wreck sites identified by the submerged cultural resources surveys of the National Park Service.

World War II sites, including wrecked aircraft, have been documented in the Aleutians and the Seward Peninsula in Alaska by the U.S. Fish & Wildlife Service and the National Park Service, respectively. The Seward Peninsula project documented a number of B-24 Liberators which made forced landings prior to reaching the Soviet Union as part of the bomber supply program. A colleague who visited one of the Liberators found intact the papers and personal effects of the pilots (women in this case).

But identifying any theoretical underpinnings in the arena of aerospace archaeology generally and professionally is another matter altogether, for the sub-field is enduring the kind of slow infancy in many ways reminiscent of the maritime and industrial archaeologies of the 1950s and 1960s. Aviation archaeology in the late 1970s and 1980s proceeded on the notion that the study of wrecked aircraft is a form of archaeological research. Yet the hopeful employment of the word "archaeology" has not served to make this work anything more than antiquarianism — the collection of old things for personal pleasure — albeit antiquarianism in a highly entertaining form.

This infancy of aviation archaeology is being followed by an adolescence that still includes a preponderant focus on individual aircraft wrecks, but is witnessing a new focus on more broad-based studies of contextual sites and base camps and the relation of these aeronautical sites to larger historical and anthropological themes. The term "aerospace archaeology" was appropriate during this phase of the field's development, if for no other reason than it was hoped that we would eventually include the study of sites from the space age, which are increasingly important to the study of modern man as the technological possibilities continue their course of altering the possibilities of human evolution.

But the challenge for archaeologists who would study wrecked aircraft or aerospace sites is a large one. Thousands of sites exist where operational aircraft have been brought to earth by accident, warfare, or obsolescence. Equivalent numbers of abandoned air *ports* testify to the base camps necessary to operate in the aerospace environment. These concepts are critical for the study of aerospace artifacts. The closest analogs we have to the deposit of spacecraft on other celestial bodies are those aeronautical remains that survive in the polar regions. But these remains vary widely in their level of preservation. While there are similarities in the states of environmental preservation as well as destruction of artifacts and sites in space and the polar regions, we are only now contemplating the beginnings of a space tourism industry. It is therefore instructive to add a few words about the historic transformation of sites in the Arctic and Antarctic, where tourists and hunters and scientists have modified the material culture of exploration for well over a century.

The sheer tonnage of aeronautical and other supplies, structures, fuels, chemicals, and means of transport emplaced by Wellman on the Virgo shoreline has made an inviting target for systemic behaviors like salvage and reuse by hunters and trappers, and relic collecting and trampling by tourists, journalists, and scientific parties. In a natural and cultural resource-scarce environment (cultural resource used here in a systemic context), the abundant wood and metalwork on the site made it practically a warehouse for winter trappers.

Visiting Virgo Harbor in 1912, Fridtjof Nansen gazed upon the remains of Wellman's base camp and remarked that they were the "ruins of that great humbug…. The workshop where they made hydrogen gas was still standing. Most of the things of value, especially those made of metal, had been stolen, but a lot was still left. The trappers and the tourists did not have time to get it all yet."[3]

Yet, even given the extensive reuse, looting, and other formation processes at work on aerospace base camps, they remain the foundational databases of aerospace archaeology. Explorations of air and space in the accelerated twentieth century required such intensive and elaborate base camps, a gathering of resources in a single location in order to project technological explorers on episodic voyages into unexplored regions. These camps can be examined with a view toward eliciting broad patterns that may hold across cultures, to generate testable hypotheses regarding human behavior as it is fundamentally changed by the use of aerospace technology.

These camps can also provide archaeological screens through which to filter lingering historically particular questions regarding the motives, seriousness, and innovations of early polar explorers. In this way, while we cannot ask questions of the creators of sites from the heroic age of polar aerial exploration as directly as a Finney can interview a modern-day astronaut or observe the launch of a space vehicle, we can use both documentary and material investigations of polar aerial base camps to reshape our view of mankind's earliest attempts to lift itself forcibly into the third dimension. Controlled use of documentary sources, sifted through a screen of archaeological data, must invariably produce truer baselines with which to write historical particulars, construct cultural chronology, and offer the basis for a truer analysis of cultural change.

As Richard Gould pointed out, however, the trick at any archaeological site is to determine not just how a site has been changed but, conversely, how the formation processes at work on both the material residues and the contextual surround may have frozen aspects of the site essentially in place. In other, more classical terms, we can describe this process as the evaluation of Rome versus Pompeii, sites disrupted and disturbed, salvaged, rebuilt, and reused (Rome), versus sites where whole contexts have been preserved as they existed at a particular time and place (Pompeii).

For example, we earlier mentioned the wreck of the USS *Macon*, sunk off the coast of California in the Pacific in 1935 and later disturbed in order to retrieve one of its Sparrowhawk aircraft. Yet, in light of Gould's cautionary words, we can say that at least these sites undeniably exist. The ocean may — indeed does — work on them, with oceanographic forces the late underwater archaeologist Keith Muckleroy identified as filters and scramblers.

Yet the ocean has also, in large measure, preserved them. Witness, to the contrary, the formation processes that worked, and worked very quickly, on a similar U.S. Navy airship, the USS *Shenandoah*, brought out of the sky in two pieces by a line squall over Ohio, in September 1925:

> First came the rescuers. They did everything they could to make it easier for the stunned survivors. Then the officers, leaving the enlisted men to guard the wreckage, hurried … to set up emergency headquarters.
>
> Soon came the looters. They came in buggies, buckboards, and broken-down Model-T Fords. Within hours curious thousands had crossed the rutted back roads to the [farms where the airship had crashed].
>
> By lunchtime souvenir hunters had torn almost all the covering off both large sections of the ship. Women, carrying yards and yards of fabric from the envelope, left the wrecked fragments of the *Shenandoah*, staggering under their loads. The looters were armed with knives, hatchets, pliers, and even wrenches. They went away with logbooks, girders eight feet long, blankets, and valuable instruments.
>
> Nothing was too small or too large. One man was seen leaving with a huge piece of twisted piping and an armful of girders. A single house slipper was sticking out of his pocket.
>
> At the crew space a man found an aluminum locker. It was locked, but a hammer soon opened it. Half a dozen enterprising men and women quickly cleaned out canned soup, condensed milk, and other supplies.
>
> They worked while the surviving enlisted men tried to keep guard. Still dazed, the men didn't know how to stop the pillage. Soon the two main sections of the ship — miles apart — looked like skeletons picked to the bones....
>
> At nightfall, in spite of National Guardsmen who threatened to open fire, the looting continued. By morning the control car had been picked clean. Every instrument had been stripped from it, all the toggles ripped out, everything movable torn free. Just the naked hull was left, and even that had been moved twenty yards from the place where it had come to rest. The Annapolis class ring was missing from [*Shenandoah* captain] Zachary Lansdowne's finger.[4]

Until recently, such episodes in aerospace history as the *Shenandoah* saga — along with such fixed remains as the base camps of polar exploration — were ignored as sources of information on human evolution and behavior. Perhaps they were ignored because they contain no native interactive component, or because of the intellectual leap required to see problems seemingly unconnected to the primitive world as connected to the study of all humans. But in the end there is no real intellectual boundary between the primitive and the modern; and polar explorers can tell us as much about human behavior as can a tribe in New Guinea.

Because the technology developed by those who sought the Pole through the air was exclusively Euro-American, it removed the necessity of consultations or cooperation with natives. Indeed, in the case of Spitsbergen, no native population existed. At the time of the Andrée and Wellman expeditions, the islands were terra nullius, a no man's land open to exploration or exploitation by all. Was this removal of any need to interact with natives a consideration of European or American explorers? Probably not an active one. But subconsciously? Perhaps. It was — and to some extent remains — an indelibly racist time, and nineteenth century explorers owed their triumphs in much of Africa in the south and Greenland in the north to the landscape knowledge and logistic skills of native guides. Walter Wellman, for one, preferred the company of Norwegians to that of native Greenlanders, although it is not certain he ever met a member of the latter group, save through the writings of Robert Peary.

Instead, after the polar aerial expeditions of Andrée and Wellman, aerospace technology became the native guide for Western man. In just seventy-three years, that optimistic grouping had accelerated from Salomon Andrée's ignominious failure to launch his hydrogen balloon from Virgo Harbor toward the Pole in the summer of 1896 to Neil Armstrong's giant leap on the lunar surface in the summer of 1969. It is difficult today to know how Wellman might have reacted to the lunar landings. He might have said that humans had merely become more machine-like in their explorations, shedding the muscular infirmities of the human shell for the supposed silicon precision of the computer. More likely he would have seen his efforts as the first in a mightily struggle to take humankind to the deep regions both over the polar sea and into outer space.

It is there that one finally finds the link between the locations of these aerospace remains and the history of archaeological theory. For these remains can be thought of as the very first "planetary artifacts." In other words, they are the first tools fashioned by *Homo sapiens* that can theoretically be found at any point on this or any other planet. This means that the human behavior behind these artifacts is the first truly global human adaptation.

5. The First Planetary Artifacts

As we have noted, it is often the case that traditional histories written about aeronautical polar exploration are almost endlessly jumbled and superficial, so that even a correct chronology, much less a true representation of events, is almost a rare event. As to general questions of cultural and behavioral response in the face of rapid technological progress, accounts of aeronautical polar explorations are almost always unsatisfactory. Turning to primary archival sources as an ameliorative to codified misstatements, as all historians must, can help to clarify some historical particulars. But even here, in many cases, the primary archival record only compounds the inconsistencies and contributes to the curtain of mist that surrounds specific historical events.

Archaeologists are traditionally trained to look for general principles that hold across individual cases, while historians are trained to examine the details of specific events. In the case of aeronautical history and its developing archaeology, these twin complimentary disciplines must shed the preconceptions that handicap the historian as a specifier, and the archaeologist as a generalizer. The historical record cannot be accepted as "the final word," and instead must be tested, or filtered, through "screens" constructed by the material remains left behind by the aeronauts and explorers themselves. Then (and only then) can new avenues of investigations be opened, investigations "triggered" in many instances by individual artifacts that bear on particular historical or culturally general questions.

Once we establish that we can use particular historical data to look at broad questions, and generalizing archaeological data to look at tiny historical specifics, it then becomes possible to use "the widest-possible definition of archaeology [with] the use of a great range of documents." After the survey of Wellman's airship base and after relating the material residues there to the historical record, this method became the most direct means to reach under the surface of traditional aerospace and polar history and approach something like credible historical truth. Perhaps more significantly, this method not only allows for the correction of the historical record, but leads the way to new interpretations of that record as well.

In this regard, while "aerospace archaeology" served as an appropriate name for our infant sub-field for the past twenty years, it now seems clear that it has only laid the methodological groundwork for a new field of interdisciplinary research in anthropology and history that we should now refer to as "planetary archaeology." Our aerospace archaeology examined questions of where, how and why the human species uses air and space technology. The "where" question has now been answered: aerospace artifacts are the first and thus far only "planetary artifact," the only material culture of *Homo sapiens* that can be found anywhere on this or any other planet. With such a theoretical basis, the field must now broaden in turn to behavioral questions of humankind as an exploring animal.

As interesting as the particular sites of wrecked aircraft can be, as aviation enthusiasts and historians and archaeologists, we must begin to employ this larger framework and examine these larger questions for several reasons. It forces us to think in new and novel ways about our role in history, and our role in producing, finding, recovering, and preserving the material remains that are the components of the archaeological record that we leave for future generations. But, on a more fundamental level, it enlarges the scope of our efforts and makes them a part of a global effort to understand not only the fossil path of human evolution but it harnesses the explanatory potential of archaeology to speculate on the future course of techno-organic evolution.

And with that we enter a whole new field of enquiry. Aerospace exploration increasingly is conducted remotely, marking a turning point in the traditional theoretical considerations of our biocultural adaptation. Andrée and Wellman took the first steps in removing the burden of expedition transport from the backs of men and elevating the human senses over the polar sea.

Now the human senses have been removed from the equation altogether and replaced by the pure intellect of an individual in front of a computer or a telemetric monitoring station. We must now begin to consider the potential archaeological record created by the actions of machines that in some cases operate on the other side of the solar system from the hand and mind that presumably control them. The AMASE expedition series in Svalbard has already examined a tangential corollary to this notion, by "launching" terrain rovers across the Mars-like surfaces of Svalbard while these rovers are accompanied by human observers. These observers then can match their human observations with the remote, machine-created observations of the machine controller back at the expedition base.

Implicit in this research is the notion that a machine "experiences" a new landscape in a much different way than a human, and that difference must be accounted for if anything like a true representation of an alien landscape is to be returned to Earth by robotic probes. This has implications for all who study human evolution, implications that may not be terribly comfortable to consider at first. It is an anthropological axiom that human behavior must be studied in relation to the environment the humans are occupying. Space probes and remotely operated oceanographic probes operate in environments beyond human adaptability as we now conceive it. By effectively removing the environment as a calculation in the adaptive value of technology, we have taken the first step in developing a theoretical basis for the study, not of human behavior, but the — for want of a better term — behavior of the machines that have begun to explore for us, and how that behavior reflects an originating culture that in future years may exist many light years distant.

These are considerations that go far beyond one individual or one expedition, and lead into general considerations of the courses of technological development and human expansion, and the kinds of imaginative notions that contribute either to success or failure in all explorations of hostile environments. And that brings us to the elusive confluence of location and archaeology: Aerospace artifacts, be they aircraft or spacecraft, are the first tools fashioned by *Homo sapiens* that can theoretically — and for all intents and purposes literally — be found anywhere on the planet.

Such artifacts are unique in that they can be found in archaeological context from the highest mountains to the deepest oceans to the most remote taiga forests. The stone hand axes known as Acheulian tools, for example, are limited in their geographic distribution by the Movius Line, a techno-geographic concept discovered by the American archaeologist Hallam Movius in 1948. Beyond the limits of the Movius Line, one does not excavate Acheulian technology.

While the archaeological features of aerospace culture, the space ports and runways, can generally be traced to a set of environmental characteristics (for example, proximity to the equator for simpler escape from Earth's gravity well for space launch facilities), aerospace artifacts — especially those aircraft and spacecraft used in exploration — have no theoretical limit to their distribution. There is no Movius Line for aerospace archaeology; planetary artifacts nullify all previous attempts to define the limits of human technologies. We can state this principle as a theorem: Planetary artifacts exhibit no definable geographic range; therefore, any artifact whose geographic range cannot be defined is a planetary artifact.

This classification principle has important implications for archaeologists who would study the material culture of *Homo sapiens* on Earth as well as in space, along with the potential for the study of the archaeology of intelligent life elsewhere in the galaxy. As we saw earlier with the vast collection of artifacts on the Moon, *Homo sapiens*'s only planetary artifacts — aerospace technologies — cannot be fit into the same kinds of clusters or ranges or industries that archaeologists traditionally use to split other technologies into comparable categories.

While it is true that we might properly categorize the various and associated facilities required of aircraft and spacecraft — everything from vehicle assembly buildings, runways and launch pads to tracking stations, service, rescue and recovery vehicles — the aircraft and spacecraft themselves, while constructed and fueled and launched from a specific and formal place, can make their transition to their archaeological context literally anywhere on this or any other celestial body in either controlled or uncontrolled landings. For the first time in the history of archaeology, this unique characteristic forces the archaeologist to contemplate a class of artifacts on a planetary scale.

In this section, we will look at the histories, technologies, and archaeological natures of these planetary artifacts scattered throughout the solar system. In so doing we will reach the edge of geography as a calculation in the matrices of archaeological objects. And once we are beyond geography, we enter interstellar space where, once again, the nature of aerospace artifacts will force us to reevaluate even our planetary archaeology, and enter the even more spectacular realm of interstellar archaeology.

5

Artifacts on the Martian Surface

Introduction

Mars, named for the Roman god of war, is a rust-colored neighbor of Earth that holds so many fascinations for humans that it is currently orbited by no less than three different spacecraft (more than any planet save for Earth itself) along with three different probes operating on its surface (including two roving craft creating a series of unique pathways across the planet) that are at work collecting geographic, geologic, and atmospheric data. The remains or wrecks of eleven other spacecraft (or, in archaeological terms, composite tools) sent from Earth to explore Mars form the known archaeology of Mars.

The size, proximity, and desiccated similarities of Mars to a suddenly depopulated Earth-like desert have all combined to give the planet the inescapable character of a landscape intimately entwined with the destiny of *Homo sapiens*. From Percival Lowell's turn-of-the-century theory of non-natural canals on Mars to Brian DePalma's *Mission to Mars* (2000)—and all of the immense body of robotic exploration and Martian-themed literature in between, from the Viking missions to Bradbury's *Martian Chronicles,* from the idea that Phobos might be artificial to Kim Stanley Robinson's spectacular Mars Trilogy—Mars has preoccupied both astronautic mission planners, exobiologists, exoarchaeologists, and science fiction writers and filmmakers for over a century.

Speculative landforms such as the famous "face" in the Cydonia region of the planet, photographed at low resolution during the Viking missions in the 1970s, led to decades of speculation that an advanced civilization once existed there. Such speculation followed, quite naturally, an existing body of writings of which Lowell's planetary canal system was only the most famous.

Given the human fascination with Mars, *Homo sapiens* have been surprisingly slow to send one or more of their fellows there to explore the landscape firsthand. A planned American mission that would have used existing Apollo technology to reach Mars in the early 1980s following the successful manned exploration of the Moon was replaced with the rather desultory development of the space shuttle. Simultaneously, the Saturn V rockets that allowed the human entry into space went unused. They were quickly transformed from their systemic heavy-lift use into a post–primary-use life as museum exhibits.

Figure 5.1. The Mars exploration rover *Spirit* took this unique photograph of its own roadway 16 July 2004. This image is cropped from a wider photomosaic comprised of 364 images called the "Santa Anita Panorama." Like the tracks made by the human-driven rover on the Moon, these robot-created tracks reflect the human tendency to drive in straight lines across unobstructed surfaces. (Credit: NASA/JPL/Cornell.)

In this sense at least, the American exploration of space regressed for twenty-five years until the heavy-lift challenge was taken up by Russia and more recently China.

So the archaeological evidence of the human exploration of Mars is exclusively robotic. Unlike the Moon, where an abundance of sites offers a comparative database between the human and the robotic, on Mars there is only the evidence of composite tools that are operated remotely from Earth. Now, in the year 2010, with the increasing likelihood of micro-organic life on or under the surface of Mars, direct human exploration of the surface may be indefinitely postponed until all of the protocols for the protection and preservation of that life are established.

The archaeological evidence of unmanned missions to Mars begins with the hard impact of the Soviet Union's *Mars 2* lander on the surface of the planet on 27 November 1971. Since that moment, eleven more unmanned expeditions to Mars have (or, in some case, are thought to have) achieved impact on the surface. Seven of these missions were undertaken by the United States and another three by the former Soviet Union. Some, like the 1999 *Mars Polar Lander*, carried additional probes to be deployed simultaneously with the main lander. In 2003, the United Kingdom attempted to land a small probe called *Beagle 2* on Mars, but it is not known whether the spacecraft reached the surface.

This situation truly stretches the definition of composite tool. There is the main bus that carried the lander to Mars, along with all of the entry components required to get the lander from the orbiter to the surface: retro-rockets, heat shields, parachutes, and so forth. This means that many of these entry components exist on the surface of Mars along with the landers, creating a landscape of artifacts scattered according to their mission role and their respective success within those roles. This very assemblage was photographed by the *Mars Global Surveyor* when it located not only the landing of the *Opportunity* probe, but also the associated elements of the *Opportunity*'s landing: the backshell and parachute in one area, the impact site of the heat shield in another, the area where the lander bounced upon impact and its final impact site in a small crater.

Many if not most of these artifacts would not have burned up before or after entry into the Martian atmosphere because that atmosphere is about one-tenth as thick as Earth's. Each of the entry components were jettisoned at a predetermined level and then crashed onto the Martian surface, their systemic purpose complete and their archaeological lives begun.

The Archaeological Catalog

1) *MARS 2*[1]

Along with its near-twin, *Mars 3*, *Mars 2* was designed as a combined bus/orbiter module with an attached descent/lander module. The objective of both missions was basic science on Mars. The goals were to collect imagery of the Martian surface and clouds, begin a study of the topography, composition and physical properties of the surface and gauge its temperature, collect data on the composition of the atmosphere and the strength of the solar wind and the interplanetary and Martian magnetic fields and, finally, to act as a communications relay for transmitting signals from the lander on the Martian surface back to Earth.

The *Mars 2* probe was launched atop a Proton rocket from Baikonur Cosmodrome on 19 May 1971. After attaining Earth orbit, it was launched towards Mars. After mid-course corrections were made in the summer and fall of 1971, the spacecraft arrived in Martian orbit in late November of that year. Four and a half hours before reaching the Red Planet on 27 November 1971, *Mars 2* released its descent module.

As the descent module entered the Martian atmosphere, it came in steeper than planned, suffered a malfunction when its parachutes failed to deploy, and then crashed into the surface. As this was going on, the orbiter was placed into an orbit 1,380 kilometers above the surface of the planet. The Soviet Union announced that the *Mars 2* and *3* missions had ended on 22 August 1972, after the two probes had sent back a total of sixty pictures. These images and the data that accompanied then gave scientists their first glimpse of a planet where mountains were higher than any on Earth, where surface temperatures ranged from -110 Celsius to +13 Celsius, and where water vapor concentrations were 5000 times less than in Earth's atmosphere.

Technical Notes

The attached orbiter/bus and descent module had a mass of approximately 4,650 kilograms at launch (including fuel) and was 4.1 meters high, 5.9 meters across the two solar panel wings, and had a base diameter of two meters. The mass of the orbiter/bus was about 3,440 kilograms fully fueled, and the fueled mass of the descent/lander module was about 1,210 kilograms. The propulsion system was situated at the bottom of the cylindrical spacecraft body and was the main structural element of the orbiter. It consisted of a cylindrical fuel tank divided into separate compartments for fuel and oxidizer. The central part of the main body was composed primarily of this fuel tank. The engine was mounted on a gimbal on the lower surface of the tank. The descent module was mounted on top of the orbiter bus. The two solar arrays extended from the sides of the cylinder and a 2.5-meter-diameter parabolic high-gain communications antenna and radiators were also mounted on the side. The instruments and navigation system were located around the bottom of the craft. Antennas for communications with the lander were affixed to the solar panels. Three low-power, directional antennas extended from the main body near the parabolic antenna.

For scientific experiments (most mounted in a hermetically sealed compartment) the *Mars 2* orbital bus carried a one-kilogram infrared radiometer with an 8- to 40-micron range to determine the temperature of the Martian surface to -100 degrees Celsius; a photometer to conduct spectral analysis by absorption of atmospheric water vapor concentrations in the 1.38-micron line; an infrared photometer; an ultraviolet photometer to detect atomic hydrogen, oxygen, and argon; a Lyman-alpha sensor to detect hydrogen in the upper atmosphere; a visible range photometer covering six narrow ranges between 0.35 and 0.70 microns; a radiotelescope and radiometer instrument to determine the reflectivity of the surface and atmosphere in the visible (0.3 to 0.6 microns) and the radio-reflectivity of the surface in the 3.4-centimeter range and the dielectric permeability to give a temperature estimate to a depth of thirty to fifty centimeters below the surface; and an infrared spectrometer to measure the 2.06-micron carbon dioxide absorption band, allowing an estimate of the abundance along a line of sight to determine the optical thickness of the atmosphere and hence the surface relief.

During the flight to Mars, measurements were made of galactic cosmic rays and solar corpuscular radiation. Eight separate narrow-angle electrostatic plasma sensors were on board to determine the speed, temperature, and composition of the solar wind in the range of thirty to 10,000 eV. A three-axis magnetometer to measure the interplanetary and Martian fields was mounted on a boom extending from one of the solar panels.

Archaeology

The *Mars 2* lander crashed at 45° S, 313° W on 27 November 1971, and at that moment entered its archaeological context. It carried the Soviet Union coat of arms on the body of the lander. It is the first artifact from Earth to reach the surface of Mars.

2) *Mars 3*[2]

History

The *Mars 3* spacecraft was launched atop a Proton rocket from the Baikonur Cosmodrome in the former Soviet Union on 28 May 1971. Like the *Mars 2* mission, the *Mars 3* orbiter was to photograph and study the Red Planet and act as a communications relay to send signals to Earth from a lander that would descend to the surface and conduct further scientific work.

The descent module was released from the main spacecraft on 2 December 1971, about four and a half hours before it reached Mars. It achieved a soft landing but within a matter of seconds the probe's instruments ceased to function.

Technical Notes

The attached orbiter/bus and descent module had a mass of approximately 4,650 kilograms at launch (including fuel) and was 4.1 meters high, 5.9 meters across the two solar panel wings, and had a base diameter of two meters. The mass of the orbiter/bus was about 3,440 kilograms fully fueled, and the fueled mass of the descent/lander module was about 1,210 kilograms. The propulsion system was situated at the bottom of the cylindrical spacecraft body and was the main structural element of the orbiter. It consisted of a cylindrical fuel tank divided into separate compartments for fuel and oxidizer. The central part of the main body was composed primarily of this fuel tank. The engine was mounted on a gimbal on the lower surface of the tank. The descent module was mounted on top of the orbiter bus. The two solar arrays extended from the sides of the cylinder and a 2.5-meter-diameter parabolic high-gain communications antenna and radiators were also mounted on the side. Telemetry was transmitted by the spacecraft at 928.4 MHz. The instruments and navigation system were located around the bottom of the craft. Antennas for communications with the lander were affixed to the solar panels. Three low-power directional antennas extended from the main body near the parabolic antenna.

For scientific experiments (most mounted in a hermetically sealed compartment) the *Mars 3* orbital bus carried a 1-kilograms infrared radiometer with an 8- to 40-micron range to determine the temperature of the Martian surface to -100 degrees Celsius; a photometer to conduct spectral analysis by absorption of atmospheric water vapor concentrations in the 1.38-micron line; an infrared photometer; an ultraviolet photometer to detect atomic hydrogen, oxygen, and argon; a Lyman-alpha sensor to detect hydrogen in the upper atmosphere; a visible range photometer covering six narrow ranges between 0.35 and 0.70 microns; a radiotelescope and radiometer instrument to determine the reflectivity of the surface and atmosphere in the visible (0.3 to 0.6 microns) and the radio-reflectivity of the surface in the 3.4-cm range and the dielectric permeability to give a temperature estimate to a depth of 35 to 50 cm below the surface; and an infrared spectrometer to measure the 2.06-micron carbon dioxide absorption band, allowing an estimate of the abundance along a line of sight to determine the optical thickness of the atmosphere and hence the surface relief.

Radio occultation experiments were also performed when communications transmissions passed through the Martian atmosphere in which the refraction of the signals gave information on the atmospheric structure. During the flight to Mars, measurements were made of galactic cosmic rays and solar corpuscular radiation. Eight separate narrow-angle, electrostatic plasma sensors were on board to determine the speed, temperature, and composition of the solar wind in the range 30 to 10,000 eV. A three-axis magnetometer to measure the interplanetary and Martian fields was mounted on a boom extending from one of the solar panels. The *Mars 3* orbiter also carried a French-built experiment which was not carried on *Mars 2*. Called *Spectrum 1*, the instrument measured solar radiation at metric wavelengths in conjunction with Earth-based receivers to study the cause of solar outbursts. The *Spectrum 1* antenna was mounted on one of the solar panels.

Archaeology

The *Mars 3* lander soft-landed on the Martian surface at 45° S, 158° W, from where it deployed and began to operate. As with the *Mars 2* lander, *Mars 3* contained a small roving vehicle called the Prop-M. This vehicle had two parallel ski-like legs that allowed it to "walk" away from the lander for a total distance of fifteen meters, which was the length of the cable that kept the robot tethered to the lander. The Prop-M robot had a mass of 4.5 kilograms. An arm on the lander would place the rover on the surface, while television cameras on the lander recorded its progress across the surface.

The total mass of the descent module was 1,210 kilograms. The total mass of the landing capsule was 358 kilograms. When the lander made contact with the surface, four pedals unfolded to expose the internal workings of the lander. The craft was sterilized prior to launch to prevent contamination and contained a plaque with the Soviet coat of arms.

The rover never had the chance to deploy, however. A minute and a half after touching down, the lander began to transmit data via the orbiter to Earth. However, just 20 seconds later, the lander shut down for reasons that are still unknown. At the moment it ceased to function, the lander entered its archaeological context. The lander consisted of three main parts: a spherical 1.2-meter diameter landing capsule, a 2.9-meter-diameter conical breaking shield, and a parachute and retro rockets. The parachute, retro rockets, and conical breaking shield were jettisoned from the spacecraft, but may still be located on the Martian surface.

3) MARS 6[3]

History

The Soviet *Mars* probes *4–7* were an associated group of spacecraft launched towards the Red Planet in July and August 1973. The *Mars 6* spacecraft was comprised of a probe that would drop off a descent lander and then continue on past Mars and into heliocentric orbit. It was launched atop a Proton rocket from Baikonur Cosmodrome in the former Soviet Union on 5 August 1973.

Mars 6 reached the Red Planet on 12 March 1974 and released its lander as it passed on by. As the lander descended through the Martian atmosphere, it transmitted data to Earth via the bus that had transported it. All signs pointed to a successful landing, but data transmission abruptly ceased as the lander reached the surface. The transmitted data also turned out to have a flaw in it that caused it to be unreadable.

Technical Notes

The *Mars 6* descent module carried a panoramic telephotometer to image the Martian surface around the lander, atmospheric temperature, pressure, density, and wind sensors; an accelerometer to measure atmospheric density during the descent; a mass spectrometer to estimate atmospheric composition; a radio altimeter; an activation analysis experiment to study soil composition; and mechanical properties soil sensors. The flyby module contained a telephotometer to image the planet, a Lyman alpha sensor to search for hydrogen in the upper atmosphere, a magnetometer, an ion trap and narrow-angle electrostatic plasma sensor to study the solar wind and its interaction with Mars, solar cosmic ray sensors, micrometeorite sensors, and a French-supplied solar radiometer to measure solar long-wavelength radio emissions. It was also equipped to perform a radio occultation experiment to profile the atmosphere and ionosphere.

Archaeology

The *Mars 6* descent/lander transmitted just over 220 seconds of data as it descended, before its impact with the surface and the end of its systemic life. The impact point of the *Mars 6* lander was at 23.90° S, 19.42° W, in the Margaritifer Sinus region of Mars.

4) VIKING 1[4]

History

Viking 1 was part of a twin spacecraft expedition to explore Mars. Each exploratory probe had both an orbital vehicle and a lander. Given the long fascination with Mars as a potential location for extraterrestrial life, the lander was placed inside a bioshield at launch to prevent contamination by terrestrial organisms.

Viking 1 was launched atop a Titan IIIE-Centaur rocket from Cape Canaveral on 20 August 1975. It took ten months to reach Mars. The spacecraft was placed into orbit around the Red Planet on 19 June 1976. From its height of slightly more than 1,500 km above the surface, the probe began to image the planet and from these images a suitable landing site was chosen.

On 20 July 1976, the lander separated from the orbiter and made a descent to the surface, the first spacecraft to make a successful soft-landing on Mars. The orbiter went on to study the Martian moon Phobos in a close flyby in February 1977. By 1980, with its fuel running low, the orbiter was placed in an orbit some 56,000 km above the surface. There it is thought to be safe from hitting and possibly contaminating the surface until the year 2019.

After its descent to Mars, the lander deployed its scientific instruments and began transmitting images of the surface just 25 seconds after landing. The seismometer and sampler arm did not function properly at first, but the other scientific experiments all deployed as planned. The mission of this probe was complex and multi-layered: it acted as a data-collection station for the specific question of whether life existed on Mars and the more fundamental problem of the origins and evolution of life itself; and it was a research station for specific questions of the geology and atmosphere of Mars and the more generalized planetary questions of the formation and development of the solar system itself. Until it ceased operation, the lander returned over 3,000 images of the Martian surface, from scanning cameras that could photograph not just the immediate area around the lander but also the Martian sky and its moons.

Technical Notes

The lander consisted of a six-sided aluminum base with an alternate 1.09 meters and .56 meters for the sides, supported on three extended legs attached to the shorter sides. The leg footpads formed the vertices of an equilateral triangle with 2.21-meter sides when viewed from above, with the long sides of the base forming a straight line with the two adjoining footpads. Instrumentation was attached to the top of the base, elevated above the surface by the extended legs. Power was provided by two radioisotope thermal generator (RTG) units containing Plutonium 238 affixed to opposite sides of the lander base and covered by wind screens. Each generator was twenty-eight centimeters tall, fifty-eight centimeters in diameter, had a mass of 13.6 kilograms and provided 30 watts of continuous power at 4.4 volts. Four wet-cell sealed, nickel-cadmium, eight-amp-hour, twenty-eight-volt rechargeable batteries were also onboard to handle peak power loads.

Propulsion was provided for deorbit by a monopropellant hydrazine ($N2H4$) rocket with twelve nozzles arranged in four clusters of three that provided 32 N thrust, giving a delta-V of 180 meters per second. These nozzles also acted as the control thrusters

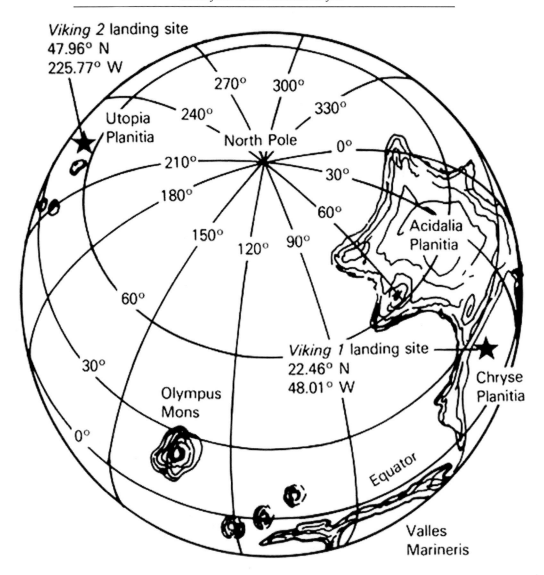

Figure 5.3. A view from above the Martian North Pole showing the locations of the landing sites of the Viking probes. (Credit: Ezell and Ezell, p. 356.)

for translation and rotation of the lander. Terminal descent and landing was achieved by three monopropellant hydrazine engines (one affixed on each long side of the base, separated by 120 degrees). The engines had eighteen nozzles to disperse the exhaust and minimize effects on the ground. The hydrazine was purified to prevent contamination of the Martian surface. The lander carried eighty-five kilograms of propellant at launch, contained in two spherical titanium tanks mounted on opposite sides of the lander beneath the RTG windscreens, giving a total launch mass of 657 kilograms. Control was achieved through the use of an inertial reference unit, four gyros, an aero-de-celerator, a radar altimeter, a terminal descent and landing radar, and the control thrust-ers.

A steerable two-axis high-gain parabolic antenna was mounted on a boom near one edge of the lander base. An omnidirectional low-gain S-band antenna also extended from the base. This antenna allowed for communication directly with Earth. A UHF (381-MHz) antenna provided a one-way relay to the orbiter using a thirty-watt relay radio. Data storage was on a tape recorder, and the lander computer had a 6,000-word memory for command instructions.

The lander carried instruments to achieve the primary scientific objectives of the lander mission: to study the biology, chemical composition (organic and inorganic), mete-orology, seismology, magnetic properties, appearance, and physical properties of the Mar-tian surface and atmosphere. Two 360-degree cylindrical scan cameras were mounted near one long side of the base. From the center of this side extended the sampler arm, with a collector head, temperature sensor, and magnet on the end. A meteorology boom, holding temperature, wind direction, and wind velocity sensors, extended out and up from the top of one of the lander legs. A seismometer, magnet and camera test targets, and magnifying mirror were mounted opposite the cameras, near the high-gain antenna. An interior, environmentally controlled compartment held a biology experiment and a gas chromatograph mass spectrometer. The X-ray fluorescence spectrometer was also mounted within the structure. A pressure sensor was attached under the lander body. The scientific payload had a total mass of approximately 91 kilograms.

Archaeology

After separation and landing, the lander had a mass of about 600 kilograms and the orbiter 900 kilograms. The *Viking 1* lander touched down in western Chryse Planitia at 22.697° N latitude and 48.222° W longitude. After landing, the spacecraft retained approximately twenty-two kilograms of propellants. Components of the spacecraft that were jettisoned during the landing included the bioshield, aeroshell and heat shield, and the parachutes.

The probe continued returning data to Earth until contact was lost on 13 November 1982 and it entered its archaeological context. Earlier that year, the *Viking 1* lander had been re-named the Thomas Mutch Memorial Station, to honor of the leader of the Viking imaging team.

5) *VIKING 2*[5]

History

Viking 2 was launched atop a Titan IIIE-Centaur from Cape Canaveral, Florida, on 9 September 1975. As with *Viking 1*, this spacecraft consisted of an orbiter and a lander, and the lander was encased in a bioshield at launch to prevent contamination by terrestrial

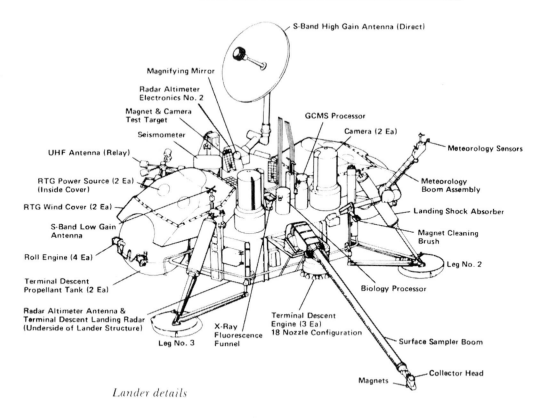

S-Band High Gain Antenna (Direct)

Magnifying Mirror

Radar Altimeter
Electronics No. 2

Magnet & Camera
Test Target

GCMS Processor

Seismometer

Camera (2 Ea)

Meteorology Sensors

UHF Antenna (Relay)

RTG Power Source (2 Ea)
(Inside Cover)

Meteorology
Boom Assembly

RTG Wind Cover (2 Ea)

Landing Shock Absorber

S-Band Low Gain
Antenna

Magnet Cleaning
Brush

Roll Engine (4 Ea)

Leg No. 2

Terminal Descent
Propellant Tank (2 Ea)

Biology Processor

Radar Altimeter Antenna &
Terminal Descent Landing Radar
(Underside of Lander Structure)

X-Ray
Fluorescence
Funnel

Terminal Descent
Engine (3 Ea)
18 Nozzle Configuration

Leg No. 3

Surface Sampler Boom

Collector Head

Magnets

Lander details

Figure 5.4. The main components of the Viking landers. (Credit: Ezell and Ezell, p. 246.)

organisms. After a voyage to Mars that lasted more than 330 days, the probe began to image the Red Planet before it was placed into Mars orbit on 7 August 1976.

Using the imagery collected from *Viking 1* along with its own data, a landing site was selected for the *Viking 2* lander. The orbiter and lander separated on 3 September 1976 and three and a half hours later the lander made a successful soft-landing on the surface of Mars and the second such landing in just six weeks, following the *Viking 1* landing on 20 July.

During its descent to the surface, the aeroshell and its heat shield slowed the spacecraft. When it was about six kilometer above the planet, the lander parachutes deployed and a few seconds later the aeroshell was jettisoned. The three lander legs extended and, at a kilometer and a half above the surface, retro-rockets ignited and fired until the lander hit the surface forty seconds later. The landing rockets were designed to spread the hydrogen and nitrogen exhaust over a wide area. This, it was hoped, would limit the amount of heating the surface would undergo in the landing process and the amount of surface material that might be displaced.

As the lander began operations on the surface, the orbiter made a close approach to the Martian moon Deimos in October 1977 and returned nearly 16,000 images to Earth. The orbiter continued to operate until 25 July 1978, when a leak in its propulsion system vented the probe's attitude-control gas. It was then placed in a higher orbit and turned off on 25 July 1978.

Technical Notes

The lander consisted of a six-sided aluminum base with alternate 1.09-meter- and .56-meter-long sides, supported on three extended legs attached to the shorter sides. The leg footpads formed the vertices of an equilateral triangle with 2.21-meter sides when viewed from above, with the long sides of the base forming a straight line with the two adjoining footpads. Instrumentation was attached to the top of the base, elevated above the surface by the extended legs. Power was provided by two radioisotope thermal generator (RTG) units containing Plutonium 238 affixed to opposite sides of the lander base and covered by wind screens. Each generator was twenty-eight centimeters tall, fifty-eight centimeters in diameter, had a mass of 13.6 kilograms and provided 30 watts of continuous power at 4.4 volts. Four wet-cell sealed, nickel-cadmium, eight-amp-hour, twenty-eight-volt rechargeable batteries were also onboard to handle peak power loads.

The twelve deorbit nozzles acted as the control thrusters for translation and rotation of the lander. Terminal descent and landing was achieved by three monopropellant hydrazine engines (one affixed on each long side of the base, separated by 120 degrees). The engines had eighteen nozzles to disperse the exhaust and minimize effects on the ground. The hydrazine was purified to prevent contamination of the Martian surface. The lander carried eighty-five kilograms of propellant at launch, contained in two spherical titanium tanks mounted on opposite sides of the lander beneath the RTG windscreens, giving a total launch mass of 657 kilograms. Control was achieved through the use of an inertial reference unit, four gyros, an aerodecelerator, a radar altimeter, a terminal descent and landing radar, and the control thrusters.

A steerable two-axis, high-gain parabolic antenna was mounted on a boom near one edge of the lander base. An omnidirectional low-gain S-band antenna also extended from the base. Both these antennas allowed for communication directly with Earth. A UHF (381-MHz) antenna provided a one-way relay to the orbiter using a thirty-watt relay radio. Data storage was on a tape recorder and the lander computer had a 6,000 word memory for command instructions.

The lander carried instruments to achieve the primary scientific objectives of the lander mission: to study the biology, chemical composition (organic and inorganic), meteorology, seismology, magnetic properties, appearance, and physical properties of the Martian surface and atmosphere. Two 360-degree cylindrical scan cameras were mounted near one long side of the base. From the center of this side extended the sampler arm, with a collector head, temperature sensor, and magnet on the end. A meteorology boom, holding temperature, wind direction, and wind velocity sensors extended out and up from the top of one of the lander legs. A seismometer, magnet and camera test targets, and magnifying mirror were mounted opposite the cameras, near the high-gain antenna. An interior, environmentally controlled compartment held the biology experiment and the gas chromatograph mass spectrometer. The X-ray fluorescence spectrometer was also mounted within the structure. A pressure sensor was attached under the lander body. The scientific payload had a total mass of approximately ninety-one kilograms.

Archaeology

After separation and landing, the orbiter had a mass of 900 kilograms and the lander a mass of about 600 kilograms. The *Viking 2* lander touched down about 200 kilometers west of the crater Mie in Utopia Planitia at 48.269° N and 225.990° W. About twenty-two kilograms of propellants were left in the lander after it reached the surface. The precautions taken to avoid disturbing the surface through the spread of the landing thruster exhaust were compromised when radar misread the distance to the planet and caused the thrusters to fire for half a second longer than planned. The surface cracked and the lander settled onto the planet with one leg on a rock, tilted at an angle of 8.2°.

The *Viking 2* lander operated on the surface of Mars for 1,281 Mars days when its batteries failed. It was turned off on 11 April 1980 and entered its archaeological context. The materials left behind by both of the Viking landers as they descended include the following:

Bioshield Cap and Base: This two-piece shield measured 3.7 meters in diameter and 1.9 meters deep. The shield was sterilized and fused to the spacecraft on Earth to prevent bio-contamination. It was made of coated, woven fiberglass .13 mm thick and attached to an aluminum support structure. The shield was jettisoned following atmospheric entry and presumably lies some distance from the lander site itself and possibly under a layer of sand if it has been subjected to sandstorms.

Aeroshell: The heat shield was made of aluminum alloys, cone-shaped and stiffened with concentric rings. It was placed between the lander and the bioshield. It measured 3.5 meters in diameter and the aluminum skin was 0.86 mm thick. The exterior was covered with a cork-like material that protected the lander during atmospheric entry, when temperatures climbed as high as 1,500 degrees Celsius or 2,730 degrees Fahrenheit. The aeroshell was fitted with twelve small control engines (four clusters of three) that were fitted around the edge of the aeroshell. Fuel for the engines was provided by two spherical tanks of hydrazine propellant. The electric umbilical, which connected the lander to the orbiter during its voyage from Earth, ran through the aeroshell.

The aeroshell contained two of the Viking science instruments: the Upper Atmosphere Mars Spectrometer (UAMS) and the Retarding Potential Analyzer as well as pressure and temperature sensors. The aeroshell was jettisoned from landing array around 6,400 meters and, like the bioshield, its location is unknown.

Base Cover and Parachute: The base cover and parachute fit between bioshield cap and the lander. It was made of aluminum and fiberglass and covered the parachute and ejection mortar, and protected the lander during the atmospheric entry.

The parachute was made of lightweight Dacron polyester and weighed fifty kilograms and had a diameter of sixteen meters. It was packed in a mortar that measured .38 meters in diameter. The mortar was mounted to the base cover. When the mortar fired, the parachute accelerated to about 139 kilometers per hour.

The parachute was attached to Base Cover via extra long suspension lines thirty meters in length. It was jettisoned at about 1,215 meters and, like the bioshield and the aeroshell, its location on the surface is unknown.

The materials that comprised the main body of both of the Viking landers include the following:

LANDER SUBSYSTEMS: The lander subsystems comprised six major categories: descent engines, communications equipment, power sources, landing radars, data storage, and guidance and control. Photographic images were taken by two identical cameras located 0.8 meters apart and mounted 1.3 meters above the surface of Mars. The cameras were capable of viewing two footpads and most of the area covered by the surface sampler. Taken together, the cameras produced three-dimensional imagery of the surface. A grid was painted within both cameras' lines of sight, which, when continuously photographed, determined whether sediment was moving. Internal camera components included a scanning mirror and elevation drive, optics, photo-sensor array, a dust cover, entrance windows, an azimuth drive, insulation, and the main electronic unit.

The science experiments carried out by the landers included a biology series designed to search for the presence of life on Mars. A meteorology series included using a boom attached to the lander to analyze the environment close to the surface. Equipment to detect any seismic activity on Mars was based on triangulating the results between the two landers, but the *Viking 1* seismometer failed to engage, so the experiment was deemed a failure. A surface sampler was used to dig trenches, pile dirt on the grid, drop rocks on the surface, press the sampler head into the dirt, and use the collector head sensor to measure temperature.

The sites of the Viking landers were imaged by the *Mars Reconnaissance Orbiter* after its arrival at Mars in 2005. As can be seen in Figure 5.5, the entire area of the landing, from the spot of the presumed impact of the heat shield, as well as the parachute and other associated elements, are seen in the same area as the lander itself, creating a unified archaeological area.

6) *MARS PATHFINDER*[6]

History

Mars Pathfinder was designed to test the proposition that a relatively low-cost spacecraft could be successfully soft-landed on Mars and deploy a roving vehicle from a stationary lander on the surface. The spacecraft was launched atop a specially modified Delta rocket from Cape Canaveral, Florida, on 4 December 1996. Thirty minutes before reaching Mars, the cruise stage of the probe was jettisoned and the spacecraft entered the Martian atmosphere on 4 July 1997 directly, without going into orbit around the planet.

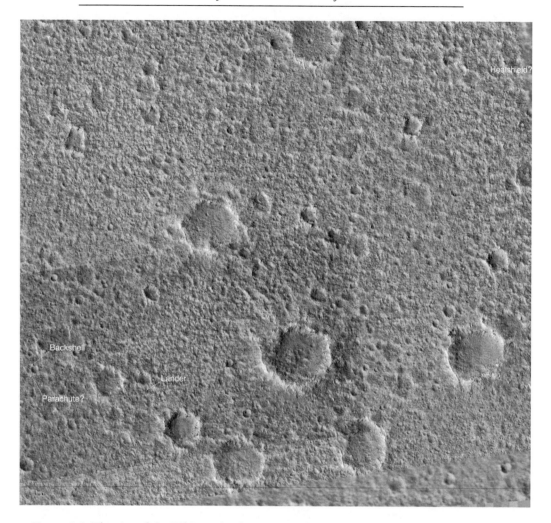

Figure 5.5. The site of the Viking 1 landing. Image from the *Mars Reconnaissance Orbiter.* (Credit: NASA/JPL-Caltech/University of Arizona.)

As the lander descended, the vehicle's heat shield slowed it from over 7,000 meters per second to 400 meters per second. Then a 12.5-meter parachute was deployed, slowing the craft to about seventy meters per second. The heat shield was released twenty seconds after parachute deployment, and the bridle, a twenty-meter-long braided Kevlar tether, deployed below the spacecraft. The lander separated from the backshell and slid down to the bottom of the bridle over about twenty-five seconds. At an altitude of about 1.6 km, the radar altimeter acquired the ground, and about ten seconds before landing, four air bags inflated to form a 5.2-meter-diameter protective "ball" around the lander. Four seconds later, at an altitude of ninety-eight meters, the three solid rockets, mounted in the backshell, fired to slow the descent, and about two seconds later the bridle was cut

117

when the spacecraft was just 21.5 meters above the ground, releasing the airbag-encased lander.

About four second later, the lander dropped to the ground in 3.8 seconds and impacted on 4 July 1997. The lander bounced about twelve meters into the air, and then bounced at least another fifteen times and rolling before coming to rest about two and a half minutes after impact and about one kilometer from the initial impact site.

After landing, the airbags deflated and were retracted. *Pathfinder* opened its three metallic triangular solar panels about an hour and a half after landing. With a few hours, the lander was transmitting to Earth views of the rover and immediate surroundings and a panoramic view of the landing area. Two days later, after operations to clear one of the landing airbags out of the way, the rover was deployed down its ramps and rolled onto the surface.

As the rover went to work, the lander conducted meteorological research and obtained imagery of its operations and relayed these data to Earth. The primary objectives were scheduled for the first seven sols (1 Martian day = 24.6 Earth hours), all within about ten meters of the lander.

Technical Notes

The lander was also equipped with more than two and a half meters of solar cells on its deployed petals that, in combination with rechargeable batteries, powered the lander. The lander's onboard computer was based on 32-bit architecture with four million bytes of static random access memory and sixty-four million bytes of mass memory for storing images. The main lander components were held in a tetrahedral-shaped unit in the center of the three petals, with three low-gain antennas extending from three corners of the box and a camera extending up from the center on a 0.8-meter-high pop-up mast.

The rover, which was named *Sojourner*, was a six-wheeled vehicle, 280 millimeters high, 630 millimeters long, and 480 millimeters wide with a ground clearance of 130 millimeters. The rover was stowed on the lander at a height of 180 millimeters. At deployment, the rover extended to its full height and rolled down a deployment ramp on 6 July 1997. The rover was controlled by an Earth-based operator who used images obtained by both the rover and lander systems. The delay in transmitting data from Mars and commands from Earth varied between ten and fifteen minutes depending on the relative position of Earth and Mars over the course of the mission. This required some autonomous control of the rover, which was mitigated by a hazard avoidance system on the rover. The onboard control system was an Intel 80C85 8-bit processor that ran about 100,000 instructions per second. The computer was capable of compressing and storing a single image onboard.

The rover was powered by 0.2 square meters of solar cells, which provided energy for several hours of operations per sol. Non-rechargeable lithium thionyl chloride (LiSOCl2) D-cell batteries provide backup. All rover communications were done through the lander.

The rover was equipped with black and white and color imaging systems which were used to image the lander in order to assess its condition after touchdown. The goal was to acquire three black and white images spaced 120 degrees apart of the lander. Images of the surrounding terrain were also acquired to study size and distribution of soils and rocks, as well as locations of larger features. Imaging of the rover wheel tracks will be used to estimate soil properties. Imaging of the rover by the lander was also done to assess rover performance and soil and site properties. The rover's performance was monitored to determine tracking capabilities, drive performance, thermal behavior, and sensor performance. UHF communications between the rover and lander were studied to determine the effectiveness of the link between the rover and lander. Assessments of rock and soil mechanics will be made based on abrasion of the wheels and adherence of dust. An alpha-proton-X-ray spectrometer (APXS) was onboard the rover to assess the composition of rocks and soil. Images of all samples tested were transmitted to Earth.

Archaeology

The landing site of *Mars Pathfinder* is in the Ares Vallis region of Mars at 19.33° N, 33.55° W. The lander site was subsequently named the Sagan Memorial Station to memorialize the astronomer Carl Sagan. The Ares Vallis region of Mars is one of the largest outflow channels on Mars, the result of a massive flood over a short period of time flowing into the Martian northern lowlands.

The systemic work of the *Mars Pathfinder* mission went on until 27 September 1997, when communications were lost for reasons that are unknown. At that moment, the probe and its rover entered their archaeological contexts. The other associated materials, such as the heat shield and descent parachute, had entered their archaeological contexts as soon as they were discarded from the active descent operation. All of these components, taken as a unified industry, along with the pathways created by the operations of the *Sojourner* rover, comprise the material culture of *Pathfinder*.

7) *MARS POLAR LANDER/MARS CLIMATE ORBITER*[7]

History

The Mars Surveyor '98 program was comprised of two spacecraft that were launched from Earth separately: the *Mars Climate Orbiter* and the *Mars Polar Lander*. The two missions were designed to study the Martian weather, climate, and water and carbon dioxide, in order to study long-term and episodic climate changes. The mission was a double technological failure: *Mars Climate Orbiter* was destroyed when a navigation error caused it to miss its target altitude at Mars by nearly 100 kilometers, instead entering the Martian atmosphere at an altitude of fifty-seven kilometers during the orbit insertion maneuver. Besides its own science mission, the orbiter was to have served as a data relay satellite for the *Mars Polar Lander* and other future NASA and international lander missions to Mars.

Mars Climate Orbiter was launched atop a modified Delta rocket from Pad A of

Launch Complex 17 at Cape Canaveral Air Station in Florida on 11 December 1998. The spacecraft reached Mars on 23 September 1999. It passed behind Mars and was to have re-emerged and established radio contact with Earth. Contact was never re-established and no signal was ever received from the spacecraft. A failure review board decided that a navigation error resulted when some of the spacecraft commands had been sent from Earth in English units instead of being converted to metric. At this low altitude, the spacecraft would have been destroyed by atmospheric stresses and friction.

The *Mars Climate Orbiter* was to have acted as a relay for the *Mars Polar Lander* after the latter's planned landing on 3 December 1999 to the end of the lander's primary mission on 29 February 2000. The orbiter was to have passed over the lander site ten times each Martian day for five or six minutes each time. Following this work, the orbiter was to have initiated a (Martian)-year-long mapping expedition. At the conclusion of this research, the orbiter was to have been placed in a stable orbit and function as a UHF relay for the Mars 2001 mission.

With the loss of the *Mars Climate Orbiter*, researchers awaited the arrival of the *Mars Polar Lander* in December 1999. However, as the lander reached Mars, it sent its last telemetry just prior to entering the Martian atmospheric on 3 December 1999. No further signals were ever received from the lander, and the cause of this loss of communication was never discovered.

Technical Notes

The *Mars Climate Orbiter* was a box-shaped spacecraft about 2.1 meters high, 1.6 meters wide and two meters deep, consisting of stacked propulsion and equipment modules. The total spacecraft had a launch mass of 629 kilograms that included 291 kilograms of propellant. An eleven-square-meter solar array wing, measuring 5.5 meters tip to tip, was attached by a two-axis gimbal to one side and a 1.3-meter-diameter high-gain dish antenna was attached by two-axis gimbal to a mast at the top of the propulsion module.

Spacecraft power was provided by three panels of solar cells on the 5.5-meter-long single-wing solar array which provided 1,000 watts of power at Earth and 500 watts at Mars. Power was stored in nickel hydride (NiH2) common pressure vessel batteries. Communications with Earth were in X-band using Cassini Deep Space Transponders and solid-state power amplifiers through the 1.3-meter high-gain antenna for both uplink and downlink, a medium-gain transmitting antenna, and a low-gain receiving antenna. A ten-watt UHF system was used for two-way communications with the *Mars Polar Lander*.

The *Mars Polar Lander* consisted of a hexagonal base composed of aluminum honeycomb with composite graphite epoxy face sheets supported on three aluminum landing legs. The lander stood 1.06 meters tall and approximately 3.6 meters wide. The launch mass of the spacecraft was approximately 583 kilograms, including sixty-four kilograms of fuel, an eighty-two-kilogram cruise stage, a 140-kilogram aeroshell/heat shield, and two 3.5-kilogram microprobes. A thermally regulated interior component deck held temperature-sensitive electronic components and batteries and the thermal control system. Two solar panels extended out from opposite sides of the base. Mounted on top of the base were the robotic arm, the stereo imager and mast, a UHF antenna, the LIDAR, the MVACS electronics, the meteorology mast and the medium-gain dish antenna. The MARDI was mounted at the base of the lander, and the propellant tanks are affixed to the sides. During the cruise to Mars, the lander was attached to the cruise stage and enclosed in the 2.4-meter-diameter aeroshell.

Also attached to the lander were two small surface probes called *Deep Space 2*. Since their mission was to explore near to the Martian South Pole, they were named *Amundsen* and *Scott*, after the Norwegian explorer Roald Amundsen and the British captain Robert F. Scott, leaders of the first two expeditions to reach the geographic South Pole on Earth.

The *Deep Space 2* probes had a total mass of 3.572 kilograms each and consisted of three parts. The aeroshell, 275 millimeters high and 350 millimeters in diameter, encased the probe and was designed to protect it from the heat of atmospheric entry. The aeroshell was made of a ceramic material designed to shatter on impact with the surface and had a mass of 1.165 kilograms. The probe itself consisted of two parts, an aftbody and a forebody. The aftbody was a short cylinder, 105.3 millimeters high and 136 millimeters in diameter, which contained the primary batteries, pressure sensors, atmospheric accelerometer, and communications equipment, including a 127-millimeter-high antenna. The aftbody was designed to remain above the surface after impact to provide radio communications. The forebody, or penetrator, was a long, thin cylinder (105.6 millimeters long, 35 millimeters in diameter) with a mass of .670 kilograms. One set of thermal properties equipment, including a temperature sensor, was housed near the front of the cylinder. Above this at the center of the cylinder was the drill motor, surrounded by the electronics and microcontroller. Over these was another set of thermal properties equipment. Above this were the drill apparatus, soil-sample chamber, and the heating and ice and water vapor detection equipment. At the top of the penetrator was a three-axis impact accelerometer. The forebody fit in the aftbody in its stowed position and was designed to separate on impact with the surface. It had a rounded front end in order to penetrate into the ground. The aftbody and forebody were connected after impact by a flexible cable. Both parts of the probe were designed to withstand extreme decelerations.

Before deployment the probes were mounted on the cruise stage of the *Mars Polar Lander* under the solar panels. They were self-contained and had no electrical connection to the lander itself. The probes were each powered by two non-rechargeable lithium-thionyl chloride batteries of 600 milliamp hours. The batteries were expected to provide six to fourteen volts nominally from one to three days, but may have lasted longer. The probes were designed to transmit data at 7,000 bits per second on a UHF band.

The probes had no active control or propulsion systems, but were designed to passively orient themselves during free fall with the forebody front forward. Impact was expected to occur at 160 to 200 meter per second with an angle of attack of less than twelve degrees. On impact, the aeroshell would shatter and the forebody separate from the aftbody and penetrate to a third- to one meter below the surface depending on the constitution of the underlying material. The three-axis accelerometer was designed to measure the deceleration of the forebody, which would help determine the depth of probe penetration and provide data on the hardness and layering of the material.

The aeroshell was made of a brittle silicon carbide, which shattered on impact. The heat shield was made of a material called SIRCA-SPLIT (Silicon Impregnated Reusable Ceramic Ablator-Secondary Polymer Impregnated Technique). It was capable of withstanding temperatures up to 2000° Celsius. The aesroshell measured 275 millimeters high and 350 millimeters in diameter. The device would have passively oriented itself— no need for parachutes, or airbags. The aeroshell weighed 1.2 kilograms.

Communications between Earth and the spacecraft during cruise to Mars were via X-band using two solid-state power amplifiers and a fixed medium-gain antenna mounted on the cruise stage and backed up by a receive-only low-gain antenna. Surface operations communications (downlink and uplink) were to have been via the UHF antenna on the lander to the orbiter, which would then function as a relay to Earth. Eight to ten relay passes over the lander would have been available from the orbiter each day, but the number of communications sessions would be limited by power demands. Uplink-only communications to Earth were to have been provided by the DTE (direct to Earth) medium-gain two-axis articulated antenna.

Power was provided during cruise phase by two gallium arsenide solar array wings with a total area of 3.1 square meters attached to the cruise stage. After landing, two gallium arsenide solar array wings with a total area of 2.9 square meters would have been deployed. Power was to have been stored in sixteen-amp-hr, nickel-hydride, common pressure vessel batteries for peak load operations and nighttime heating.

Archaeology

The *Mars Polar Lander* was to have touched down on the southern polar region of the Red Planet on 3 December 1999, at a point between 73° S and 76° S, less than 1,000 kilometers from the South Pole and near the edge of the carbon dioxide ice cap. The upper cruise stage of the lander was to have been jettisoned at about 20:05 UT, and about eighteen seconds later, the two *Deep Space 2* microprobes were to be dropped from the cruise stage into the Martian atmosphere. These were also targeted at the southern polar layered terrain, where they would fall and penetrate beneath the Martian surface and send back data on its sub-surface properties. The lander itself was to have made a direct entry into the Martian atmosphere at 6.8 kilometers per second about five minutes after separation from the upper cruise stage.

In addition, a Mars Descent Imager (MARDI) was planned to capture regional views from parachute deployment at about eight kilometers altitude down to the landing. The Russian Space Agency had also provided a laser ranger (LIDAR) package for the lander, which was to have been used to measure dust and haze in the Martian atmosphere. A miniature microphone on board was intended to record the sounds of the Martian surface.

At an altitude of about 7.3 kilometers, the parachute was to have been deployed by a mortar, followed by heat-shield separation. Just before heat-shield separation, the descent imager (MARDI) was to have turned on. The landing legs were to have been deployed between seventy to 100 seconds before landing and the descent engines warmed up with short pulses. Then the parachute would be jettisoned and the descent engines fired, regulated by the spacecraft control system and the Doppler radar. The backshell would separate from the lander at about 1.4 kilometers altitude and the descent engines turned on to slow the descent and turn the flight path to vertical.

At twelve meters altitude, the final descent phase was to have begun. Engine shutoff was to have occurred when one of the landing legs touched the ground. The lander was to have touched down at approximately 20:15 UT Earth received time (3:15 p.m. EST) in the late southern spring season, during which the Sun would always be above the horizon at the landing site.

With the subsequent disruption in contact, it is not known whether any of these steps that followed Earth's final contact with the probe were executed, nor whether any of the descent plan took place as planned. The terrain where the lander wreck may lie is apparently composed of alternating layers of clean and dust-laden ice, where researchers have thought that they might extract a long-term record of the climate.

Immediately after landing the solar panels were to have been deployed. The first signal from the lander was scheduled to reach Earth twenty-four minutes after landing, but no signal was ever received at that moment or subsequently. The first sounds from the microphone were to have been released as early as the day following the landing, while the first soil and/or ice samples were scheduled to be collected by the robot arm on 7 December. The science program was planned to last for three months, with an extended program planned, depending on the performance of the lander as it would be evaluated at that time.

The impacts of the two *Deep Space 2* probes were planned to occur about fifteen to twenty seconds before the *Mars Polar Lander* touchdown, on 3 December 1999. However, no signals were received from the probes by *Mars Global Surveyor* after landing or over the following days. As with the lander and the orbiter, the reason or reasons for the failure of the probes is not known.

The jettisoned components of the lander included the heat shield, backshell and parachute. Atmospheric entry components included a 2.4-meter ablator heat shield, similar to the design of the *Mars Pathfinder*. An onboard navigator velocity estimator determined when parachute should have been fired. Once the parachute had deployed, the heat shield would have detached from backshell. The parachute was 8.4 meters in diameter and was fired by a mortar. The MARDI instrument would have begun operation after the heat shield was jettisoned. Following descent, flight software attitude-control algorithms would have determined the time for backshell and parachute jettison.

The question of the fate of the *Mars Polar Lander* and the *Amundsen* and *Scott Deep Space 2* probes has occupied NASA and the National Imagery and Mapping Agency (NIMA) ever since the loss of the mission in 1999. *Mars Global Surveyor* searched unsuccessfully for the lander in 2001. NASA then planned to train the *Mars Reconnaissance Orbiter*'s High Resolution Imaging Science Experiment (HiRISE) camera at the edge of the polar plains, 800 kilometers from the pole, where *Mars Polar Lander* was supposed to have descended. But as of 2010 the lander had not been found.

8) *BEAGLE 2*[8]

History

The *Beagle 2* probe, a project to gather high-resolution imagery of Mars, was developed by scientists in the United Kingdom for the European Space Agency (ESA). The name was a tribute to the vessel on which Charles Darwin made his famous five-year voyage of discovery in the nineteenth century. The probe was carried to the Red Planet by the *Mars Express Orbiter*. The mission of the expedition was to study the geology, mineralogy, and geochemistry in the area around the landing site, research the physical properties of the atmosphere and surface layers, collect data on Martian meteorology and climatology, and search for possible signatures of life.

The probe was launched atop a Soyuz/Fregat rocket configuration from the Baikonur Cosmodrome on 2 June 2003. The bus, called the *Mars Express Orbiter*, and the booster were put into a 200-kilometer Earth parking orbit where the Fregat was fired again to put the spacecraft into a Mars transfer orbit before the Fregat and the orbiter were separated. The solar panels were deployed and a trajectory correction maneuver performed on 4 June to aim the orbiter towards Mars and allow the Fregat booster to coast into interplanetary space.

The *Mars Express Orbiter* arrived at Mars after a 400-million-kilometer journey in December 2003. The *Beagle 2* lander was released and placed on a ballistic cruise towards the surface on 19 December. On 20 December, the orbiter fired a short thruster burst to put it into position to orbit the planet, where it was expected to operate for one Martian year (687 Earth days).

The *Beagle 2* coasted for five days after release and entered the Martian atmosphere on the morning of 25 December.

Technical Notes

The *Beagle 2* was designed to be a small, light space probe. It was a clam-shaped structure consisting of a lid and base connected with a cable-driven hinge. Its diameter was 0.65 meters and the depth was 0.25 meters. The outer shell provided energy absorption and thermal insulation while the inner shell was made of a carbon-fiber skin and an aluminum honeycomb core. The whole assemblage weighed 33.2 kilograms.

Power derived from four deployable panels that were to have folded out from the top of the lander. The four panels charged a forty-two-cell battery package made from lithium ion technology. The batteries were charged by the solar panels and the experiments ran off of the batteries. The total area of the solar array was one square meter.

The command and data management system consisted of five circuit boards and batteries are situated on top of each other. These were mounted directly to the base of the lander. The central computer was a 32-bit processor and the whole system was called the "Common Electronics." The "Common Electronics" provided the lander with power management and conditioning, power converters, the central processing, descent electronics, pyrotechnical supplies, motor devices, data handling, and experiment interfaces.

Telecommunications was via a UHF antenna which was to have unfolded and deployed with lander. This antenna was not powerful enough to communicate directly with Earth, but had to relay data to the orbiter which would then have relayed it on to Earth.

Other instruments included a Damien Hirst Calibration Target, which was made of aluminum and mounted on one of the ribs of the lander and used to calibrate the instruments. It measured 8 × 8 centimeters and weighed 26.5 grams. A robotic arm was 0.75 meters long and equipped with a grinder and corer, a device designed to collect core samples of nearby rocks. A Mossbauer and X-ray spectrometer, stereo cameras, and the microscope were located on the end of the arm. Taken together, these components were part of a scientific package called the PAW (position adjustable workbench) located at the end of the arm.

Scientific instruments included a microscope mounted on the end of the arm and part of the PAW package; the Mossbauer spectrometer that was designed to provide data on iron content of mineral samples; an X-ray fluorescence spectrometer designed to measure elements in rocks by bombarding samples with four radioactive sources; panoramic stereo and wide-angle cameras; a gas-analysis package designed to search for organic material, determine light element content and speciation, and analyze atmospheric gases; seven environmental sensors to detect air temperature, thermocouples to detect air temperature, pressure sensors, horizontal wind gauges, dust sensors, and a three-axis accelerometer; and "The Mole," which was designed to crawl several meters across the surface and, once it reached a boulder, it would have burrowed underground to collect samples.

The *Mars Express Orbiter* that carried the *Beagle 2* was a cube-shaped spacecraft with two solar panel wings extending from opposite sides. The launch mass of 1,123 kilograms included a main bus with 113 kilograms of payload, the sixty-kilogram lander, and 457 kilograms of propellant. The main body was 1.5 meters × 1.8 meters × 1.4 meters in size, with an aluminum honeycomb structure covered by an aluminum skin. The solar panels measured about twelve meters tip to tip. A 1.8-meter-diameter high-gain antenna was mounted on one face, pointing in the same direction as the solar panels. Two twenty-meter-long wire dipole antennas extended from opposite side facing perpendicular to the solar panels as part of the radar sounder. A four-meter tubular monopole low-gain antenna extended from the upper face. The body was built around the main propulsion system, with two 267-liter propellant tanks with a capacity of 595 kilograms. Approximately 370 kilograms were needed for the mission. Pressurized helium from a thirty-liter tank was used to force fuel into the engine. Trajectory corrections were made using a set of eight thrusters, attached to each corner of the spacecraft bus. Attitude control (three-axis stabilization) was achieved using two three-axis inertial measurement units, a set of two star cameras and two Sun sensors, gyroscopes, accelerometers, and four reaction wheels. Thermal control was maintained through the use of radiators, multi-layer insulation, and actively controlled heaters. The spacecraft configuration was optimized for a Soyuz/Fregat launch vehicle rocket, but was also compatible with a Delta II launch vehicle if necessary.

The spacecraft's power was provided by the solar panels which contained 11.42 square meters of silicon cells. The originally planned power was to be 660 watts but a faulty connection reduced the amount of power available by 30 percent, to about 460 watts. Power was stored in three lithium-ion batteries with a total capacity of 64.8 Ah for use during eclipses.

Two lander relay UHF antennas were mounted on the top face for communication with the *Beagle 2*. The spacecraft was run by two control and data management units with a ten-gigabit solid-state mass memory for storage of data and housekeeping information for transmission.

The science payload consisted of seven experiments. A high-resolution stereoscopic camera (HRSC) was mounted inside the spacecraft body, aimed through the top face of the spacecraft for Mars operations. A visible and near-infrared spectrometer (OMEGA), infrared spectrometer (PFS) and ultraviolet spectrometer (SPICAM) were also mounted inside, pointing out the top face. Neutral and charged particle sensors (ASPERA) were mounted on the top face. The subsurface radar and altimeter were mounted in the body and incorporated two twenty-meter antennas. The total mass budgeted for the science payload was 116 kilograms.

Archaeology

The *Beagle 2* entered the Martian atmosphere on the morning of 25 December 2003. Landing was expected to occur that morning, but no signals were ever received and the lander was declared lost. The landing site was planned to be at 10.6° N, 270° W, on the Isidis Planitia, a large, flat, low-lying region located by ancient highlands. It was hypothesized that the region was most likely the basin from a meteor or comet impact with the planet.

The components of the mission that entered the Martian environment weighed sixty-nine kilograms. The components that might exist in archaeological context on the surface include the ejection mechanism, chute deployment mechanism, a heat shield, two parachutes, three gas bags, and the stowed lander. The heat shield was to have been jettisoned about 200 meters above the surface. At or just before the surface impact, the main parachute was to have been jettisoned. The lander would then have bounced about a dozen times, encased in its gas bags, before coming to a rest. Once the lander came to a rest, the gas bags were to have deflated and the lander deployed. If the lander made it to the surface, the components that were to have been jettisoned — such as the heat shield and the parachutes — should exist in close proximity to the remains of the lander.

9) MARS EXPLORATION ROVERS: *SPIRIT* AND *OPPORTUNITY*[9]

History

The *Spirit* and *Opportunity* rovers (Mars Exploration Rover A or MER-2, and the Mars Exploration Rover B or MER-1) were both launched towards Mars in mid–2003. The rovers were designed to travel about 100 meters per day for about ninety days across the surface of the planet in support of scientific goals that included determining if life ever arose on Mars, characterizing the climate and geology of Mars, and preparing for human exploration of Mars.

Spirit was launched atop a standard Delta II rocket from Cape Canaveral on 10 June 2003 while *Opportunity* was launched on a heavy Delta II rocket on 8 July 2003. The *Spirit*'s cruise phase to Mars ended on 20 November 2003, 45 days before Mars entry, while cruise of the *Opportunity* ended on 11 December 2003. *Spirit* entered the Martian atmosphere on 4 January 2004, and *Opportunity* followed on 25 January 2004.

Both rovers are still in operation as of 2010, but the *Spirit* rover became stuck in a patch of soil in early 2009 and operators on Earth were still working on a solution in early 2010. As of late 2009, *Spirit* had traversed over 7,700 meters of Martian territory, while the *Opportunity* had logged almost 19,000 meters.

Technical Notes

The Mars Exploration Rovers *Spirit* and *Opportunity* consist of a box-like chassis mounted on six wheels. The chassis contains the so-called warm electronics box (WEB).

Figure 5.11. The landing station of the *Opportunity* rover in its archaeological context in Eagle Crater. The lander was photographed by the rover as it exited the crater. (Credit: NASA.)

On top of the WEB is the triangular rover equipment deck, on which is mounted a Pancam mast assembly, high-gain, low-gain, and UHF antennas, and a camera calibration target. Attached to the two forward sides of the equipment deck are solar arrays which are level with the deck and extend outward with the appearance of a pair of swept-back wings. Attached to the lower front of the WEB is the instrument deployment device, a long-hinged arm which protrudes in front of the rover.

The wheels are attached to a rocker-bogie suspension system and each wheel has its own motor and the two front and two rear wheels are independently steerable. The rovers have a top speed of five centimeters per second, but the average speed over time on flat, hard ground would be one centimeter per second or less due to the hazard avoidance protocols. The rovers are designed to withstand a tilt of forty-five degrees without falling over, and are programmed to avoid exceeding tilts of thirty degrees.

The warm electronics box houses the computer, batteries, and other electronic components. The box is designed to protect these components and control their temperature. Thermal control is achieved through the use of gold paint, aerogel insulation, heaters, thermostats, and radiators. Power is provided by the solar arrays, generating up to 140 watts of power under full Sun conditions. The energy is stored in two rechargeable batteries.

Communications with Earth are in X-band via the high-gain directional dish antenna and the low-gain omni-directional antenna. Communications with orbiting spacecraft are through the UHF antenna. The onboard computer has 128 Mb RAM and an inertial measurement unit provides three-axis information on position.

The rovers carry a suite of instruments for science and navigation. The panoramic camera (Pancam) and navigation cameras are mounted on top of the Pancam mast assembly, at a height of about 1.4 meters from the base of the wheels. The mast, mounted at the front of the equipment deck, also acts as a periscope for the Miniature Thermal Emission Spectrometer (Mini-TES). Attached to the end of the instrument deployment device are the Alpha Particle X-Ray Spectrometer (APXS), Mossbauer Spectrometer (MB), Microscopic Imager (MI), and Rock Abrasion Tool (RAT). A magnet array is attached to the front of the equipment deck. Two hazard avoidance cameras are mounted on the front of the rover and two on the rear. The group of science instruments (Pancam, Mini-TES, APXS, MB, MI, and RAT) are known as the Athena science package.

Archaeology

The cruise-stage mass of the rovers was 193 kilograms and propellant mass was fifty kilograms. The rovers were compactly stowed in a tetrahedron-shaped landing platform and encased in an aeroshell consisting of a heat shield and a backshell for launch, cruise, and atmospheric entry. The lander platform has a mass of 348 kilograms, the backshell and parachute 209 kilograms, and the heat shield seventy-eight kilograms.

Upon entry into the Martian atmosphere, the lander and components had a mass of 827 kilograms and were traveling at 19,300 kilometers per hour. The aeroshell decelerated the lander in the upper Martian atmosphere for about four minutes to a velocity of 1,600 kilometers per hour, followed by deployment of a parachute. The parachute slowed the spacecraft to about 300 kilometers per hour. A series of tones was transmitted by the spacecraft during entry and after landing to indicate the successful completion of each phase. Just prior to impact, at an altitude of about 100 meters, retrorockets slowed the descent and airbags were inflated to cushion the impact. The craft hit at roughly fifty kilometers per hour and bounced and rolled along the surface. After it stopped the airbags deflated and retracted, the petals opened, and the rover deployed its solar arrays.

The *Opportunity* rover landed in an area called the Terra Meridiani at a position of 2.07° S, 6.08° W. The site is rich in coarse-grained hematite, an iron-rich material formed in water, and selected because of its smooth surface — even though the rover eventually bounced into a small crater upon settling to the surface. The *Spirit* rover landed in the Gusev Crater at a position of 14.82° S, 184.85° W. It was thought that the sediment on the bottom of this crater lakebed might be of marine origin.

The atmospheric entry components of the rovers include the rovers themselves, along with the following artifacts which would have entered their archaeological context as soon as they reached the Martian surface:

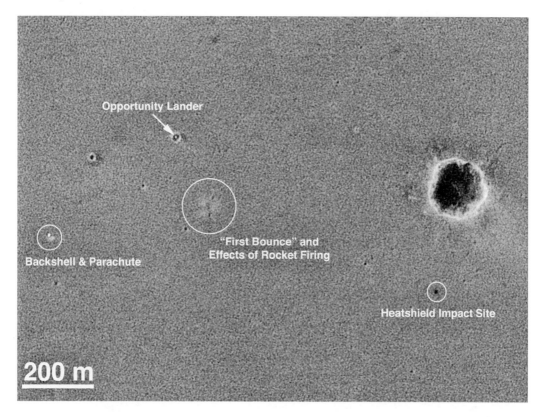

Figure 5.12. A view of the landing area of the *Opportunity* rover, taken from the *Mars Global Surveyor*. (Credit: NASA.)

THE AEROSHELL: The aeroshell, which was made of two separate components, the heat shield and backshell. The heat shield protected the craft and slowed it during atmospheric entry and weighed 78 kilograms. The backshell was cone-shaped and enclosed the lander, and was connected to the heat shield. The backshell contained several components including the parachute, the electronics and batteries, a Litton LN-200 Inertial Measurement Unit, which monitored and reported orientation of the backshell during descent, three RAD (Rocket Assisted Descent) rockets, which rapidly slowed the craft prior to impact, and three small rockets (aimed horizontally out of the backshell) that oriented the craft vertically during RAD burn.

THE BACKSHELL AND PARACHUTE: The backshell and parachute weighed 209 kilograms. The aeroshell was made of an aluminum honeycomb structure with graphite-epoxy face sheets and the outside was covered with a layer of a sterile material made from benzene called phenalic. The honeycomb structure was filled with an ablative material made from cork wood, binder, and silica glass spheres. Both the heat shield and backshell contained ablator, but the heat shield had a thicker layer of it. The backshell was coated with an aluminized mylor blanket that burnt up during entry.

The parachute was located in the backshell and was made of polyester and nylon. Three Kelvar bridles connected it to the backshell. The heat shield was jettisoned ten kilometers above the surface using six separation nuts and springs. The lander then descended a metal tape by using a centrifugal breaking system built into one of the petals. The lander was placed on a position at the end of another bridle made of twenty-meter-long braided Zylon, which provided room for airbag deployment, distance from RAD exhaust, and increased stability. A radar altimeter was mounted on the lander tetrahedron that determined when the Zylon bridle should be cut, when airbags were to inflate, and when RAD rockets would fire.

THE AIRBAGS: The airbags were the same as the airbags used on the *Mars Pathfinder* and made of the synthetic material Vectron. Each rover used four airbags with six lobes each, while ropes crisscrossed the lander and held the bags to it. Three gas generators were stowed with the bags.

THE LANDER: The lander itself was a tetrahedron shape with a mass of 348 kilograms. It contained three petals and one base. The three petals unfolded to reveal the rover. The beams of the petals were made of carbon-based layers of graphite fiber woven into fabric. Titanium fittings were bonded onto the beams that allowed them to be bolted together. Special nuts and bolts held the Rover inside. Small explosives released the Rover from the nuts and bolts. Hinges connect the petals to the base and each of the hinges was connected to a powerful motor capable of lifting the entire weight of the lander in the event that it did not land upright. The petals also contained a retraction system that reeled in the airbags so they would not obstruct the rover. Small ramps made of Vectron cloth were connected to the petals to provide a pathway for the rover to exit the lander.

An extraordinary photograph taken by the *Mars Global Surveyor* shows not only the small crater into which the *Opportunity* probe came to a landing, but also the associated elements of the landing: the backshell and parachute in one area, the impact site of the heat shield in another, the area where the lander bounced upon impact and its final impact site in a small crater subsequently named Eagle Crater. The rover later investigated the area around the impact site of its own heat shield, which can be considered the first instance of robotic archaeological research on Mars.

10) PHOENIX MARS LANDER[10]

History

The *Phoenix Mars Lander* was designed to study the surface and near-surface environment of a landing site in the high northern area of Mars. In this sense, its mission was similar to that of the lost *Mars Polar Lander*, which was to have searched the South Polar Region. The *Phoenix* was launched atop a Delta II rocket from Cape Canaveral Air Force Station on 4 August 2007. It arrived at Mars ten months later, and landed on the Red Planet on 25 May 2008. Fourteen minutes before touchdown, and about seven minutes before atmospheric entry (about 125 kilometers above the surface) the cruise stage was jettisoned.

The spacecraft entered the atmosphere and the heat shield initially slowed the craft. After about three minutes the parachute deployed, followed by ejection of the heat shield fifteen seconds later, then deployment of landing legs ten seconds after that, and radar activation fifty seconds later. At one kilometer altitude the parachute was released and a powered descent and soft-landing was achieved using a pulsed propulsion system with eight thrusters, which turned off when footpad sensors detected touchdown.

Communications were maintained through the relays on the orbiting Mars spacecraft *Mars Reconnaissance Orbiter* and *Mars Express* throughout the descent and for about one minute after touchdown, after which there was no communications with *Phoenix* for about an hour and a half. The solar panels were deployed after allowing fifteen minutes for the dust to settle.

When communications resumed, the first images, along with spacecraft health telemetry, were relayed back to Earth. All instruments were deployed in the first two days after landing, followed by a week-long period to check out all systems. After this, the first surface soil samples were collected for analysis, followed by analysis of deeper layers in two- to three-centimeter increments. Ice is expected to be two to five centimeters deep.

Technical Notes

The spacecraft comprised an octagonal base supported on three landing legs. Two octagonal solar panel wings extended from the base to provide power. Communication was primarity through UHF relay via the *Mars 2001 Odyssey* orbiter, and *Phoenix* had a steerable medium gain X-band antenna to provide communications directly with Earth.

The science experiments and a robotic arm were mounted on the base. The experiments are the Microscopy, Electrochemistry, and Conductivity Analyzer (MECA), the

Robotic Arm Camera (RAC), the Surface Stereo Imager (SSI), the Thermal and Evolved Gas Analyzer (TEGA), and the meteorological station (MET). The total science payload mass is fifty-five kilograms. The primary science objectives for *Phoenix* were to determine polar climate and weather, interaction with the surface, and composition of the lower atmosphere around 70° north for at least ninety sols; determine the atmospheric characteristics during descent through the atmosphere; characterize the geomorphology and active processes shaping the northern plains and the physical properties of the near-surface regolith focusing on the role of water; determine the aqueous mineralogy and chemistry as well as the adsorbed gases and organic content of the regolith; characterize the history of water, ice, and the polar climate; and determine the past and present biological potential of the surface and subsurface environments.

Archaeology

Landing occurred just before the northern summer solstice, at 68° N latitude, in the North Polar Region of Mars. The landing site is in a relatively boulder-free area with a high (30–60 percent) ratio of ice to rock. Surface temperatures in this region range between about 190 and 260 Kelvin. At the time of touchdown, Mars was 275 million kilometers from Earth, a light travel time of about fifteen minutes. As the summer ended, the mission had less solar energy to operate and *Phoenix* made its last transmission on 2 November 2008 before power was depleted and the lander entered its archaeological context.

Conclusions

Two of the landers discussed in this chapter—*Spirit* and *Opportunity*—remain in systemic context, meaning that they still being used for that which they were designed. But they are included here because they will make their transition to archaeological context within the next months or years. *Mars 2, Mars Polar Lander* and its *Deep Space 2* probes were all systemic failures—achieving their archaeological context as soon as they reached the Red Planet, since the probes never regained contact with Earth after entering the Martian atmosphere. A separate lander named *Mars 7*, which was identical to *Mars 6*, missed Mars completely and went into heliocentric orbit where—like the other heliocentric objects *Homo sapiens* have lost or discarded—they exist as museum-quality artifacts in a vast mobile gallery.

The challenges of the survey, preservation, and protection of spacecraft discarded on the surface of Mars will be a great one. Dust storms could damage the landers or even bury them beneath the red Martian soil. And since Mars has no protective ozone layer, ultraviolet energy from the Sun could damage the spacecraft. It may be necessary to deploy shields over such sites to protect them from the continual abrasion and decay caused by extreme temperatures, radiation, wind, and dust.

Eventually, the Viking landers, the *Mars Pathfinder*, and the *Spirit* and *Opportunity* rovers will need to be shielded from this intense ultraviolet solar radiation that penetrates the ozone-deficient Martian atmosphere. The *Opportunity* rover can even be seen to have conducted the first archaeological research on Mars, when it investigated the area around the impact site of its own heat shield.

And, of course, field survey teams — human or robotic — will need to be dispatched to the South Pole of Mars to answer the mystery of whatever became of NASA's lost 1999 *Mars Polar Lander* and its associated *Deep Space 2* probes, and to the Isidis Planitia basin in search of the European Space Agency's ill-fated *Beagle 2*. A direct search will almost certainly be required for the *Mars Polar Lander*, given its small size and the resolution limits of space-based imaging systems.

The question of the fate of the *Mars Polar Lander*, in particular, has occupied NASA and the National Imagery and Mapping Agency (NIMA) ever since it vanished on arrival at the Red Planet. The first approach was to use the *Mars Global Surveyor* spacecraft that reached Mars three years before the disappearance of the *Polar Lander* and its associated components such as the protective aeroshell, heat shield and parachute. The lander itself was only a bit larger than the smallest objects the orbiter's camera can see on the surface, making a direct archaeological expedition perhaps the only way the mystery of this catastrophic mission failure may ever be solved.

6

Artifacts on Other Planets and Moons in the Solar System

Humans have been attempting to robotically explore other planets in the solar system — and, in the case of the gas giants, their moons — for half a century. With the exception of Mars, however, actual landings on these other celestial bodies have been few. The *Galileo* spacecraft sent to Jupiter released a probe into the atmosphere in 1995; however, the pressure of that gas giant likely completely obliterated the probe. The *Galileo* spacecraft itself was deliberately destroyed in the atmosphere of Jupiter in 2003 to prevent it from possibly colliding with and contaminating Europa, one of Jupiter's moons that could contain life forms. Of the fifteen exploratory robotic probes sent from Earth that actually reached planets or moons other than Mars, fourteen of them have attempted landings on Venus, and the fifteenth landed recently on the Saturnian moon Titan.

The archaeology of the exploration of Venus belongs nearly exclusively to the former Soviet Union, which had attempted to land a robot probe, *Venera 1*, on the planet as early as 1961, and finally succeeded in 1966 with *Venera 3*. The experience gained from these expeditions led to further robotic spacecraft that became gradually more resistant to the harsh conditions of Venus, where intense pressures and temperatures make the survival of composite tools from Earth problematic at best. While *Venera 3* was the first craft to reach the surface of Venus, it was likely crushed as it descended through the Venusian atmosphere. It was not until *Venera 7* in 1970 that the Soviet space program was able to both land on the surface and then successfully transmit data from Venus. During this developmental phase, the spacecraft bound for Venus became progressively heavier and more sophisticated.

After the Venera missions, the Soviet Union launched two final probes toward Venus called *Vega 1* and *Vega 2*. The most notable thing about these crafts is that they deployed weather balloon aerostats to monitor the conditions of the planet and it is possible that evidence of these explorations could still be found on the surface of the planet, despite temperatures of nearly 500 degrees Celsius and ninety atmospheres of pressure. In 1978, NASA also launched a craft to Venus. The *Pioneer Venus 2* split into five different parts on entry into the Venusian atmosphere, and left behind four different probes on the surface, each on a different specific part of Venus.

Besides Venus, the only other place in the solar system where humans have discarded a composite tool that may still survive on the surface is on the moon of Saturn called Titan. There, in early 2005, the European Space Agency's *Huygens* probe descended through Titan's atmosphere. It remained in operation for a few hours, transmitting data to Earth via the orbiting *Cassini* spacecraft, before entering its archaeological context on the surface of Titan.

The Archaeological Catalog

1) *VENERA 3*[1]

History

Venera 3 was launched atop a modified SS-6 Sapwood rocket from Baikonur Cosmodrome on 16 November 1965. The mission of this spacecraft was to land on the surface of Venus.

Technical Notes

The spacecraft had a mass of 960.0 kilograms. The entry body contained a radio communication system, scientific instruments, electrical power sources, and medallions bearing the coat of arms of the U.S.S.R.

Archaeology

The station impacted Venus on 1 March 1966. This event made *Venera 3* the first spacecraft to impact on the surface of another planet. Communications systems failed before any planetary data could be returned, suggesting that the probe entered its archaeological context the moment it touched down on Venus.

2) *VENERA 4*[2]

History

Venera 4 was launched from Baikonur Cosmodrome on 12 June 1967, to conduct direct atmospheric studies. On 18 October 1967, the spacecraft entered the Venusian atmosphere and released two thermometers, a barometer, a radio altimeter, and atmospheric density gauge, eleven gas analyzers, and two radio transmitters operating in the DM waveband.

Technical Notes

The main bus, which had carried the capsule to Venus, carried a magnetometer, cosmic ray detectors, hydrogen and oxygen indicators, and charged particle traps.

Archaeology

Signals were returned by the spacecraft, which braked and then deployed a parachute system after entering the Venusian atmosphere, until it reached an altitude of 24.96 kilometers.

3) *VENERA 5*[3]

History

Venera 5 was launched from Baikonur Cosmodrome on 5 January 1969. Its mission was to obtain atmospheric data from Venus. During satellite descent towards the surface of Venus, a parachute opened to slow the rate of descent. For fifty-three minutes on 16 May 1969, while the capsule was suspended from the parachute, data from the Venusian atmosphere were returned.

Technical Notes

The spacecraft was very similar to *Venera 4*, although it was of a stronger design. When the atmosphere of Venus was approached, a capsule weighing 405 kilograms and containing scientific instruments was jettisoned from the main spacecraft.

Archaeology

The spacecraft carried a medallion bearing the coat of arms of the Soviet Union and a bas-relief of V.I. Lenin to the night side of Venus.

4) *VENERA 6*[4]

History

Venera 6 was launched from Baikonur Cosmodrome on 10 January 1969 to obtain atmospheric data from Venus. When the atmosphere of Venus was approached, a capsule weighing 405 kilograms was jettisoned from the main spacecraft. This capsule contained scientific instruments. During descent towards the surface of Venus, a parachute opened to slow the rate of descent. For fifty-one minutes on 17 May 1969, while the capsule was suspended from the parachute, data from the Venusian atmosphere were returned.

Technical Notes

The spacecraft was very similar to *Venera 4* although it was of a stronger design.

Archaeology

The spacecraft carried a medallion bearing the coat of arms of the Soviet Union as well as a bas-relief of V.I. Lenin to the night side of Venus.

5) VENERA 7[5]

History

Venera 7 was launched from Baikonur Cosmodrome on 17 August 1970 to study the atmosphere and other phenomena of Venus. *Venera 7* entered the atmosphere of Venus on 15 December 1970, and a landing capsule was jettisoned. After aerodynamic braking, a parachute system was deployed. The capsule antenna was extended, and signals were returned for thirty-five minutes.

Archaeology

Venera 7 continued to transmit data—albeit in very weak signals—to Earth for twenty-three minutes after it landed on the surface of Venus. It thus became the first human artifact to return data after landing on another planet.

6) VENERA 8[6]

History

Venera 8 was a Venus atmospheric probe and lander that launched from Baikonur Cosmodrome on 27 March 1972. The spacecraft reached Venus on 22 July 1972 where the lander separated from the bus and entered the atmosphere. Descent speed was reduced from 41,696 kilometers per hour to about 900 kilometers per hour by aerobraking. The two-and-a-half-meter diameter parachute opened at an altitude of sixty kilometers, and a refrigeration system was used to cool the interior components, as the lander continued to transmit data during the descent. At around thirty to thirty-five kilometers altitude, the lander entered into an increasingly dark layer of the atmosphere and then, below ten kilometers, into a layer where wind speeds of less than one meter per second were measured.

Technical Notes

The instrumentation on board *Venera 8* included temperature, pressure, and light sensors as well as an altimeter, gamma-ray spectrometer, gas analyzer, and radio transmitters.

Archaeology

Venera 8 landed at a position of 10° S, 335° W. The lander mass was 495 kilograms. It continued to send back data for more than fifty minutes before failing due to the harsh surface conditions. The probe confirmed earlier data on the high Venus surface temperature and pressure (470° Celsius, 90 atmospheres of pressure) returned by *Venera 7*, and also measured the light level as being suitable for surface photography, finding it to be similar to the amount of light on Earth on an overcast day with roughly one kilometer of visibility.

7) VENERA 9[7]

History

Venera 9 was launched from Baikonur Cosmodrome on 8 June 1975. The lander separated from the orbiter on 20 October 1975 and made a landing on the surface of Venus two days later. During descent, heat dissipation and deceleration were accomplished sequentially by protective hemispheric shells, three parachutes, a disk-shaped drag brake, and a compressible, metal, doughnut-shaped landing cushion.

Technical Notes

A system of circulating fluid was used to distribute the heat load. This system, plus pre-cooling prior to entry, permitted operation of the spacecraft for fifty-three minutes after landing.

Archaeology

The surface temperatures around the landing site were registered at 485 degrees Celsius. With light levels comparable to those of the mid-latitudes of Earth on a cloudy summer day, television photography revealed a landscape of shadows, with no apparent dust in the air, and a variety of thirty to forty centimeter-sized rocks which were not eroded.

8) VENERA 10[8]

History

Venera 10 was an orbiter/lander combination that was launched from Baikonur Cosmodrome on 14 June 1975. The lander separated from the orbiter on 23 October 1975 and landed on the surface of Venus two days later. During descent, heat dissipation and deceleration were accomplished sequentially as on Venera 9, by protective hemispheric shells, three parachutes, a disk-shaped drag brake, and a compressible, metal, doughnut-shaped landing cushion. As it descended, the lander returned data indicating that at forty-two kilometers altitude the pressure was 3.3 Earth atmospheres and the temperature was 158° Celsius; at an altitude of fifteen kilometers the pressure was thirty-seven Earth atmospheres and the temperature was 363° Celsius; and that on the surface the pressure was ninety-two Earth atmospheres and the temperature was 465° Celsius.

Technical Notes

A system of circulating fluid was used to distribute the heat load. This system, plus pre-cooling prior to entry, permitted operation of the spacecraft for sixty-five minutes after landing.

Archaeology

The landing took place about 2,200 kilometers distant from *Venera 9*, which had landed on the surface three days earlier. Television photography revealed a landscape of large pancake rocks with lava or other weathered rocks in between, with surface wind speeds of 3.5 meters per second.

9) *VENERA 11*[9]

History

Venera 11 was an orbiter/lander combination launched from Baikonur Cosmodrome on 14 June 1975. The lander separated from its flight platform on 23 December 1978 and entered the atmosphere of Venus two days later.

Technical Notes

The *Venera 11* descent craft carried instruments designed to study the detailed chemical composition of the atmosphere, the nature of the clouds, and the thermal balance of the atmosphere.

Archaeology

The *Venera 11* lander made a soft landing on the surface on 25 December after a descent that lasted approximately one hour. Data was transmitted to the flight platform for transmittal to Earth until it moved out of range ninety-five minutes after the lander touched down. The lander returned evidence of lightning and thunder and the discovery of carbon monoxide at low altitudes before it ceased to transmit and entered its archaeological context.

10) *PIONEER VENUS PROBE*[10]

History

The *Pioneer Venus Probe* was launched atop an Atlas-Centaur rocket from Cape Canaveral, Florida, on 8 August 1978. This expedition sent four instrumented, atmospheric entry probes to the vicinity of Venus to be released for descent through the atmosphere to the planet's surface. The bus carrying the probes reached Venus in mid–November of 1978. A simultaneous mission, *Pioneer Venus Orbiter*, placed an orbiting spacecraft around Venus five days before the probes entered the atmosphere.

The large probe separated from the bus on 16 November and the small probes on 20 November. Two of the small probes entered on the night side of the planet, while one small probe and the large probe entered on the day side.

Archaeology

The bus was targeted to enter the Venusian atmosphere at a shallow entry angle and transmit data to Earth until it was destroyed by the heat of atmospheric friction during its descent. The large probe had a mass of 300.0 kilograms, and took one and a half hours to descend through the atmosphere. The three smaller probes, with masses of 75.0 kilograms, reached the surface of Venus seventy-five minutes after entry.

11) VENERA 12[11]

History

The *Venera 12* probe of Venus launched from Baikonur Cosmodrome on 14 September 1978. The probe separated from its flight platform on 19 December 1978, and entered the planet's atmosphere two days later and made a soft landing on the surface on 21 December. The lander then transmitted data to Earth via the flight platform until it moved out of range 110 minutes after the lander touched down.

Technical Notes

The descent craft carried instruments designed to study the detailed chemical composition of the atmosphere, the nature of the clouds, and the thermal balance of the atmosphere.

Archaeology

Like *Venera 11*, the probe reported evidence of lightning and thunder and the discovery of carbon monoxide at low altitudes.

12) VENERA 13[12]

History

The *Venera 13* probe of Venus launched from Baikonur Cosmodrome on 30 October 1981. *Venera 13* and *14* were identical spacecraft built to take advantage of the 1981 Venus launch opportunity and launched five days apart. *Venera 13* mission consisted of a bus and an attached descent craft. The descent vehicle separated from the bus and entered the atmosphere of Venus on 1 March 1982.

Technical Notes

The *Venera 13* descent craft/lander was a hermetically sealed pressure vessel, which contained most of the instrumentation and electronics, mounted on a ring-shaped landing platform and topped by an antenna. The design was similar to the earlier *Venera 9–12* landers. It carried instruments to take chemical and isotopic measurements, monitor the spectrum of scattered sunlight, and record electric discharges during its descent phase through the Venusian atmosphere. The spacecraft utilized a camera system, an X-ray fluorescence spectrometer, a screw drill and surface sampler, a dynamic penetrometer, and a seismometer to conduct investigations on the surface.

Archaeology

After entering the atmosphere, a parachute was deployed and then released at an altitude of forty-seven kilometers. *Venera 13* landed about 950 kilometers northeast of *Venera 14* at 7° 30' S, 303° E, just east of the eastern extension of an elevated region known as Phoebe Regio. The area was composed of bedrock outcrops surrounded by dark, fine-grained soil. After landing an imaging panorama was started and a mechanical drilling arm reached to the surface and obtained a sample, which was deposited in a hermetically sealed chamber, maintained at 30° C and a pressure of about .05 atmospheres, where it was then analyzed. The lander survived for 127 minutes (the planned design life was thirty-two), during which time it transmitted data to the bus, which acted as a data relay as it flew by Venus. On the 128th minute, the lander entered its archaeological context.

13) *VENERA 14*[13]

History

The *Venera 14* probe of Venus launched from Baikonur Cosmodrome on 4 November 1981. *Venera 13* and *14* were identical spacecraft built to take advantage of the 1981 Venus launch opportunity and launched five days apart. Each consisted of a bus and an attached descent craft. The descent vehicle separated from the bus and entered the atmosphere of Venus on 5 March 1982.

Technical Notes

The *Venera 14* descent craft/lander was a hermetically sealed pressure vessel, which contained most of the instrumentation and electronics, mounted on a ring-shaped landing platform and topped by an antenna. The design was similar to the earlier *Venera 9–12* landers. It carried instruments to take chemical and isotopic measurements, monitor the spectrum of scattered sunlight, and record electric discharges during its descent phase through the Venusian atmosphere. The spacecraft utilized a camera system, an X-ray fluorescence spectrometer, a screw drill and surface sampler, a dynamic penetrometer, and a seismometer to conduct investigations on the surface.

Archaeology

After entering the atmosphere a parachute was deployed and then released at an altitude of about fifty kilometers. *Venera 14* landed about 950 kilometers southwest of *Venera 13* near the eastern flank of Phoebe Regio at 13° 15' S by 310° E on a basaltic plain. After landing an imaging panorama was started and a mechanical drilling arm reached to the surface and obtained a sample, which was deposited in a hermetically sealed chamber, maintained at 30 degrees C and a pressure of about .05 atmospheres where its composition could be analyzed.

The lander survived for fifty-seven minutes (the planned design life was thirty-two), during which time it transmitted data to the bus, which acted as a data relay as it flew by Venus. Once the lander systems failed after an hour on the surface, the artifact entered its archaeological context.

14/15) *VEGA 1*[14] AND *VEGA 2*[15]

History

In perhaps the Soviet Union's most remarkable robotic exploration of another planet, two identical spacecraft, *Vega 1* and *Vega 2*, were launched from Baikonur Cosmodrome on 15 and 21 December 1984, respectively. After carrying their Venus entry probes to the vicinity of the planet, the two spacecraft used the gravity field of Venus to sail toward a 1986 rendezvous with the Comet Halley and then into heliocentric orbits. The Venus probes consisted of both a (by now) traditional surface lander, and also a helium balloon aerostat that would deploy and inflate in the atmosphere and circulate around the planet.

The *Vega 1* lander/balloon assembly entered the atmosphere of Venus at approximately 125 kilometers altitude on 11 June 1985. Fifteen seconds later, a parachute opened at an altitude of sixty-four kilometers and was then released fifteen seconds after that. The balloon package was pulled from its compartment by parachute forty seconds later at an altitude of sixty-one kilometers, at a position of 8° 1' N, 176° 9' E. A second parachute opened at an altitude of fifty-five kilometers, extracting the balloon itself. It took 100 seconds and another kilometer of descent before the balloon was inflated and at that point the parachute and inflation system were discarded.

At this point, the ballast was jettisoned and the balloon rose to its operational altitude of around fifty-four kilometers above the surface. At this height, the balloon was floating in a layer of the Venusian atmosphere where the temperatures were about 28° Celsius. The balloon drifted westwards at a speed of about seventy meters per second and at a constant altitude, crossing the terminator from night to day on 12 June after cruising for 8,500 kilometers.

The entry of the *Vega 2* combined probe entered the atmosphere of Venus four days after *Vega 1* and executed a similar descent plan to the earlier probe. *Vega 2*'s balloon crossed the terminator from night to day on 16 June after a flight of some 7,400 kilometers.

Technical Notes

Each of the Vega spacecraft was three-axis stabilized. Their main features were large solar panels, a high-gain antenna dish, and an automatic pointing platform carrying those experiments that required pointing at the comet nucleus. Approximately half of the Vega spacecraft was devoted to the Halley module and the other half to the Venus lander package.

The Venus Descent Module consisted of a sphere 240 centimeters in diameter, which separated two days before arrival at Venus and entered the planet's atmosphere on an inclined path, without active maneuvers, as was done on previous Venera missions. The lander probe was identical to those of *Venera 9* through *14* and similarly had two objectives, the study of the atmosphere and the study of the superficial crust. In addition to temperature- and pressure-measuring instruments, the descent probe carried an ultraviolet spectrometer for measurement of minor atmospheric constituents, an instrument dedicated to measurement of the concentration of H_2O, and other instruments for determination of the chemical composition of the condensed phase: a gas-phase chromatograph; an X-ray spectrometer observing the fluorescence of grains or drops; and a mass spectrograph measuring the chemical composition of the grains or drops. The X-ray spectrometer separated the grains according to their sizes using a laser-imaging device, while the mass spectrograph separated them according to their sizes using an aerodynamic inertial separator. After landing, a small surface sample near the probe was to be analyzed by gamma spectroscopy and X-ray fluorescence. The ultraviolet spectrometer, the mass spectrograph, and the pressure- and temperature-measuring instruments were developed in cooperation between French and Soviet investigators.

The aerostat's balloon probes were comprised a 3.4-meter-diameter balloon and a gondola, suspended below the balloon by a thirteen-meter-long tether strap. The total mass of the deployed balloon probe was 21.5 kilograms: 12.5 kilograms for the balloon and tether, 6.9 kilograms for the gondola, and 2.1 kilograms of helium in the balloon. The balloon, gondola, parachute, ballast, tanks of helium, and timing electronics and pyrotechnic release devices with a total mass of 120 kilograms were stored in a compartment surrounding the lander antenna before deployment.

The balloon was made of a Teflon cloth matrix coated with Teflon film and filled with helium. The diffusion of helium from the balloon was slow enough that the balloon would outlast the probe battery lifetime, losing less than 5 percent of its helium and 500 meters of altitude. The balloon itself was transparent to the downlink radio frequency used.

The gondola was 1.2 meters high and had three parts, connected by straps. The upper section, connected to the tether, was a thirty-seven-centimeter-long antenna, fourteen centimeters in diameter at its base. The middle section was connected by two straps to the upper section with dimensions approximately 40.8 × 14.5 × 13.0 centimeters. The upper part of the section contained a radio transmitter and modulator, data-handling system, and signal-processing and power-regulating electronics. The lower part had pressure and illumination sensors and a deployable arm which held temperature sensors and an anemometer. The lower section was 9.0 × 14.5 × 15.0 centimeters, and was also connected to the middle section by two straps, and held the batteries and a nephelometer, an instrument for measuring suspended particulates in a liquid or gas. The gondola was painted with a white coating that resisted corrosion by sulfuric acid and increased the surface albedo.

The radio-transmitter power supply consisted of one kilogram of lithium batteries with 250 watt hours' capacity and an expected life of forty-six to fifty-two hours. Twenty ground stations were used for Very Long Baseline Interferometry (VLBI) tracking of the balloons. Six of these stations were on territory of the Soviet Union and were coordinated by the Soviet space agency. The other fourteen antennas were coordinated by CNES (France) and included three NASA Deep Space Network antennas and eleven radio astronomy observatories.

The aerostats floated at approximately fifty kilometers' altitude in the middle and most active layer of the Venus three-tiered cloud system, recording atmospheric dynamics, pressure and temperature, and lightning and illumination levels on both the day and night sides of Venus. Data from the balloon instruments were transmitted directly to Earth for the forty-seven-hour lifetime of the mission, indicating that horizontal winds were of 240 kilometers per hour and downward gusts were one meter per second.

Archaeology

The *Vega 1* lander touched down on the surface of Venus on 11 June 1985, at a position of 7° 5' N, 177° 7' E. The pressure at the landing site was recorded as ninety-five atmospheres and the temperature was 466° Celsius. The *Vega 2* lander touched down on 15 June 1985 at a position of 8° 5' S, 164° 5' E. Pressure at this site was recorded as ninety-one atmospheres and the temperature as 463° Celsius. When they ceased their data transmissions to Earth, both sites entered their archaeological contexts.

The final transmission from the *Vega 1* balloon occurred on 13 June 1985, when the balloon was at a position of 8° 1' N, 68° 8' E, after a cruise of 11,600 kilometers. The final transmission from the *Vega 2* balloon occurred on 17 June 1985, when the balloon was at a position of 7° 5' S, 76° 3' E, after a cruise of 11,100 kilometers. It is not known how much farther either of the balloons traveled, or if or where it came down on the surface. It is possible, given that the Teflon-based aerostat would have been impervious to most chemicals and stable over a wide range of temperatures, that they could have survived their eventual descents to the surface and exist in there in their archaeological contexts. Other components of the overall Vega material cultural would include the parachutes, inflation systems, and ballast all discarded during the landing procedures of both probes.

16) CASSINI-HUYGENS[16]

History

The *Cassini* space probe to Saturn was launched atop a Titan IV-Centaur rocket from Cape Canaveral, Florida, on 10 October 1997. To compensate for the absence of an appropriate deep-space propulsion rocket, the probe instead made two flybys of Venus (in April 1998 and June 1999), one of Earth in August 1999, and then one of Jupiter in December 2000 in order to gain the momentum to reach Saturn. The probe reached orbit around Saturn in mid–2004, where it prepared to deploy a probe of the moon Titan.

After the probe was released, the two craft maintained separate orbits for about three weeks. The *Cassini* was then positioned above the surface of Titan in order to receive transmissions from the probe as it entered Titan's atmosphere, about two hours prior to *Cassini*'s approach to the Saturnian moon.

The probe of Titan was called *Huygens* and was designed by the European Space Agency to make in situ observations of Titan. The *Huygens* probe's objectives were to (1) determine the physical characteristics (density, pressure, temperature, etc.) of Titan's atmosphere as a function of height; (2) measure the abundance of atmospheric constituents; (3) investigate the atmosphere's chemistry and photochemistry, especially with regard to organic molecules and the formation and composition of aerosols; (4) characterize the meteorology of Titan, particularly with respect to cloud physics, lightning discharges, and general circulation; and (5) examine the physical state, topography, and composition of the surface.

The probe landed on Titan on 14 January 2005, the most distant robotic landing from Earth that humans have ever achieved. In its few minutes of systemic life before its batteries failed, *Huygens* returned an image of a world that looks eerily similar to the frozen, rock-filled soil of Rudolf Island in Franz Josef Land in the Russian Arctic where we located and surveyed the Soviet-era aircraft in 2006.

Technical Notes

The *Cassini* was equipped with two recorders, each of which had a capacity of two gigabits of data in the form of dynamic random access memory (DRAM). Because such memory is vulnerable to radiation effects, the recorders were encased in half-inch-thick aluminum. Recorded data was periodically transmitted to Earth via the high-gain antenna and erased. *Cassini*'s scientific instrumentation consisted of a radar mapper, a CCD imaging system, a visible/infrared mapping spectrometer, a composite infrared spectrometer, a cosmic dust analyzer, a radio and plasma wave experiment, a plasma spectrometer, an ultraviolet imaging spectrograph, a magnetospheric imaging instrument, a magnetometer, an ion/neutral mass spectrometer. Telemetry from the communications antenna as well as other special transmitters (an S-band transmitter and a dual frequency Ka-band system) were used to make observations of the atmospheres of Titan and Saturn and to measure the gravity fields of the planet and its satellites.

The *Huygens* probe consisted of the probe and the probe support equipment (PSE). The probe itself consisted of two elements: the aeroshell to protect the instruments during the high-velocity entry into Titan's atmosphere, and the descent module, which contained the scientific instrumentation. The descent module was enclosed in the aeroshell. They were mechanically attached to each other at three locations.

The aeroshell was comprised of two parts: a front shield and a back cover. The front shield was a 79-kilogram, 2.75-meter-diameter, 60-degree half-angle coni-spherical surface. Tiles of ablative material provided protection against the heat of entry into Titan's atmosphere. The supporting structure was a carbon-fiber-reinforced plastic honeycomb shell, also designed to protect the descent module from the heat generated during entry.

The tiles were attached to the supporting structure by an adhesive. A suspension of hollow silica spheres was sprayed directly on the aluminum structure of the rear surface of the front shield to further insulate the surface. The back cover, which was projected to experience far less heating during atmospheric entry, carried multi-layer insulation to protect the probe during the cruise phase to Saturn and during the coast phase. A hole in the cover allowed for depressurization during launch and allowed for re-pressurization during entry.

The descent module consisted of a forward dome and an after cone which surrounded the experiment platform. A top platform completed the enclosure. The forward dome and the top platform contained a variety of ports to permit experiment sensors access to the atmosphere and to provide a means for deployment of the parachutes.

The PSE, although a part of the *Huygens* system, remained attached to the *Cassini* orbiter. Its purpose was to support the probe and provide power to the probe prior to separation and to provide communications between the probe and orbiter both prior to and after separation. It also provided the spin given to the probe during the separation process.

Archaeology

As it descended into the atmosphere of Titan, the aeroshell surrounding the *Huygens* probe acted to decelerate it from six kilometers per second to 400 meters per second in about two minutes. A parachute was then deployed and the aeroshell jettisoned. The probe floated down through the atmosphere, making measurements as it went. A swivel on the parachute harness enabled the module to spin during descent to allow camera to scan its surroundings. The parachute was released at an altitude of around forty kilometers and the probe free-fell through the lower atmosphere. The duration of the parachute descent was estimated at 120–150 minutes whereupon the *Huygens* was estimated to have about a half-hour to operate on the surface before its batteries ran low and the probe entered its archaeological context, along with the earlier jettisoned components, the aeroshell and the parachute.

Conclusions

The violent nature of the atmosphere of Venus, with its extreme temperatures and pressures, would prevent any direct field archaeology. The lengths to which *Homo sapiens* planning the Venus probes had to go to construct an artifact that could survive such conditions — if even for a few seconds — is a testament to human creativity and perseverance. The effort required to successfully imagine, build, and launch from Earth, then reach, orbit, and land successfully on a neighboring planet, all for a few seconds or minutes of data about that other world, speaks to a level of curiosity that is fundamental to the success of the human species over two million years of evolution.

The one artifact that is certain to gain some eventual attention from archaeologists and cultural resource managers is the *Huygens* probe on Titan. In part, this process has already begun. In 2007, the landing site of the *Huygens* was named in memory of a former head of the European Space Agency, Hubert Curien (1924–2005), a reminder that of the human need to memorialize the past even as the species engages in the exploration of geographies of the future.

Huygens is the first exploration of the outer planets to leave an archaeological assemblage that survived contact with the moon it was to explore and that should still exist in its archaeological context. As a location that holds frozen water, liquid hydrocarbon lakes in its polar regions, a dense atmosphere and Earth-like surface features of sand dunes and shorelines, Titan is certain to be visited innumerable times in future years as the search for extraterrestrial life extends beyond the surface of Mars.

PART III:
INTERSTELLAR ARCHAEOLOGY

The *Pioneer* probe during its rendezvous with Jupiter. After this encounter, the probe moved on into interstellar space. (Credit: NASA-Ames.)

7

Interstellar Archaeology

Aerospace archaeology and cultural resource management conducted on the Moon and Mars will form the methodological and theoretical basis for the survey and stabilization of similar sites in the solar system (our new "planetary archaeology") as well as the search for potential signatures of intelligent life throughout the universe. In this chapter, we examine larger related points that derive directly from the earlier consideration of the study and preservation of planetary sites from the history of aerospace exploration. These larger considerations — which form the basis for a kind of interstellar archaeology — encompass the potential for intelligent life elsewhere in the universe, the possible archaeological signatures of such life, and the parameters by which such signatures might be recognized and archaeological surveys conducted on them on several levels: galactic, planetary, area, and site.

1. Soul Searching: Intelligent Life in the Galaxy and Its Archaeology

"Where is everybody?" asked Enrico Fermi over lunch at Los Alamos Laboratory in the summer of 1950.[1] Fermi's three colleagues at lunch — Emil Konopinski, Herbert York and Edward Teller — understood right away what he was referring to. If popular estimates of thousands of extraterrestrial civilizations are accurate, why don't we see evidence of such alien civilizations in the form of communications, spacecraft and other alien artifacts, or even visits to Earth?

A decade after Fermi formed what has since become known as his universal paradox, astronomer Frank Drake[2] created an equation to estimate the number of technological civilizations that reside in our galaxy.

$$: N = R f_p \, n_e f_l f_i f_c \, L$$

In Drake's equation, N is the number of civilizations that share the universe with us; R the average rate of star formation; f_p the fraction of those stars that have planets; ne the number of planets capable of sustaining life; f_l the planets where life actually develops; f_i those planets that evolve intelligent life; f_c where civilization develops that is capable of releasing evidence of its presence into space; and, finally, L the length of time those civilizations actually release messages into space (in other words, the amount of time between the start of a civilization's radio age to the time of that civilization's [assumed] destruction).

The mechanical aspects of such a construct are no doubt sound. Perhaps inevitably, however, they also contain several human conceits. Among these are a general overestimation of the number and longevity of civilizations as well as the cultural constraints on the technologies of exploration. Such overestimations led physicists to calculate that the numbers of civilizations capable of contacting Earth ranged anywhere from handfuls to thousands.

The main conceit in such constructions, perhaps, is the assumption that if intelligent life has developed something similar to *Homo sapiens'* civilization, such a civilization exists now, in real time, somewhere in the galaxy, in a mode capable of contacting Earth. It is this conceit upon which the notion of contact with exo-cultures (the SETI project, for example) is predicated. Not only do such cultures with advanced technological civilization exist now — in this way of imagining cultures in the universe — but they are capable of transmitting data in some pattern or form recognizable by *Homo sapiens* as the definable signature of extraterrestrial civilization.

It was Isaac Asimov who first explored this notion as it might relate directly to aero-space archaeology. Asimov used a more reasonable approximation of the lengths of the stages of technological development in human civilization to calculate the probability that similar such civilizations exist in our own galaxy.

As in all such constructs, one makes a few dramatic assumptions. For Asimov, writing in the Cold War era of the 1970s, it was that a civilization such as *Homo sapiens* destroys itself within, at most, several generations of developing nuclear power. Asimov further assumed that every habitable planet with a life-bearing span of 12 billion years developed an intelligent species after 4.6 billion years, which then developed an increasingly sophisticated and lethal civilization over the ensuing 600,000 years.

He continued:

> Since 600,000 is 1/20,000 of 12 billion, we can divide the 650 million habitable planets in our Galaxy by 20,000 and find that only 32,500 of them would be in that 600,000-year period in which a species the intellectual equivalent of *Homo sapiens* is expanding in power.
>
> Judging by the length of time human beings have spent at different stages in their development and taking that as an average, we could suppose that 540 habitable planets bear an intelligent species that, at least in the more advanced parts of the planet, are practicing agriculture and living in cities.
>
> In 270 planets in our Galaxy, intelligent species have developed writing; in 20 planets modern science has developed; in 10 the equivalent of the industrial revolution has taken place; and in 2 nuclear energy has been developed, and those 2 civilizations are, of course, near extinction.
>
> Since our 600,000 years of humanity occur near the middle of the Sun's lifetime, and since we are taking the human experience as average, then all but 1/20,000 of the habitable planets fall outside that period, half earlier and half later. That means that

on about 325 million such planets no intelligent species has as yet appeared, and on 325 million planets there are signs of civilizations in ruins. And nowhere is there a planet with a civilization not only alive but substantially father advanced than we are.

If all this is so, then even though ... hundreds of millions of civilizations [may have arisen] in our Galaxy ... it is no wonder that we haven't heard from them.[3]

Asimov's analysis may be dispiriting to exobiologists hoping to make contact with an intelligent form of extraterrestrial life. For archaeologists, however, the calculation that "on 325 million planets there are signs of civilizations in ruins" is a notion to stagger the imagination. Not even the National Historic Preservation Act of 1969 could have envisioned a requirement for 325 million cultural resource professionals, much less the need to equip each of them with survey and transport equivalent of the Apollo program.

To this potential planetary database we need to add two additional considerations. The first is obvious: on Earth there is evidence not just of one civilization in ruins but several. So while we might speak of 325 million planets with signs of civilization in ruins, such a reality would translate to actual ruins numbering in the *billions.*

Second, we need to consider the possible forms such ruined civilizations might take if they managed to achieve, prior to their destruction, a level of technological development far beyond anything contemplated in the near-term cultural evolution of *Homo sapiens.* Freeman Dyson suggested the possibility that potentially massive engineering works might exist in the universe when he proposed a galactic search for sources of infrared radiation as a necessary corollary to the search for radio communications.[4] Dyson assumed that, given the enormous scales of time and distance in the universe, any technological civilization observable from Earth would have been in existence for many millions of years longer than comparable civilization on Earth. (Dyson was [again] assuming a living civilization, but the argument holds perhaps even more closely for a civilization that survives only as an archaeological entity.) Such an advanced civilization would have long ago outstripped its planetary resources. In response, it would have developed solar system–scale technological structures to provide for its post–Malthusian energy requirements and, as Dyson wrote, its *lebensraum.*

Dyson proposed such an artifact in the form of a shell or sphere that would surround a Solar System's star, effectively capturing all of its radiant energy and enabling the material resources of all the planetary and asteroid bodies in the system to be mined. Using our Solar System as a model, Dyson conceived of an industrial operation that, over the course of 800 years, would disassemble the planet Jupiter and reassemble its mass as a two- to three-meter-thick shell at a distance of twice the distance from Earth from the Sun. People occupying the inside surface of this sphere would have access to the entire output of the Sun's energy. Presumably, given this constant energy source, this entire inside surface would resemble a tropical rain forest.

In terms of a galactic archaeological survey, such a notion would require archaeologists to search not just for those places most visible to radio telescopes, but those dark areas where the light of an entire solar system is being harnessed for occupants living on the inside edge of a Dyson sphere. In terms of cultural anthropology, the magnitude of such an effort, both in terms of technology and time, would require the concentrated efforts of an entire planet over the course of forty generations or more.

There are no international Earth corollaries to such an effort, although national structures such as the Egyptian pyramids or the Great Wall of China perhaps come closest to predicting what a planetary-scale effort would require. The former, a response to a spiritual requirement, and the latter, a response to security threats, would suggest the difficulty of predicting the precise rationale for an undertaking of this magnitude.

In the end, the implication of Azimov's calculations and, to a lesser extent, Dyson's conjecture, is evident. SETI stations are hearing only static through their radio telescopes because they are, in effect, listening for a message from the Mayans, or the Sumerians, or any of dozens of dead civilizations who can speak to us now only through their archaeology.

2. Orbital Archaeology: Is There Intelligent Life Down There?

Given the time spans and likely cultural resistance (and/or *résistance*) such an effort as a Dyson sphere would generate, it is more likely that a long-term project in cultural survival would result in a loose federation of hundreds of smaller outposts. And this, of course, is assuming that such an advanced technological society, upon completing such a structure, would then retreat to a band-level tropical rain forest existence that its forbears presumably walked away from millions of years earlier. Each of these scattered outposts, given the time and distances involved even in solar system–level travel, would within several generations have developed a variety of distinctive cultural adaptations and the different dialects or distinct languages that evolve with them.

An Earth corollary to such a planetary scenario would be the Norse colonization of the North Atlantic.[5] A mother culture for a variety of reasons spins perhaps 10 percent of its population away from the fjords of Norway, with some of the voyagers settling Iceland. Once this area became too crowded, 10 percent of this Icelandic population eventually settles even further to the west, in Greenland. Explorers from this population push on to Vínland, but are as quickly pushed back when Native Americans oppose the new colonization. A combination of factors then besets the Greenland colony over the course of several hundred years until it is finally cut off from its originating cultures of Norway and then Iceland. Eventually, the Greenland colony vanishes, leaving the barest trace of written records, none of which testifies to their fate. With no or with indecipherable written records, as in the Norse Greenland colony or the civilization of Mohenjo Daro, the archaeological record then becomes the primary means of studying the vanished civilization.

Such material records of past civilization have been proposed even within our own Solar System. Highly speculative landforms like the unexplained linear markings on the Tharsis plateau of Mars,[6] or "The Face" and the pyramidal shapes in the Cydonia region of Mars,[7] which eventually were identified as ancient buttes worn down by sandstorms, have in the past been advanced as sites to be examined as potential artifacts of intelligence.

The "scientific politics" of discussing such notions is evident from an article by a professor of physics, describing the *Mars Pathfinder* probe as it was being readied to explore for fossil life on Mars.[8] Faculty and graduate students in the Department of Geophysical Sciences at the University of Chicago gathered to discuss the more speculative aspects of the mission. Like Enrico Fermi, they only felt comfortable bringing the subject up outside the formal parameters of a scheduled seminar. Questions of life on Mars were brought into the open only after the scientists had consumed large quantities of beer — and this even though their multi–million dollar mission was already an accomplished fact.

Such fears are increasingly unfounded. The sub-field of "exobiology" has been commonplace for half a century, and consistently generates news from its mostly hypothetical undertakings. The icy Jovian moon of Europa, with an apparent frozen ocean similar to Earth's Arctic Ocean, is now under study by such biologists who, with intensive planning by spacecraft engineers, seek to burrow an oceanographic-style probe through Europa's pack ice in search of microbial life.[9]

Carl Sagan suggested that the search for evidence of intelligent life in the universe had to begin by first verifying the criteria for intelligent life with the corollary of Earth.[10] Sagan who, unlike Asimov, believed there were more than a million currently active galactic civilizations, expressed his optimism in a chapter called "Is There Intelligent Life on Earth?" He argued that, with 1970s-era satellite imagery of one-mile resolution, one could stare for hours at the entire eastern seaboard of the United States and see no sign of life, intelligent or otherwise.

Without finer resolution imagery, one would fall back on basic requirements for life in general: water and oxygen. To this add carbon dioxide to warm the planet, and the presence of methane as an indicator of life. Chlorophyll or some other mechanism for absorbing solar radiation and transmuting it into a form necessary to both sustain life and produce oxygen would also be present. Such life would also vent methane into the atmosphere, another sign.

The search for intelligent life on Earth begins with the search for radio wave transmissions that are sequential, irregular, and travel along predictable frequencies. With space-borne imagery of less than 100 meters' resolution, one would begin to see a planetary penchant for geometric shapes and linear settlements and pathways. Perhaps one would mistake modes and means of transportation as intelligent life rather than its byproduct.

For archaeologists, this raises the question that if structures similar to the Jonglei Canal or the Aswan High Dam exist on Alpha Centauri, would we be able to recognize them as artifacts of intelligence? If in fact what we will find in space is not life, but the traces of past life, not civilization, but the traces of past civilization, it makes sense for us to start discussing what forms such life and such remains might take based on existing terrestrial analogues. As notes, this process is well along in the biological sciences, but has been all but ignored in archaeology.

At a minimum, existing satellite imagery of Earth could be used to create analogues for the kinds of artifacts and structures that might be encountered on future exploratory space missions, analogues that could begin by drawing upon examples of similar such work already accomplished.[11] Constructing such a database of structural analogues for potential signatures of advanced civilizations is well within the province of aerospace archaeology.

It seems appropriate — not least given its unique place amid discussions of extraterrestrial visits to Earth — to apply here a cautionary note from Easter Island (Rapa Nui). During his 1955–56 archaeological expedition to the island, the Norwegian explorer Thor Heyerdahl discovered a sub-culture of Rapa Nui culture that had gone underground, living a cave-like existence.[12] A society under the stress of resource depletion, external security threats, climate change, overpopulation, pollution, or any combination of the above, might well radically reduce its planetary archaeological footprint to a problematic level for external space-based sensors. In such a case, the absence of a planetary surface archaeological signature does not rule out a cultural adaptation that exists (or existed) on the outer edges of our theoretical constructs and is all but invisible to much of the current methodology and technology of our remote sensing.

3. Concentration on Concentrations: Remote Sensing of Areas

As noted above, given the limitations on direct human exploration of the universe, archaeological expeditions to search, survey and study interplanetary or intergalactic sites will of necessity be conducted through the techniques and technologies of remote sensing. Given the requirements of water and oceans as essential to life, and current models such as the planning of the "Icepick" mission to Europa, these remote sensing techniques will owe as much to the history of underwater archaeology as to aerial archaeology.

The shift toward remote sensing of archaeological sites began in the 1970s, as one method to elevate archaeology from its reliance on "the limited observational capacity of the human senses."[13] It took on greater momentum in the latter part of the twentieth century not only from the accelerating refinement of survey technology but also because of encroaching political considerations that threaten to overwhelm traditional archaeology.

As early as 1975, Americanist archaeologists began to acknowledge the potential for political limits on their global historical explorations stemming from foreign nationalism. Since such an admission implied that excavations would be limited in both their scope and content — if they were allowed at all — it was suggested that Americanist archaeologists, "who tend to be intensive excavators rather than observers of surface remains,"[14] begin to systemically adopt two underemployed methods, one well-established and one relatively new and emerging.

The first was the British technique of noninvasive "field archaeology" espoused by O.G.S. Crawford. In the years before World War I, Crawford "longed to see [archaeological sites] not obliquely but in plan, as would be possible in an aeroplane"[15] or balloon, and after the war he went on to invent and refine the techniques of aerial photography of archaeological sites. The second method, one that relied on modern high technology inventions, was to adopt, adapt, and develop sophisticated scientific technologies, similar to those already employed by investigators in other "hard" sciences, for archaeological investigations.

In addition to Crawford's classic methods of field archaeology and aerial photogram-metry, these techniques included proton magnetometry to measure magnetic anomalies, soil resistivity to measure electrical resistance, and ground-penetrating radar. At the high end of the technological spectrum, advocated methods included thermal and infrared remote sensing by aircraft and satellites.

For underwater sites, exploration with submersibles like Jacques-Yves Cousteau's *Soucoupe*, or archaeologist George Bass' *Asherah*, a submersible developed specifically for archaeological research in 1964, could be combined with manned undersea field stations like the Conshelf Two station envisioned and constructed in the Red Sea by Cousteau and, since the 1960s, with unmanned, remotely operated undersea research vehicles like those under continuing development at the Woods Hole Oceanographic. Remotely oper-ated instruments have been placed around artifact concentrations in northern Europe to monitor currents, salinity and other processes affecting wreck sites.[16]

These "alternative[s] to the traditional approach to archaeological exploration, dis-covery and investigation ... emphasize the acquisition and sophisticated analysis of a vari-ety of remotely sensed imagery and data as the *primary* tools of exploration, discovery and recording."[17] With the biosphere, geosphere and archaeosphere thus delineated, tra-ditional field surveys and excavations would automatically revert to a status as secondary methods for verifying, or "ground-truthing," the data collected with the primary remote sensors.

Exploration techniques that have been used elsewhere in the world but not applied to specific archaeological problems in the undersea Arctic, for example, should proceed with a view toward their corollary development for space archaeology research. A side-scan sonar system was fitted to the nuclear submarine HMS *Sovereign* for a voyage beneath the sea ice of the Arctic Ocean as early as October 1976.[18] The narrow beam upward-looking sonar profiles produced features that could be seen clearly on the under-ice maps, including open water, thin ice, pressure ridges, hummock fields, first-year floes and multi-year ice. Such remote sensing techniques comprise at present the only way archaeologists can cover the vast distances required to explore and resolve historical and archaeological questions in extreme ice ocean environments.

The dependence on such massive technological infrastructure such as nuclear sub-marines and the bases and personnel they require will obtain until the perfection of inde-pendent undersea/space archaeology robotic probes. The array of such an "archaeoprobe," equipped with real-time telemetry capability and a miniature terrain rover, could be modified, like its oceanographic cousins, to meet virtually any exigency in the field. More, such a probe could be sent to a planetary site and operated remotely by a single explorer.

Such technological development will proceed alongside a long-running debate in oceanographic technology circles over the course of subsea exploration. As Travis made clear, there has been a long-running debate on how oceanographic subsurface technology should proceed, whether with submarines, submersibles, ROVs or AUVs, or some combination of all of them.[19]

What is clear is that there is a core of scientific explorers who do not want to leave exploration solely to robotic sensors. Willard Bascom, one of the most famous of American oceanographers, acknowledges this same human yearning when he writes in his autobiography of using satellites to study the oceans, remarking at one point that "in recent years my interest [in satellite oceanography] has waned again, probably because this is not a very adventurous form of oceanography. Although the scientific findings can be intellectually exciting, it takes a special sort of person to sit at a computer all day long sorting the data from a big dish antenna pointed at the sky or to spend years figuring out algorithms for converting the millions of data bits into useful information about what the ocean is doing."[20]

The equation for archaeologists is simple: either develop post-doctoral programs at oceanographic and space research centers to get us up to speed on the latest survey technology and simultaneously develop new technologies for our own research designs, or see archaeological exploration descend into arbitrary deconstructionism, "a kind of literary criticism, in which equally stimulating and internally consistent interpretations abound, but where no basis exists for deciding which one best approximates the historical reality of the past."[21] New and effective combinations of already available technologies, combined with the development of autonomous vehicles, employed in a research design that frees the archaeologist from reliance on the technological debates of oceanographers, will provide the necessary data for the application of the scientific method by archaeological explorers.

More than twenty-five years ago George Bass entered the technological end of this controversy when the paradigm was manned versus unmanned exploration of space, and he seemed to endorse the conception of technological archaeology, in this case a sonar/ROV-equipped, long-range, lock-out submarine for archaeology, one that could also serve as either a supply vessel for an underwater habitat for archaeologists, or as the habitat itself. Wrote Bass:

> Submarines will allow archaeologists to map the visible remains with stereophotography and to clear away the sand with portable, neutrally buoyant air lifts directed by remotely controlled manipulators attached to the submarines....
>
> Only one thing is missing, and that is the sure touch of the archaeologist's hand on the site. The present scientific controversy over whether manned or unmanned vehicles are more practical in the exploration of outer space is easily answered for the archaeological exploration of inner space: only a vast array of the most delicate manipulators imaginable could clean and raise the fragile and fragmentary pieces of wood which are so easily and gently handled by human divers.
>
> Probably as important for the future of underwater archaeology are the underwater houses now being developed.[22]

158

It has now been more than forty years since Bass commissioned *Asherah*, the first (and only) submarine constructed specifically for archaeology. While some might see a submarine for archaeology as an expensive luxury, Bass notes that more has been paid by museums for a single work of Classical art than was spent on his submarine, which held the potential for revealing entire shiploads of such art.

Yet, within two years, *Asherah* was not exploring archaeological sites, but was instead in the service of oceanographers and, since the mid–1970s, has been in storage for want of an operating budget. Both of these problems would have been ameliorated if *Asherah* had been operated, not from an anthropology or classical archaeology department, but from a department of archaeological engineering and exploration attached to an oceanographic institute, which would have provided the technical, financial, and historical basis of long-term mission planning, logistics, and operations.

4. Site Level: The Base Camp of the Imagination

The twentieth century stands as the first in which the human species rose above the earth both to study its own habitat and its capability to visit and potentially inhabit other worlds. Questions of where, how, and why humankind first sought to use air and space technology for scientific and geographic exploration have a direct bearing on behavioral questions of why we have become perhaps the "most inquisitive, exploring animal."[23] Defining the archaeological signatures by which this cultural transformation took place will provide a comparative model for similar cultural responses by extraterrestrial civilizations.

If remote survey technologies can be combined with techniques for identifying such surface remains in extreme environments, they will provide the basis for site evaluation without the requirements of surface survey. The current avenue for such remote evaluation of extreme environment sites is satellite photography on the order of high-altitude (150 miles perigee) advanced KH-11 satellite imagery.[24] The fine-spatial resolution (less than one meter) of KH-11 imagery and its use of metric markings for use as maps, combined with more recent VEGA satellites that employ imaging radar for use through cloud cover, would make it possible to draw plans for virtually any small-scale site.

The current pathway of such research is clear. Part of the mission profile of the *Mars Reconnaissance Orbiter* was to search for archaeological traces of the lost *Mars Global Surveyor*, the *Mars Polar Lander* and the British *Beagle 2*.[25] The expedition has thus far succeeded in capturing provided high-resolution images of the *Spirit* rover that has been exploring the surface of Mars as well as the two Viking probes that reached Mars in the 1970s.[26]

This human requirement to search for traces of former expeditions is a prosaic necessity of accident investigation. But it is also an almost spiritual need to relocate familiar human landmarks along expansionary pathways. It means that future space missions will devote significant energies not just to pioneering new routes through space, but to rediscovering the techniques and technologies of earlier explorers.

With the emerging capabilities of archaeologists to combine digital photography and photogrammetry in a regional GIS context in a Google Earth environment,[27] it will be possible to delineate the exploratory archaeosphere, both topographically and, eventually, bathymetrically, in such a way as to enable provenance maps and charts of artifact clusters, sites, and site environments, as well as site and regional archaeological histories.

The requirement of water for life, along with the proposed mission to the potential frozen ocean of Europa, highlight the necessity to consider undersea sensing systems for archaeological research in a space context. Corollaries to human space missions, such as those that have established model Mars bases in the Arctic,[28] should be developed to test the requirements for similar archaeological missions. Moreover, what aerospace archaeology currently lacks in direct access for the archaeologist it can make up both in such corollary experiments, and in the massive volume of historical, technological, and planetary data available for synthesis into a catalog of structural signatures of intelligent life.

Conclusions

Given the vastness of space, the chances of real-time communication with other civilizations are small; on the other hand, the chances of excavating or otherwise remote sensing traces of other civilizations seems, by comparison, rather high. The role of archaeology in space exploration in the near-term, then, is twofold.

The first is to shape the currently available raw material of historical, technological and planetary data into a catalog of analogs for defining the presence of extraterrestrial civilizations. This catalog should be both methodological and theoretical, and center on notions of *Homo sapiens* as an exploratory, migratory species.

Secondly, a department of archaeological engineering, co-located perhaps with departments with similar mission sets such as those for ocean engineering, should develop a model of a remote probe to be employed throughout the galaxy to explore for traces of these signatures of civilization. With this mixture of anthropological theory and technological experience, an archaeoprobe can be designed and developed even though it might not see its first deployment for fifteen generations or more. Operating in a sense as medieval monks, we can at least prepare a sort of illuminated manuscript for the edification of researchers not yet born, and within it a blueprint for the machine required to explore for the traces of galactic civilization defined by that manuscript.

8

Mobile Artifacts in the Solar System and Beyond

Among the examples we used to start this book were space probes like the *Voyager* and *Pioneer* series. It feels a bit odd for an archaeologist to consider objects that are still in motion as part of their material culture database, since the image we have of archaeological research centers upon the careful excavation of objects that have been fixed within the soil or rock of Earth, oftentimes for millions of years. Whole new categories of archaeological methodology seem to be called for if we are to consider the possibilities of fieldwork on the now dead — or soon-to-be dead — spacecraft we have launched on their way to distant stars.

But there is first the issue of whether or not a mobile artifact is in fact an object for archaeological study. This definition rests on whether or not the artifact is still being used for that which it was designed. As we mentioned earlier, several distant-traveling spacecraft have not yet become strictly archaeological objects. These include the two *Voyager* probes, the *Galileo* probe to Jupiter, and the *New Horizons* probe to Pluto. Each of these spacecraft is scheduled to break contact with Earth in the year 2015. Until then, they still exist as part of a living human cultural system.

Once the spacecraft no longer responds to signals from Earth, it ceases to be used for the original mission for which it was designed, and becomes instead a discarded, and hence, archaeological, object. This is the case with the *Pioneer 10* space probe, which ceased "speaking" with Earth in 2003, and is now headed on a two-million-year journey toward the red star Aldebaran.

But these strict categories of systemic and archaeological context are not absolute. It is possible for an object to move in and out of context. For example, a ship that wrecks along a coastline and breaks apart has ceased to the things humans designed for it to do. It has entered its archaeological context. But pieces of the ship can be salvaged by people on shore, by the company that owned the ship, by salvors and insurance companies. These fragments can be reused in other systemic contexts, like the hut that Walter Wellman's crew built from timbers and sailcloth salvaged from his ship before it sank off the coast of Waldenøya in 1894. The shipwreck itself can return in a different form to a systemic context, like the wreck of the S.S. *Ethie* that I photographed along the western coast of

Newfoundland in 2006. This site is now in systemic context as a tourist spot, complete with wayside plaque, parking lot and viewing platform.

Within the general category of mobile artifacts in the solar system and beyond, there are a few sub-categories. The first would be those artifacts that are on their way from Earth to some undetermined place in interstellar space; the second would be those objects that, either deliberately or as the result of a mission failure, now orbit around the Sun (heliocentric orbit); and, finally, the vast archaeological space "midden" that currently encircles Earth.

For our purposes, we will largely leave aside the third category, but here offer a few words on it. A "midden" in archaeological terms is a feature of an archaeological site where one finds a collection of the waste products produced during the course of normal human daily life. Such features can and do accumulate for generations, and can be studied as the material signature of an entire culture. The midden of space junk that encircles Earth can similarly be thought of as a dump for domestic waste, but in this case the domestic waste of a whole planetary community.

The orbital midden is thought to comprise tens of millions of separate artifacts, none of them in systemic context. The vast majority of these artifacts are chips of paint from orbital satellites and spacecraft, slag from solid rocket motors, coolant from nuclear power plants and other such small debris. Some of this material will fall from its Earth orbit and burn up in the atmosphere. But collisions between these small fragments create more small fragments, an increasing problem for attempts to track these objects so that they do no damage to new space missions.

Spacecraft can largely be protected from collisions with such debris by shielding the craft with metal foil. When a small object collides with the foil, the speed of the collision causes the debris to vaporize. However, NASA estimates that larger objects, those of ten centimeters or larger, now number some 19,000. Objects of this size coming at a spacecraft at eight kilometers per second would destroy it.

In February 2009, a functioning (systemic) satellite, *Iridium 33*, collided at a speed of more than 42,000 kilometers per hour with a defunct (archaeological) Russian Space Forces satellite, *Kosmos-2251*. The combined weight of the two satellites was about a ton and a half. Both were destroyed instantly, but at the same time produced potentially thou-

Opposite: Figure 8.1. Artist's conception of a space habitat large enough to support 10,000 *Homo sapiens*. This wheel-like structure orbits Earth in the same orbit as the Moon in a stable position that is equidistant from both Earth and the Moon, a point called the Lagrangian libration point, L5. The habitat consists of a tube 130 m (427 ft) in diametral cross section bent into a wheel 1790 m (over 1 mile) in diameter. The tube is connected by six large access routes (spokes) to a central hub where incoming spacecraft dock. These spokes are 15 m (48 ft) in diameter and provide entry and exit to the living and agricultural areas in the tubular region. To simulate Earth's normal gravity the entire habitat rotates at one revolution per minute about the central hub. A large stationary mirror suspended directly over the hub captures solar energy to power the floating village in space. (Credit: NASA painting by Rick Guidice.)

Figure 8.2. The wreck of the S.S. *Ethie* photographed along the western coast of Newfoundland in 2006, in archaeological context as a shipwreck, which in turn is in systemic context as an historic site/tourist spot. (Credit: Author.)

sands of new bits of orbital debris, each of which is a potential hazard to other orbiting satellites and spacecraft.

The second category of mobile artifacts in the solar system is those in heliocentric orbit, that is, orbit around the Sun. There are more than fifty such objects, including twenty-nine from launched from the United States, fifteen from the Soviet Union/Russian Federation, five from the European Space Agency, and five from Japan. Only seven of these missions are still active and therefore in systemic context. The remainders are artifacts that were either lost through communications failures or technical problems, those deliberately abandoned after their system use was finished, such as the *Apollo 10* Lunar Module *Snoopy*; or those that missed their original targets such as the Moon or Venus or Mercury and were subsequently captured by the gravitational pull of the Sun. Artifacts in this category include:

Luna 1 (USSR; lunar exploration; launch 2 January 1959)
Pioneer 4 (US; lunar exploration; launch 3 March 1959)
Pioneer 5 (US; destination interplanetary space; launch 11 March 1960)
Venera 1 (USSR; destination Venus; launch 19 May 1961)
Ranger 3 (US; lunar exploration; launch 26 January 1962)
Ranger 5 (US; lunar exploration; launch 18 October 1962)
Mariner 2 (US; destination Venus; launch 27 August 1962)
Mars 1 (USSR; destination Mars; launch 1 November 1962)
Mariner 3 (US; destination Mars; launch 5 November 1964)
Mariner 4 (US; destination Mars; launch 28 November 1964)
Zond 2 (USSR; destination Mars; launch 30 November 1964)
Zond 3 (USSR; destination Moon; launch 18 July 1965)
Venera 2 (USSR; destination Venus; launch 12 November 1965)
Pioneer 6 (US; solar research; launch 16 December 1965)
Pioneer 7 (US; solar research; launch 17 August 1966)
Mariner 5 (US; destination Venus; launch 14 June 1967)
Pioneer 8 (US; solar research; launch 13 December 1967)
Pioneer 9 (US; solar research; launch 8 November 1968)
Mariner 6 (US; destination Mars; launch 24 February 1969)
Mariner 7 (US; destination Mars; launch 27 March 1969)
S-IVB upper stages for *Apollo 8, 9, 10, 11* and *12* (1968–1969)
Lunar Module *Snoopy* from *Apollo 10* (1969)
Mars 4 (USSR; destination Mars; launch 21 July 1973)
Mars 7 (USSR; destination Mars; launch 9 August 1973)
Mariner 10 (US; destination Venus and Mercury; launch 3 November 1973)
Helios 1 (Joint US-ESA; solar research; launch 10 December 1974)
Helios 2 (Joint US-ESA; solar research; launch 15 January 1976)
Venera 11 (USSR; destination Venus; launch 9 September 1978)

Venera 12 (USSR; destination Venus; launch 14 September 1978)

Venera 13 (USSR; destination Venus; launch 3 October 1981)

Venera 14 (USSR; destination Venus; launch 4 November 1981)

Vega 1 (USSR; destination Venus; launch 15 December 1984)

Vega 2 (USSR; destination Venus; launch 21 December 1984)

Sakigake (Japan; destination Halley's Comet; launch 7 January 1985)

Sakigake (Japan; destination Halley's Comet; launch 18 August 1985)

Giotto (ESA; destination Halley's Comet; launch 2 July 1985)

Phobos 1 (USSR; destination Martian moon of Phobos; launch 21 July 1988)

Ulysses (Joint US-ESA; destination Jupiter; launch 6 October 1990)

Nozomi (Japan; destination Mars; launch 3 July 1998)

Hayabusa/Minerva mini-lander (Japan; destination asteroid Itokawa; launch 9
May 2003)

The first category of mobile artifacts in the solar system is of those objects that were deliberately launched from Earth into a journey into interstellar space. These special artifacts of human intelligence hold a particular fascination for archaeologists, as they represent *Homo sapiens*'s attempts to fashion a tool that can cross the barrier of space on a hopeful mission to communicate with other forms of intelligent life that may or may not exist in the galaxy. There are five such composite tools: *Pioneer 10, Pioneer 11, Voyager 1, Voyager 2,* and *New Horizons.* Each initially had a specific scientific mission to carry out within the solar system (*New Horizons* is still in its active mission phase; it will reach its target of the planet Pluto in the year 2015). Once these primary missions were concluded, the spacecraft were then directed toward the boundaries of the solar system with the expectation that they would eventually enter interstellar space and become the representatives of *Homo sapiens* to the rest of the galaxy.

In a NASA history of the Pioneer expeditions, there is an epilogue titled "Interstellar Cave Painting." It recounts how Eric Burgess of the *Christian Science Monitor* looked at the *Pioneer 10* spacecraft as it was being tested and conceptualized it as the first human object that might reach other intelligent species. This observation led to a chain of events culminating in the design and placement on the spacecraft of "a special message from mankind."[1] Carl Sagan and others designed a plaque that would attempt in symbols to represent where the object had come from and the kinds of beings who had constructed it and sent it into space.

The human representations are slender, bipedal and naked. An accompanying scale matched to the overall size of the spacecraft itself is supposed to allow an alien intelligence to discover that the woman is 162.56 centimeters — about 5'4" — tall, the male a bit taller (presumably our alien intelligence will recognize this as the long-term sexual dimorphism of the species). The male has his right arm uplifted at a right angle with the palm of his hand facing outwards in what is hoped will be interpreted as a sign of greeting. Both figures have full heads of hair but otherwise no body hair, clothes, shoes, scars, deformities, tattoos, piercings or other adornments or much in the way of body fat. The man's penis and scrotum are shown, but not the woman's vulva. Ethnically they appear white. They are relatively young, perhaps no more than twenty-five years old. They appear friendly and unthreatening; there is no suggestion of the endemic violence of their home world. There are no other representations of any other life on Earth, present or past, or any suggestion that the form of human on the plaque was the product of millions of years of evolution through natural selection and therefore constantly changing along with all other forms of life on the planet and, in fact, the planet itself. It has been said that the scientific contents of the plaque are difficult even for scientists to understand.

The NASA history explains that the "radial pattern to the left of center of the plaque represents the position of the Sun relative to 14 pulsars and to the center of the Galaxy... the binary digits on the [pulsar] lines denote time."

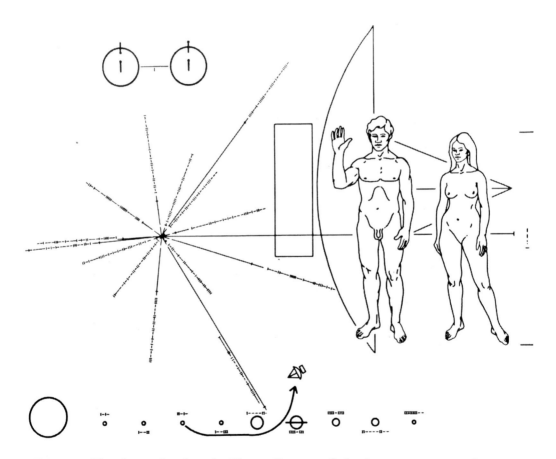

Figure 8.3. The plaque placed on the *Pioneer 10* spacecraft that is meant to communicate to an extraterrestrial intelligence that another species of intelligence exists in the universe who built this particular artifact and sent it on a very long voyage that would almost certainly outlive the species that sent it. (Credit: NASA.)

This can be deduced because they represent precision to 10 decimal digits, which is unlikely for distances to stellar objects but quite feasible for measurements of time. And from the unit of time established from the hydrogen atom, the extraterrestrial intelligence should be able to deduce that all the times are about one tenth of a second … pulsars! Since the periods of pulsars run down at well established rates they act as galactic clocks. An advanced civilization would be able to search its galactic records and identify the star system from which the spacecraft originated, even if Pioneer is not intercepted for billions of years.[2]

It is a wonderfully comforting conceit, this idea of an advanced civilization of galactic record-keepers. One envisions a planet of thoughtful Dutch archivists, as in a painting by Rembrandt, calmly discoursing on the meaning of the plaque as they examine the probe — now displayed atop the circular mahogany table of an ornate special collections room in a vast and eclectic library. It is revealing, as well, of the designer's apparent view of the essential loneliness of the human condition: *Homo sapiens* waving hopefully across a billion years of a cold universe on the infinitesimal chance someone might wave back.

A further orientation on the plaque shows our solar system, with the spacecraft leaving from the third planet from the Sun and with its antenna pointing backwards towards that planet. Presumably from this an extraterrestrial intelligence would be able to infer that only this planet held the remarkable species that sent the artifact. Would they also conclude that no life existed on any other planets in our system? Or merely that these particular beings did not communicate, or had no ability to communicate, or did not *want* to communicate, with life on other planets in the system? What if humans launched a similar probe from the surface of Mars in, say, 100 or 1,000 years from now, equipped with a similar plaque but a different point of origin. Would this be interpreted by others as representing cooperation or conflict within our solar system? Or even the death of the third planet?

Of course, all such questions rely on the intercepting extraterrestrials having a similar level of intelligence as humans, combined with a similar visual anatomy, physiology, and cognitive processing apparatus — a point that the NASA history itself makes. "If that [extraterrestrial] life possesses sufficient intelligent to detect the Pioneer spacecraft … it may also have the curiosity and the technical ability to pick up the spacecraft and take it into a laboratory to inspect it. Then the plaque with its message from Earth people should be found and hopefully deciphered."[3] If an extraterrestrial intelligence took an oceanic form — like whales, for example — then our message would not find an audience capable of even an attempt at decipherment.

As tool-using, bipedal organisms with stereoscopic vision, we have fashioned our space probes almost strictly for scientific purposes. When there is a thought given to cultural or archaeological implications of our exploration of space, as with the *Pioneer 10* plaque, the result can be seen as almost cursory — or illusory, depending on one's interpretation of the *Pioneer 10* plaque. We are asking for an intelligence elsewhere in the Galaxy to possess the ability to detect our lifeless probe and the technical skill to intercept it as it moves at perhaps ten kilometers per second or faster. The very concept of intercepting an object that appears on a set course might not be one that would even occur to another species. Or perhaps their interception would take the form of a defensive/offensive measure such as that taken seen in the Hollywood film *Star Trek V: The Final Frontier*, when the Klingons indeed intercepted a Pioneer probe with its attached plaque — only to immediately blow it up.

Assuming that the *Pioneer 10* probe and its unique representation of *Homo sapiens* are not destroyed by another species possessing some of our own aggressive tendencies, it should survive well beyond the age of humans on Earth. More than that, as the NASA history puts it, this modern cave painting "might survive not only all the caves of Earth, but also the solar system itself. It is an interstellar stela that shows mankind possesses a spiritual insight beyond the material problems of the age of human emergence."[4]

The Archaeological Catalog: Artifacts En Route from the Solar System

1) *Pioneer 10*[5]

History

Pioneer 10 was launched atop an Atlas-Centaur rocket from Cape Canaveral, Florida, on 3 March 1972. This mission was the first to be sent to the outer solar system and the first to investigate the planet Jupiter, where it achieved its closest approach on 4 December 1973. Since this encounter, *Pioneer 10* has followed an escape trajectory from the solar system that is the opposite direction from both *Voyager 1* and *2* and *Pioneer 11*. The spacecraft is heading generally towards the red star Aldebaran, which forms the eye of the constellation Taurus. This journey — a distance of sixty-eight light years — will require about two million years to complete.

Besides the plaque intended for extraterrestrial communications, the probe carried the following scientific instruments: magnetometer, plasma analyzer, charged particle detector, ionizing detector, non-imaging telescopes with overlapping fields of view to detect sunlight reflected from passing meteoroids, sealed pressurized cells of argon and nitrogen gas for measuring the penetration of meteoroids, UV photometer, IR radiometer, and an imaging photopolarimeter, which produced photographs and measured polarization.

Technical Notes

The spacecraft body was mounted behind a 2.74-meter-diameter parabolic dish antenna that was forty-six centimeters deep. The spacecraft structure was a thirty-six-centimeter-deep flat-equipment compartment, the top and bottom being regular hexagons. Its sides were seventy-one centimeters long. One side joined a smaller compartment that carried the scientific experiments. The high-gain antenna feed was situated on three struts, which projected forward about 1.2 meters. This feed was topped with a medium-gain antenna. A low-gain omnidirectional antenna extended about 0.76 meters behind the equipment compartment and was mounted below the high-gain antenna. Power for the spacecraft was obtained by four SNAP-19 radioisotope thermonuclear generators (RTG), which were held about three meters from the center of the spacecraft by two three-rod trusses 120 degrees apart. A third boom extended 6.6 meters from the experiment compartment to hold the magnetometer away from the spacecraft. The four RTGs generated about 155 watts at launch and decayed to approximately 140 watts by the time the spacecraft reached Jupiter, 21 months after launch.

There were three reference sensors: a star sensor for Canopus, which failed shortly after its Jupiter encounter, and two sun sensors. Attitude position could be calculated from the reference directions to Earth and the Sun, with the known direction to Canopus as a backup. Three pairs of rocket thrusters provided spin-rate control and changed the velocity of the spacecraft, the spin period near the end of the mission being 14.1 seconds. These thrusters could be pulsed or fired steadily by command. The spacecraft was temperature-controlled between minus 23° Celsius and plus 38° Celsius.

Archaeology

Pioneer 10 has a mass of 258.0 kilograms. The different components of the probe failed or were turned off at varying times. Some were turned off permanently and others were cycled on and off in accordance with a power sharing plan implemented in September 1989. The Asteroid/Meteoroid Detector failed in December 1973, followed by the Helium Vector Magnetometer (HVM) in November 1975 and the Infrared Radiometer in January 1974. The Meteoroid Detector was turned off in October 1980 due to inactive sensors at low temperatures. The spacecraft Sun sensors became inoperative in May 1986, and the Imaging Photopolarimeter (IPP) instrument was used to obtain roll phase and spin period information until being turned off in October 1993 to conserve power. The Trapped Radiation Detector (TRD) and Plasma Analyzer (PA) were respectively turned off in November 1993 and September 1995 for the same reason. As of January 1996 the final power cycling plan included part-time operations of the Charged Particle Instrument (CPI), the Cosmic Ray Telescope (CRT), the Geiger Tube Telescope (GTT), and the Ultraviolet Photometer (UV). As of August 2000, only the GTT instrument was still returning data.

Humans ceased routine tracking of the probe on 31 March 1997 when they could not afford to pay for it. The last successful data acquisitions through NASA's Deep Space Network (DSN) occurred on 3 March 2002, the thirtieth anniversary of *Pioneer 10's* launch date, and on 27 April 2002. The spacecraft signal was last detected on 23 January 2003. No signal at all was detected during a final attempt on 6–7 February 2003, so Pioneer Project staff at NASA Ames concluded that the spacecraft power level had fallen below that needed to power the onboard transmitter, so no further attempts would be made. It can be assumed that, soon after that moment, the spacecraft entered its archaeological context.

2) *PIONEER 11*[6]

History

Pioneer 11 was launched atop an Atlas-Centaur rocket from Cape Canaveral, Florida, on 6 April 1973, on NASA's second mission to investigate Jupiter and the outer solar system and the first to explore the planet Saturn and its main rings. Like *Pioneer 10*, *Pioneer 11* used Jupiter's gravitational field to alter its trajectory radically. It then passed close to Saturn and followed an escape trajectory from the solar system. During its closest approach to Jupiter on 3 December 1974, *Pioneer 11* passed to within 43,000 kilometers of the gas giant's cloud tops.

The science program included studies of the interplanetary and planetary magnetic fields; solar wind properties; cosmic rays; transition region of the heliosphere; neutral hydrogen abundance; distribution, size, mass, flux, and velocity of dust particles; Jovian aurorae; Jovian radio waves; the atmospheres of planets and satellites; and the surfaces of Jupiter, Saturn, and some of their satellites.

Pioneer 11 passed just 21,000 kilometers above Saturn's cloud cover on 1 September 1979. Five years after these encounters, the spacecraft began sharing power between its instruments because of declining RTG power output.

Technical Notes

The spacecraft was 2.9 meters long and contained a 2.74-meter-diameter high-gain antenna of aluminum honeycomb sandwich material whose feed was topped with a medium-gain antenna. A low-gain, omnidirectional antenna was mounted below the high-gain dish. The spacecraft contained two nuclear electric-power generators, which generated 144 watts at Jupiter, which decreased to 100 watts at Saturn. There were three reference sensors: a star (Canopus) sensor and two Sun sensors. Attitude position could be calculated from the reference direction to Earth and the Sun, with the known direction to Canopus as backup. *Pioneer 11*'s star sensor gain and threshold settings were modified, based on experience gained from the settings used on *Pioneer 10*. Three pairs of rocket thrusters provided spin-axis control (maintained at 4.8 rpm) and change of the spacecraft velocity. The thrusters could be either fired steadily or pulsed, by command.

The scientific instrument suite included a magnetometer, plasma analyzer (for solar wind), charged-particle detector, ionizing detector, non-imaging telescopes with overlapping fields of view to detect sunlight reflected from passing meteoroids, sealed pressurized cells of argon and nitrogen gas for measuring penetration of meteoroids, UV photometer, IR radiometer, and an imaging photopolarimeter, which produced photographs and measured the polarization.

171

Archaeology

Pioneer 11 has a mass of 259 kilograms. Science operations and daily telemetry ceased on 30 September 1995 when the RTG power level was insufficient to operate any experiments. It continues to heading outward from the solar system at a rate of 2.5 AU per year. (An AU is the equivalent of the mean distance between Earth and the Sun across one orbit of Earth around the Sun.) Like *Pioneer 10*, this spacecraft contains a plaque incised with a depiction of a *Homo sapiens* male and female, and a representation of the location of the Sun and Earth within the wider galaxy.

3) VOYAGER 1[7]

History

Voyager 1 was launched atop a Titan IIIE-Centaur rocket from Cape Canaveral, Florida, on 5 September 1977. The expedition was one of a pair of spacecraft launched to explore the planets of the outer solar system and then continue on to conduct research in the interplanetary environment. Each Voyager had as its major objectives at each planet to (1) investigate the circulation, dynamics, structure, and composition of the planet's atmosphere; (2) characterize the morphology, geology, and physical state of the satellites of the planet; (3) provide improved values for the mass, size, and shape of the planet, its satellites, and any rings; and (4) determine the magnetic field structure and characterize the composition and distribution of energetic trapped particles and plasma therein.

Although launched sixteen days after *Voyager 2*, *Voyager 1*'s trajectory was the quicker one to Jupiter. On 15 December 1977, while both spacecraft were in the asteroid belt, *Voyager 1* surpassed *Voyager 2*'s distance from the Sun. *Voyager 1* then proceeded to Jupiter (making its closest approach on 5 March 1979) and Saturn (with closest approach on 12 November 1980). Both prior to and after planetary encounters, observations were made of the interplanetary medium. Some 18,000 images of Jupiter and its moons were taken by *Voyager 1*. In addition, roughly 16,000 images of Saturn, its rings and moons were obtained.

After its encounter with Saturn, *Voyager 1* remained relatively quiescent, continuing to make in situ observations of the interplanetary environment and UV observations of stars. After nearly nine years of dormancy, *Voyager 1*'s cameras were once again turned on to take a series of pictures. On 14 February 1990, *Voyager 1* looked back from whence it came and took the first "family portrait" of the solar system, a mosaic of sixty frames of the Sun and six of the planets (Venus, Earth, Jupiter, Saturn, Uranus, and Neptune) as seen from outside the solar system. After this final look back, the cameras on *Voyager 1* were once again turned off.

Technical Notes

Each Voyager consisted of a decahedral bus, forty-seven centimeters in height and 1.78 meters across from flat to flat. A 3.66-meter-diameter parabolic, high-gain antenna was mounted on top of the bus. The major portion of the science instruments were mounted on a science boom extending out some 2.5 meters from the spacecraft. At the end of the science boom was a steerable scan platform on which were mounted the imaging and spectroscopic remote sensing instruments. Also mounted at various distances along the science boom were the plasma and charged particle detectors. The magnetometers were located along a separate boom extending thirteen meters on the side opposite the science boom. A third boom, extending down and away from the science instruments, held the spacecraft's radioisotope thermoelectric generators (RTGs). Two ten-meter whip antennas (used for the plasma wave and planetary radio astronomy investigations) also extended from the spacecraft, each perpendicular to the other. The spacecraft was three-axis spin-stabilized to enable long integration times and selective viewing for the instruments mounted on the scan platform.

Power was provided to the spacecraft systems and instruments through the use of three radioisotope thermoelectric generators. The RTGs were assembled in tandem on a deployable boom hinged on an outrigger arrangement of struts attached to the basic structure. Each RTG unit, contained in a beryllium outer case, was 40.6 centimeters in diameter, 50.8 centimeters in length, and weighed 39 kilograms. The RTGs used a radioactive source (plutonium 238 in the form of plutonium oxide) which, as it decayed, gave off heat. A bi-metallic thermoelectric device was used to convert the heat to electric power for the spacecraft. The total output of RTGs slowly decreases with time as the radioactive material is expended. Therefore, although the initial output of the RTGs on *Voyager* was approximately 470 watts of 30 volt DC power at launch, it had fallen off to approximately 335 watts by the beginning of 1997 (about 19.5 years post-launch). As power continues to decrease, power loads on the spacecraft must also decrease.

Because of its distance from Earth and the resulting time-lag for commanding, the Voyager spacecraft were designed to operate in a highly autonomous manner. In order to do this and carry out the complex sequences of spacecraft motions and instrument operations, three interconnected onboard computers were utilized. The Computer Command Subsystem (CCS) was responsible for storing commands for the other two computers and issuing the commands at set times. The Attitude and Articulation Control Subsystem (AACS) was responsible for controlling spacecraft attitude and motions of the scan platform. The Flight Data Subsystem (FDS) controlled the instruments, including changes in configuration (state) or telemetry rates. All three computers had redundant components to ensure continued operations. The AACS included redundant star trackers and Sun sensors as well.

Archaeology

Each Voyager spacecraft has mounted to one of the sides of the bus a twelve-inch gold-plated copper disk. Unlike the simple representation of the naked *Homo sapiens* on the Pioneer plaques, the Voyager disk has recorded on it sounds and images of Earth designed to portray the diversity of life and culture on the planet. Each disk is encased in a protective aluminum jacket along with a cartridge and a needle, which was the prevailing technology for playing recorded music at the time the Voyager spacecraft were designed and built. Instructions explaining from where the spacecraft originated and how to play the disk are engraved onto the jacket.

Electroplated onto a two-centimeter area on the cover is also an ultra-pure source of uranium 238 (with a radioactivity of about 0.26 nanocuries and a half-life of 4.51 billion years), allowing the determination of the elapsed time since launch by measuring the amount of daughter elements to remaining U238. The 115 images on the disk were encoded in analog form. The sound selections (including greetings in fifty-five languages, thirty-five sounds, natural and man-made, and portions of twenty-seven musical pieces) are designed for playback at 1000 rpm, much faster than the 33 rpm speed typical of record players of the era.

The *Voyager 1* spacecraft has a mass of 721.9 kilograms. It is speeding away from the Sun at a velocity of about 3.50 AU per year. On 17 February 1998, *Voyager 1* became the most distant man-made object from the Sun, surpassing the distance of *Pioneer 10*. It was estimated in 1998 that increasingly limited instrument operations could be carried out from *Voyager 1* at least until 2020.

4) *Voyager 2*[8]

History

Voyager 2 was launched atop a Titan IIIE-Centaur rocket from Cape Canaveral, Florida, on 20 August 1977, sixteen days before its twin, *Voyager 1*. *Voyager 2* one of a pair of spacecraft launched to explore the planets of the outer solar system and the interplanetary environment. Each Voyager had as its major objectives at each planet to (1) investigate the circulation, dynamics, structure, and composition of the planet's atmosphere; (2) characterize the morphology, geology, and physical state of the moons of the planet; (3) provide improved values for the mass, size, and shape of the planet, its moons, and any rings; and (4) determine the magnetic field structure and characterize the composition and distribution of energetic trapped particles and plasma therein.

In April 1978, *Voyager 2*'s primary radio receiver failed, automatically kicking in the backup receiver which also proved to be faulty. Attempts to recover the use of the primary receiver failed and the backup receiver was used for the remainder of the mission. Although use of the backup receiver made communication with the spacecraft more difficult, engineers were able to find workarounds. *Voyager 2* proceeded with its primary mission and flew by Jupiter, where it made its closest approach on 9 July 1979, and then Saturn, where it made its nearest approach on 5 August 1981. *Voyager 2* obtained about the same number of images at each planet as did *Voyager 1*: 18,000 at Jupiter and 16,000 at Saturn.

Voyager 2 continued on to make successful flybys of Uranus on 24 January 1986, where the probe obtained 8,000 images, and then Neptune on 25 August 1989, where

10,000 images were returned to Earth. After the encounter with Neptune, the expedition was renamed the Voyager Interstellar Mission (VIM) by NASA, as the probe began to record measurements of the interplanetary magnetic field, plasma, and charged particle environment while searching for the heliopause (the distance at which the solar wind becomes subsumed by the more general interstellar wind).

Technical Notes

Each Voyager consisted of a decahedral bus, forty-seven centimeters in height and 1.78 meters across from flat to flat. A 3.66-meter-diameter parabolic, high-gain antenna was mounted on top of the bus. The major portion of the science instruments were mounted on a science boom extending out some 2.5 meters from the spacecraft. At the end of the science boom was a steerable scan platform on which were mounted the imaging and spectroscopic remote sensing instruments. Also mounted at various distances along the science boom were the plasma and charged particle detectors. The magnetometers were located along a separate boom extending thirteen meters on the side opposite the science boom. A third boom, extending down and away from the science instruments, held the spacecraft's radioisotope thermoelectric generators (RTGs). Two ten-meter whip antennas (used for the plasma wave and planetary radio astronomy investigations) also extended from the spacecraft, each perpendicular to the other. The spacecraft was three-axis spin-stabilized to enable long integration times and selective viewing for the instruments mounted on the scan platform.

Power was provided to the spacecraft systems and instruments through the use of three radioisotope thermoelectric generators. The RTGs were assembled in tandem on a deployable boom hinged on an outrigger arrangement of struts attached to the basic structure. Each RTG unit, contained in a beryllium outer case, was 40.6 centimeters in diameter, 50.8 centimeters in length, and weighed 39 kilograms. The RTGs used a radioactive source (plutonium 238 in the form of plutonium oxide) which, as it decayed, gave off heat. A bi-metallic thermoelectric device was used to convert the heat to electric power for the spacecraft. The total output of RTGs slowly decreases with time as the radioactive material is expended. Therefore, although the initial output of the RTGs on *Voyager* was approximately 470 watts of 30-volt DC power at launch, it had fallen off to approximately 335 watts by the beginning of 1997 (about 19.5 years post-launch). As power continues to decrease, power loads on the spacecraft must also decrease.

Because of its distance from Earth and the resulting time-lag for commanding, the Voyager spacecraft were designed to operate in a highly autonomous manner. In order to do this and carry out the complex sequences of spacecraft motions and instrument operations, three interconnected onboard computers were utilized. The Computer Command Subsystem (CCS) was responsible for storing commands for the other two computers and issuing the commands at set times. The Attitude and Articulation Control Subsystem (AACS) was responsible for controlling spacecraft attitude and motions of the scan platform. The Flight Data Subsystem (FDS) controlled the instruments, including changes in configuration (state) or telemetry rates. All three computers had redundant components to ensure continued operations. The AACS included redundant star trackers and Sun sensors as well.

Archaeology

Each Voyager spacecraft has mounted to one of the sides of the bus a twelve-inch gold-plated copper disk. Unlike the simple representation of the naked *Homo sapiens* on the Pioneer plaques, the Voyager disk has recorded on it sounds and images of Earth designed to portray the diversity of life and culture on the planet. Each disk is encased in a protective aluminum jacket along with a cartridge and a needle, which was the prevailing technology for playing recorded music at the time the Voyager spacecraft were designed and built. Instructions explaining from where the spacecraft originated and how to play the disk are engraved onto the jacket.

Electroplated onto a two-centimeter area on the cover is also an ultra-pure source of uranium 238 (with a radioactivity of about 0.26 nanocuries and a half-life of 4.51 billion years), allowing the determination of the elapsed time since launch by measuring the amount of daughter elements to remaining U238. The 115 images on the disk were encoded in analog form. The sound selections (including greetings in fifty-five languages, thirty-five sounds, natural and man-made, and portions of twenty-seven musical pieces) are designed for playback at 1000 rpm, much faster than the 33 rpm speed typical of record players of the era.

The *Voyager 2* spacecraft has a mass of 721.9 kilograms. It is moving away from the Sun at a velocity of about 3.13 AU per year.

5) NEW HORIZONS[9]

History

The *New Horizons* probe was launched atop Atlas V 551 booster with a Star 48B third stage directly into an interplanetary trajectory on 19 January 2006. The expedition is designed to fly by Pluto, Charon, and Pluto's recently discovered moons, Nix and Hydra, and transmit images and data back to Earth. It will then continue on into the Kuiper Belt where it will fly by one or more Kuiper Belt Objects and return further data. The primary objectives are to characterize the global geology and morphology, map the surface composition of Pluto and Charon, and characterize the neutral atmosphere of Pluto and its escape rate. Other objectives include studying the time variability of Pluto's surface and atmosphere; imaging Pluto and Charon in stereo; mapping the terminators and composition of selected areas of Pluto and Charon at high resolution; characterizing Pluto's upper atmosphere, ionosphere, energetic particle environment, and solar wind interaction; searching for an atmosphere around Charon and characterizing its energetic particle environment; and characterizing one or more Kuiper Belt Objects.

The spacecraft passed within 101,867 kilometers of the main belt asteroid JF56 on 13 June 2006. It used the encounter as a test of its instruments and tracking and navigation sensors, and returned images of the 2.5-kilometer-diameter asteroid, which only shows as a faint dot at that distance. It reached Jupiter for a gravity assist on 28 February 2007. The flyby put the spacecraft on a trajectory towards Pluto. On 8 June 2008 *New Horizons* crossed the orbit of Saturn.

The encounter with Pluto is planned to occur on 14 July 2015. Data from the encounter will begin to flow back towards Earth about six months before *New Horizons* reaches the area. It is expected that the spacecraft will fly within 10,000 kilometers of Pluto and as close as 27,000 kilometers to Charon. Because of the limited power available at this range, the instruments will be duty-cycled during encounter. The flyby will take place at a distance of about thirty-three AU from Earth with a round-trip light time of nine hours. Given these vast distances and low powers, the data from the encounter will be transmitted to Earth at 600 bps over a nine-month period.

Technical Notes

The spacecraft has the shape of a thick triangle (0.68 × 2.11 × 2.74 meters), with a cylindrical radiothermal generator (RTG) protruding from one vertex in the plane of the triangle and a 2.1-meter high-gain radio dish antenna affixed to one flank side. An aluminum central cylinder supports surrounding honeycomb panels. The central cylinder acts as the payload adapter fitting and houses the propellant tank. The 465-kilogram launch mass included eighty kilograms of propellant. The entire structure is covered in thermal, multi-layer insulating blankets and thermal control is further achieved by electrical dissipation and RTG waste heat, thermal louvers, and external shunt plates. The RTG will provide approximately 228 watts at the time of the Pluto encounter in 2015. Star cameras are mounted on the side of the spacecraft for navigation.

The thirty-one-kilogram science payload package requires twenty-one watts of power and consists of seven scientific instruments. These include a Long Range Reconnaissance Imager (LORRI) consisting of a visible-light, high-resolution CCD Imager; the Ralph instrument is composed of two parts, a visible CCD imager (MVIC) and a near-infrared-imaging spectrometer (LEISA); and the Alice instrument is an ultraviolet imaging spectrometer.

Archaeology

The *New Horizons* space probe has a mass of 385 kilograms. After passing by Pluto, it heads toward the Kuiper Belt. This is the area of the solar system beyond the orbit of Neptune, a distance of some fifty-five AU from the Sun. There, one to three Kuiper Belt Objects with diameters exceeding thirty-five kilometers are expected to be targeted for encounter and similar measurements to those made at Pluto.

The Kuiper phase of the mission is expected to last from five to ten years, after which *New Horizons* will leave the solar system around 2029 and enter its archaeological context in interstellar space. *New Horizons* does not carry the same kind of inter-species communication devices such as the Pioneer plaques or the Voyager discs. It does, however, carry numerous cultural objects on board, including an American flag, a State of Florida quarter-dollar, a compact disc with almost half a million names on it, and some of the ashes of the discover of Pluto, Clyde Tombaugh (1906–1997).

Chapter Notes

Preface

1. Ben Finney, *From Sea to Space* (Palmerston North, New Zealand: Massey University Press, 1992), 105.
2. Ibid.
3. Alice Gorman, "The Cultural Landscape of Interplanetary Space," *Journal of Social Archaeology* 5, no. 1 (Feb. 2005): 86.

Chapter 1

1. Beth L. O'Leary, "The Cultural Heritage of Space, the Moon and Other Celestial Bodies," *Antiquity* 80, no. 307 (March 2006): 11–13.
2. Beth L. O'Leary, et al. "Lunar Legacy Project." New Mexico State University, 2003, http://spacegrant.nmsu.edu/lunarlegacies/.
3. C. S. Gillmor, "Science and Travel in Extreme Latitudes," *Isis* 85 (1994): 482–485.
4. David L. Harrowfield, "Historic Sites in the Ross Dependency, Antarctica," *Polar Record* 24, no. 151 (1988): 277–284.
5. Neville A. Ritchie, "Archaeological Techniques and Technology on Ross Island, Antarctica," *Polar Record* 26, no. 159 (1990): 257–264.
6. W. E. Burrows, *Exploring Space* (New York: Random House, 1990), 162.
7. See, for example, P. J. Capelotti, "Space: The Final (Archaeological) Frontier," *Archaeology* 57, no. 6 (Nov./Dec. 2004); or P. J. Capelotti, "A Conceptual Model for Aerospace Archaeology: A Case Study from the Wellman Site, Virgohamna, Danskøya, Svalbard," Ph.D. dissertation, Rutgers University, 1996, University Microfilms #9633681.
8. Michael Schiffer, *Formation Processes of the Archaeological Record* (Salt Lake City: University of Utah Press, 1987).
9. Ibid., 5.
10. See, for example, James P. Delgado, Daniel J. Lenihan, and Larry E. Murphy, *The Archaeology of the Atomic Bomb: A Submerged Cultural Resources Assessment of the Sunken Fleet of Operation Crossroads at Bikini and Kwajalein Atoll Lagoons* (Santa Fe: National Park Service, Southwest Cultural Resources Center Professional Papers No. 37, 1991); or Center for Air Force History, *Coming in from the Cold: Military Heritage in the Cold War* (Washington, D.C.: Center for Air Force History, 1994).
11. D. P. Dymond, *Archaeology and History: A Plea for Reconciliation* (London: Thames and Hudson, 1974).
12. James Deetz, *In Small Things Forgotten* (Garden City, NY: Anchor Books, 1977), 24.
13. Richard A. Gould, "The Archaeology of War," in *Shipwreck Anthropology*, edited by Richard A. Gould (Albuquerque: University of New Mexico Press, 1983), 117–118.
14. Richard A. Gould, *Recovering the Past* (Albuquerque: University of New Mexico Press, 1990), 178–179.
15. Richard A. Gould, "The Archaeology of War," in *Shipwreck Anthropology*, edited by Richard A. Gould (Albuquerque: University of New Mexico Press, 1983), 117–118.
16. Ben R. Finney, *From Sea to Space* (Palmerston North, New Zealand: Massey University Press, 1992), 105.
17. Ibid.

Chapter 2

1. For technical and other mission details, see the National Aeronautics and Space Administration, National Space Science Data Center (hereinafter referred to as the NSSDC), for the mission of *Apollo 10*, Nov. 2009, http://nssdc.gsfc.nasa.gov/nmc/spacecraftDisplay.do?id=1969-043A.
2. National Aeronautics and Space Administration, *Apollo 10 Mission Report; MSC-00126* (Houston: Manned Spacecraft Center, 1969).
3. Ibid., 9-18-9-19.
4. NSSDC, *Apollo 11*, Nov. 2009, http://nssdc.gsfc.nasa.gov/nmc/spacecraftDisplay.do?id=1969-059A.
5. NSSDC, *Apollo 12*, Nov. 2009, http://nssdc.gsfc.nasa.gov/nmc/spacecraftDisplay.do?id=1969-099A.

6. NSSDC, *Apollo 13*, Nov. 2009, http://nssdc.gsfc.nasa.gov/nmc/spacecraftDisplay.do?id=1970-029A.

7. NSSDC, *Apollo 14*, Nov. 2009, http://nssdc.gsfc.nasa.gov/nmc/spacecraftDisplay.do?id=1971-008A.

8. NSSDC, *Apollo 15*, Nov. 2009, http://nssdc.gsfc.nasa.gov/nmc/spacecraftDisplay.do?id=1971-063A.

9. NSSDC, *Apollo 16*, Nov. 2009, http://nssdc.gsfc.nasa.gov/nmc/spacecraftDisplay.do?id=1972-031A.

10. NSSDC, *Apollo 17*, Nov. 2009, http://nssdc.gsfc.nasa.gov/nmc/spacecraftDisplay.do?id=1972-096A.

Chapter 3

Note: All images of Soviet spacecraft are from the Soviet lunar mission website of the NSSDC, Nov. 2009, http://nssdc.gsfc.nasa.gov/planetary/lunar/lunarussr.html.

1. Beth L. O'Leary, "The Cultural Heritage of Space, the Moon and Other Celestial Bodies," *Antiquity* 80, no. 307 (March 2006).

2. *Luna 2* technical notes can be found at the NSSDC, Nov. 2009, http://nssdc.gsfc.nasa.gov/nmc/spacecraftDisplay.do?id=1959-014A.

3. *Ranger 4* technical notes from the *Lunar Prospector* website lunar exploration timeline: NASA, n.d., http://lunar.arc.nasa.gov/history/timeline/info/ranger401.htm.

4. R. Cargill Hall, *Lunar Impact: A History of Project Ranger* (Washington, D.C.: National Aeronautics and Space Administration, SP-4210, 1977), 72.

5. *Ranger 6* technical notes from the *Lunar Prospector* website lunar exploration timeline: NASA, n.d., http://lunar.arc.nasa.gov/history/timeline/info/ranger601.htm.

6. *Ranger 7* history can be found at: NSSDC, Nov. 2009, http://nssdc.gsfc.nasa.gov/nmc/spacecraftDisplay.do?id=1964-041A. *Ranger 7* technical notes from the *Lunar Prospector* website lunar exploration timeline: NASA, n.d., http://lunar.arc.nasa.gov/history/timeline/info/ranger701.htm.

7. *Ranger 8* technical notes from the *Lunar Prospector* website lunar exploration timeline: NASA, n.d., http://lunar.arc.nasa.gov/history/timeline/info/ranger801.htm.

8. *Ranger 9* technical notes from the *Lunar Prospector* website lunar exploration timeline: NASA, n.d., http://lunar.arc.nasa.gov/history/timeline/info/ranger901.htm.

9. NSSDC, *Luna 5*, Nov. 2009, http://nssdc.gsfc.nasa.gov/database/MasterCatalog?sc=1965-036A. Notes for the Luna series of probes can also be found at the excellent Zarya site maintained by Robert Christy, "Luna — Exploring the Moon," 2000, http://www.zarya.info/Diaries/Luna/Luna.php.

10. NSSDC, *Luna 7*, Nov. 2009, http://nssdc.gsfc.nasa.gov/database/MasterCatalog?sc=1965-077A.

11. NSSDC, *Luna 8*, Nov. 2009, http://nssdc.gsfc.nasa.gov/database/MasterCatalog?sc=1965-099A.

12. NSSDC, *Luna 9*, Nov. 2009, http://nssdc.gsfc.nasa.gov/nmc/spacecraftDisplay.do?id =1966-006A.

13. NSSDC, *Surveyor 1*, Nov. 2009, http://nssdc.gsfc.nasa.gov/nmc/spacecraftDisplay.do?id=1966-045A.

14. NSSDC, *Lunar Orbiter 1*, Nov. 2009, http://nssdc.gsfc.nasa.gov/nmc/spacecraftDisplay.do?id=1966-073A.

15. NSSDC, *Surveyor 2*, Nov. 2009, http://nssdc.gsfc.nasa.gov/nmc/spacecraftDisplay.do?id=1966-084A.

16. NSSDC, *Lunar Orbiter 2*, Nov. 2009, http://nssdc.gsfc.nasa.gov/nmc/spacecraftDisplay.do?id=1966-100A.

17. Bruce K. Byers, *Destination Moon: A History of the Lunar Orbiter Program* (Washington, D.C.: NASA, 1977), 255. It is in this official history that one finds the notion that *Lunar Orbiter 2* was the first spacecraft to image an archaeological site on the Moon, when it photographed the crash site of the earlier *Ranger 8* site.

18. NSSDC, *Luna 13*, Nov. 2009, http://nssdc.gsfc.nasa.gov/nmc/spacecraftDisplay.do?id=1966-116A.

19. NSSDC, *Lunar Orbiter 3*, Nov. 2009, http://nssdc.gsfc.nasa.gov/nmc/spacecraftDisplay.do?id=1967-008A.

20. NSSDC, *Surveyor 3*, Nov. 2009, http://nssdc.gsfc.nasa.gov/nmc/spacecraftDisplay.do?id=1967-035A.

21. NSSDC, *Lunar Orbiter 4*, Nov. 2009, http://nssdc.gsfc.nasa.gov/nmc/spacecraftDisplay.do?id=1967-041A.

22. NSSDC, *Surveyor 4*, Nov. 2009, http://nssdc.gsfc.nasa.gov/nmc/spacecraftDisplay.do?id=1967-068A.

23. NSSDC, *Lunar Orbiter 5*, Nov. 2009, http://nssdc.gsfc.nasa.gov/nmc/spacecraftDisplay.do?id=1969-058A.

24. NSSDC, *Surveyor 5*, Nov. 2009, http://nssdc.gsfc.nasa.gov/nmc/spacecraftDisplay.do?id=1967-084A.

25. NSSDC, *Surveyor 6*, Nov. 2009, http://nssdc.gsfc.nasa.gov/nmc/spacecraftDisplay.do?id=1967-112A.

26. NSSDC, *Surveyor 7*, Nov. 2009, http://nssdc.gsfc.nasa.gov/nmc/spacecraftDisplay.do?id=1968-001A.

27. NSSDC, *Luna 15*, Nov. 2009, http://nssdc.

gsfc.nasa.gov/nmc/spacecraftDisplay.do?id=196
9-058A.

28. NSSDC, *Luna 16*, Nov. 2009, http://nssdc.
gsfc.nasa.gov/nmc/spacecraftDisplay.do?id=197
0-072A.

29. Lawrence Van Gelder, "F.B.I. Revisits Earthly
Theft of Moon Rock," *New York Times*, December
2, 1995: 24.

30. NSSDC, *Luna 17/Lunokhod 1*, Nov. 2009,
http://nssdc.gsfc.nasa.gov/nmc/spacecraftDisplay.do
?id=1970-095A.

31. Leonard David, "Lunar Lost & Found: The
Search for Old Spacecraft," *Space.com*, 27 March
2006, www.space.com/scienceastronomy/060327_m
ystery_monday.html.

32. NSSDC, *Luna 18*, Nov. 2009, http://nssdc.gs
fc.nasa.gov/nmc/spacecraftDisplay.do?id=1971-073A.

33. NSSDC, *Luna 20*, Nov. 2009, http://nssdc.
gsfc.nasa.gov/nmc/spacecraftDisplay.do?id=1972-0
07A. Notes on the mission and recovery of the *Luna
20* ascent stage samples come as well from the Zarya
site: http://www.zarya.info/Diaries/Luna/Luna.p
hp/.

34. NSSDC, *Luna 21/ Lunokhod 2*, Nov. 2009,
http://nssdc.gsfc.nasa.gov/nmc/spacecraftDisplay.do
?id=1973-001A.

35. Andrew Chaikin, "The Other Moon Landings," *Air & Space Magazine* (February/March 2004),
http://www.airspacemag.com/space-exploration/ot
her-moon.html.

36. CollectSPACE.com, "The Astronaut Son's
Secret Sputnik," 2007, http://wwww.collectspace.
com/news/news-100207a.html.

37. NSSDC, *Luna 23*, Nov. 2009, http://nssdc.
gsfc.nasa.gov/nmc/spacecraftDisplay.do?id=1974-0
84A.

38. NSSDC, *Luna 24*, Nov. 2009, http://nssdc.
gsfc.nasa.gov/nmc/spacecraftDisplay.do?id=1976-0
81A.

39. NSSDC, *Hiten*, Nov. 2009, http://nssdc.gs
fc.nasa.gov/nmc/spacecraftDisplay.do?id=1990-00
7A.

40. NSSDC, *Lunar Prospector*, Nov. 2009, http://
nssdc.gsfc.nasa.gov/nmc/spacecraftDisplay.do?id=1
998-001A.

41. NSSDC, *SMART-1*, Nov. 2009, http://nss
dc.gsfc.nasa.gov/nmc/spacecraftDisplay.do?id=
2003-043C.

42. NSSDC, *Chang'e 1*, Nov. 2009, http://nssdc.
gsfc.nasa.gov/nmc/spacecraftDisplay.do?id=2007-0
51A.

43. D. U. Guodong, "China's Lunar Probe
Chang'e 1 Impacts Moon." *China View*, March 1,
2009, http://news.xinhuanet.com/english/2009-0
3/01/content_10923205.htm.

44. NSSDC, *Chandrayaan 1*, Nov. 2009, http://
nssdc.gsfc.nasa.gov/nmc/spacecraftDisplay.do?id=20
08-052A.

45. "India's own probe also found water on
moon: ISRO," *Times of India*, 25 Sep 2009, http://
timesofindia.indiatimes.com/news/india/Indians-o
wn-probe-also-found-water-on-moon-ISRO/artic
leshow/5054436.cms.

46. NSSDC, *LCROSS*, Nov. 2009, http://nssdc.
gsfc.nasa.gov/nmc/spacecraftDisplay.do?id=2009-0
31B.

47. Jonas Dino, "LCROSS Impact Data Indicates
Water on Moon." *NASA Press Release*, 13 November
2009.

48. For more on the Arctic Mars Analog Svalbard
expedition, see: NASA, "Arctic Mars Analog Svalbard Expedition," 23 Nov 2007, http://www.nasa.
gov/mission_pages/mars/news/amase/index.html.

49. Leonard David, "Lunar Lost & Found: The
Search for Old Spacecraft," *Space.com*, March 27,
2006, www.space.com/scienceastronomy/060327_m
ystery_monday.html.

Chapter 4

1. The full text of the *Archaeology* article can be
found at: P. J. Capelotti, "Space: The Final [Archae-
ological] Frontier," *Archaeology* 57, no. 6 (Nov./Dec.
2004), http://www.archaeology.org/0411/etc/space.
html. The preconditioning for the final conflict article can be found at: Thomas Horn, "*Stargates, Ancient Rituals, and Those Invited Through the Portal
(Pt. 10)*," *Alien Nation*, 2003, http://www.thewatche
rfiles.com/stargates/part-ten.htm.

2. Yevgeny Fedorov, *Polar Diaries* (Moscow:
Progress Publishers, 1979), 106.

3. Translated from Fridtjof Nansen, *En Ferd Til
Spitsbergen* (Kristiania: Jacob Dybwads Forlag, 1920),
145.

4. John Toland, *The Great Dirigibles* (New York:
Dover, 1972), 146–147.

Chapter 5

1. NSSDC, *Mars 2*, Nov. 2009, http://nssdc.
gsfc.nasa.gov/nmc/masterCatalog.do?sc=1971-045A.

2. NSSDC, *Mars 3*, Nov. 2009, http://nssdc.
gsfc.nasa.gov/nmc/masterCatalog.do?sc=1971-049A.
The *Mars 2/3* image comes from: V. G. Perminov,
"The Difficult Road to Mars: A Brief History of Mars
Exploration in the Soviet Union," *Monographs in
Aerospace History*, 15 (July 1999), http://klabs.org/ri
chcontent/Reports/mars/difficult_road_to_mars.pdf,
48.

3. NSSDC, *Mars 6*, Nov. 2009, http://nssdc.
gsfc.nasa.gov/nmc/masterCatalog.do?sc=1973-052A.

4. NSSDC, *Viking 1*, Nov. 2009, http://nssdc.
gsfc.nasa.gov/nmc/spacecraftDisplay.do?id=1975-0
75C.

5. NSSDC, *Viking 2*, Nov. 2009, http://nssdc. gsfc.nasa.gov/nmc/spacecraftDisplay.do?id=1975-0 83A. Additional information can be found at the following sources: NASA, "Viking Mission to Mars, *NASA Facts*, 1988, http://www.jpl.nasa.gov/news/fac t_sheets/viking.pdf; Edward C. Enzell and Linda Neuman Enzell, *On Mars: Exploration of the Red Planet, 1958–1978* (Washington, D.C.: NASA, 1984), http://www.hq.nasa.gov/office/pao/History/ SP-4212/contents.html; Robert Godwin, *Mars: The NASA Mission Reports* (Burlington, Ontario: Apogee, 2000).

6. NSSDC, *Mars Pathfinder*, Nov. 2009, htt p://nssdc.gsfc.nasa.gov/nmc/spacecraftDisplay.do?id =1996-068A.

7. NSSDC, *Mars Polar Lander*, Nov. 2009, http://nssdc.gsfc.nasa.gov/nmc/spacecraftDisplay.do ?id=1999-001A.

8. NSSDC, *Beagle 2*, Nov. 2009, http://nssdc. gsfc.nasa.gov/database/MasterCatalog?sc=2003-0 22C.

9. NSSDC, Mars Exploration Rovers, *Spirit*, Nov. 2009, http://nssdc.gsfc.nasa.gov/database/Mas terCatalog?sc=2003-027A; *Opportunity*, Nov. 2009, http://nssdc.gsfc.nasa.gov/database/MasterCatalog?s c=2003-032A.

10. NSSDC, *Phoenix Mars Lander*, Nov. 2009, http://nssdc.gsfc.nasa.gov/database/MasterCatalog?s c=2007-034A.

Chapter 6

1. NSSDC, *Venera 3*, Nov. 2009, http://nssdc. gsfc.nasa.gov/database/MasterCatalog?sc=1965-0 92A.

2. NSSDC, *Venera 4*, Nov. 2009, http://nssdc. gsfc.nasa.gov/database/MasterCatalog?sc=1967-0 58A.

3. NSSDC, *Venera 5*, Nov. 2009, http://nssdc. gsfc.nasa.gov/database/MasterCatalog?sc=1969-0 01A.

4. NSSDC, *Venera 6*, Nov. 2009, http://nssdc. gsfc.nasa.gov/database/MasterCatalog?sc=1969-0 02A.

5. NSSDC, *Venera 7*, Nov. 2009, http://nssdc. gsfc.nasa.gov/database/MasterCatalog?sc=1970-0 60A.

6. NSSDC, *Venera 8*, Nov. 2009, http://nssdc. gsfc.nasa.gov/database/MasterCatalog?sc=1972-0 21A.

7. NSSDC, *Venera 9*, Nov. 2009, http://nssdc. gsfc.nasa.gov/database/MasterCatalog?sc=1975-0 50D.

8. NSSDC, *Venera 10*, Nov. 2009, http://nssdc. gsfc.nasa.gov/database/MasterCatalog?sc=1975-0 54D.

9. NSSDC, *Venera 11*, Nov. 2009, http://nssdc.

gsfc.nasa.gov/database/MasterCatalog?sc=1978-08 4D.

10. NSSDC, *Pioneer Venus Probe*, Nov. 2009, http://nssdc.gsfc.nasa.gov/database/MasterCatalog?s c=1978-078A.

11. NSSDC, *Venera 12*, Nov. 2009, http://nssdc. gsfc.nasa.gov/database/MasterCatalog?sc=1978-0 86C.

12. NSSDC, *Venera 13*, Nov. 2009, http://nssdc. gsfc.nasa.gov/database/MasterCatalog?sc=1981-1 06D.

13. NSSDC, *Venera 14*, Nov. 2009, http://nssdc. gsfc.nasa.gov/database/MasterCatalog?sc=1981-110D.

14. NSSDC, *Vega 1*, Nov. 2009, http://nssdc. gsfc.nasa.gov/database/MasterCatalog?sc=1984-1 25A.

15. NSSDC, *Vega 2*, Nov. 2009, http://nssdc. gsfc.nasa.gov/database/MasterCatalog?sc=1984-1 28A.

16. NSSDC, *Cassini-Huygens*, Nov. 2009, http:// nssdc.gsfc.nasa.gov/database/MasterCatalog?sc=199 7-061A.

Chapter 7

1. Eric M. Jones, *"Where Is Everybody?" An Account of Fermi's Question* (Los Alamos, NM: Los Alamos National Laboratory Report LA-10311-MS, 1985).

2. F. D. Drake, "The Radio Search for Intelligent Extraterrestrial Life," in *Current Aspects of Exobiology*, edited by G. Mamikunian and M. H. Briggs, Jet Propulsion Laboratory technical report 32–428, 1965, pp. 323–346.

3. Isaac Asimov, *Extraterrestrial Civilizations* (New York: Crown, 1979), 193.

4. Freeman John Dyson, "Search for Artificial Stellar Sources of Infrared Radiation," *Science* 131 (3 June 1960): 1667–1668.

5. Kristen A. Seaver, *The Frozen Echo: Greenland and the Exploration of North America, ca. A.D. 1000–1500* (Stanford: Stanford University Press, 1996).

6. Carl Sagan, *Cosmos* (New York: Random House, 1980), 129.

7. Mark J. Carlotto, *The Martian Enigmas* (Berkeley, CA: North Atlantic, 1991).

8. James Trefil, "Ah, But There May Have *Been* Life on Mars," *Smithsonian* 26, no. 5 (1995).

9. See, for example, Douglas Isbell and Mary Beth Murrill, "Jupiter's Europa Harbors Possible 'Warm Ice' or 'Liquid Water,'" *NASA Release* (13 Aug. 1996): 96–164, http://nssdc.gsfc.nasa.gov/planetar y/text/gal_eur_water.txt.

10. Carl Sagan, *Pale Blue Dot: A Vision of the Human Future in Space* (New York: Random House, 1994), 59–79.

11. Ronald Blom, "Space Technology and the

Discovery of Ubar." *P.O.B.* 17, no. 6 (1992): 11–20.

12. Thor Heyerdahl, *Aku-Aku: The Secret of Easter Island* (London: George Allen and Unwin, 1958).

13. Thomas R. Lyons & Douglas H. Scovill, "Non-Destructive Archaeology and Remote Sensing: A Conceptual and Methodological Stance," in *Remote Sensing and Non-Destructive Archaeology*, edited by T. R. Lyons & James I. Ebert (Washington, D.C.: National Park Service, 1978).

14. Thomas R. Hester, R. F. Heizer, and J. A. Graham, *Field Methods in Archaeology* (Mountain View, CA: Mayfield, 1975), 309.

15. O. G. S. Crawford, *Archaeology in the Field* (London: Phoenix House, 1953), 46.

16. John Whitfield, "Shipwreck Network Launched: Three-Year European Project Aims to Safeguard Shipwrecks," *Nature News*, published online, 23 January 2002.

17. Thomas R. Lyons & Douglas H. Scovill, "Non-Destructive Archaeology and Remote Sensing: A Conceptual and Methodological Stance," in *Remote Sensing and Non-Destructive Archaeology*, edited by T. R. Lyons & James I. Ebert (Washington, D.C.: National Park Service, 1978).

18. P. Wadhams, "Sidescan Sonar Imagery of Sea Ice in the Arctic Ocean," *Canadian Journal of Remote Sensing* 4, no 2 (19782).

19. John Travis, "Deep-Sea Debate Pits *Alvin* Against *Jason*," *Science* 259 (1993): 1534.

20. Willard Bascom, *The Crest of the Wave: Adventures in Oceanography* (New York: Harper & Row, 1998), 314.

21. Richard A. Gould, *Recovering the Past* (Albuquerque: University of New Mexico Press, 1990), 239.

22. George Bass, *Archaeology Under Water* (Baltimore: Penguin Books, 1970), 152.

23. Ben R. Finney, *From Sea to Space* (Palmerston North, New Zealand: Massey University Press, 1992), 105.

24. Jeffrey T. Richelson, "U.S. Satellite Imagery, 1960–1999," *National Security Archive Electronic Briefing Book No. 13* (1990).

25. Leonard David, "Orbiter to Look for Lost-to-Mars Probes," Space.com, 1 November 2006.

26. Sara Goudarzi, "Mars Orbiter Photographs Three Old Spacecraft," 2006, http://www.space.com/news/061205_mars_reconnaissance.html.

27. See, for example, Brian Handwerk, "Google Earth, Satellite Maps Boost Armchair Archaeology," *National Geographic News* (7 Nov 2006), http://news.nationalgeographic.com/news/2006/11/061107-archaeology.html.

28. William L. Fox, *Driving to Mars: In the Arctic with NASA on the Human Journey to the Red Planet* (Emeryville, CA: Shoemaker & Hoard, 2006).

Chapter 8

1. R. O. Fimmel and William Swindell, *Pioneer Odyssey* (Washington, D.C.: NASA, 1977), 183.

2. Ibid., 184.

3. Ibid.

4. Ibid., 186.

5. NSSDC, *Pioneer 10*, Nov. 2006, http://nssdc.gsfc.nasa.gov/database/MasterCatalog?sc=1972-012A.

6. NSSDC, *Pioneer 11*, Nov. 2006, http://nssdc.gsfc.nasa.gov/database/MasterCatalog?sc=1973-019A.

7. NSSDC, *Voyager 1*, Nov. 2006, http://nssdc.gsfc.nasa.gov/database/MasterCatalog?sc=1977-084A.

8. NSSDC, *Voyager 2*, Nov. 2006, http://nssdc.gsfc.nasa.gov/database/MasterCatalog?sc=1977-076A.

9. NSSDC, *New Horizons*, Nov. 2006, http://nssdc.gsfc.nasa.gov/database/MasterCatalog?sc=2006-001A.

Bibliography

Asimov, Isaac. *Extraterrestrial Civilizations.* New York: Crown, 1979.

Bascom, Willard. *The Crest of the Wave: Adventures in Oceanography.* New York: Harper & Row, 1988.

Bass, George. *Archaeology Under Water.* Baltimore: Penguin Books, 1970.

Blom, Ronald. "Space Technology and the Discovery of Ubar." *P.O.B.* 17, no. 6 (1992): 11–20.

Burrows, W. E. *Exploring Space.* New York: Random House, 1990.

Byers, Bruce K. *Destination Moon: A History of the Lunar Orbiter Program.* Washington, D.C.: NASA, 1977.

Capelotti, P. J. "Space: The Final (Archaeological) Frontier," *Archaeology* 57, no. 6 (Nov./Dec. 2004).

_____. *A Conceptual Model for Aerospace Archaeology: A Case Study from the Wellman Site, Virgohamna, Danskøya, Svalbard.* Ph.D. dissertation. Rutgers University, 1996. University Microfilms #9633681.

Carlotto, Mark J. *The Martian Enigmas.* Berkeley, CA: North Atlantic Books, 1997.

Center for Air Force History. *Coming in from the Cold: Military Heritage in the Cold War.* Washington, D.C.: Center for Air Force History, 1994.

Chaikin, Andrew. "The Other Moon Landings." *Air & Space Magazine* (Feb./Mar. 2004). http://www.airspacemag.com/space-exploration/other-moon.html.

CollectSPACE.com. 2007. "The Astronaut Son's Secret Sputnik." 2007. http://www.collectspace.com/news/news-100207a.html.

Crawford, O. G. S. *Archaeology in the Field.* London: Phoenix House, 1953.

David, Leonard. "Lunar Lost & Found: The Search for Old Spacecraft." *Space.com.* 27 March 2006. www.space.com/scienceastronomy/060327_mystery_monday.html.

_____. "Orbiter to look for Lost-to-Mars Probes." Space.com. 1 November 2006.

Davies, M. E., and T. R. Colvin. "Lunar Coordinates in the Regions of the Apollo Landers." *Journal of Geophysical Research* 105, no. E8 (Aug. 2000): 20277–20280.

Deetz, James. *In Small Things Forgotten.* Garden City, NY: Anchor Books, 1977.

Delgado, James P., Daniel J. Lenihan, and Larry E. Murphy. *The Archaeology of the Atomic Bomb: A Submerged Cultural Resources Assessment of the Sunken Fleet of Operation Crossroads at Bikini and Kwajalein Atoll Lagoons.* Santa Fe: National Park Service, Southwest Cultural Resources Center Professional Papers No. 37, 1991.

Dino, Jonas. "LCROSS Impact Data Indicates Water on Moon." *NASA Press Release*, 13 November 2009. http://www.nasa.gov/mission_pages/LCROSS/main/prelim_water_results.html.

Drake, F. D. "The Radio Search for Intelligent Extraterrestrial Life." In *Current Aspects of Exobiology*, edited by G. Mamikunian and M. H. Briggs. Jet Propulsion Laboratory Technical Report 32–428 (1965).

Dymond, D. P. *Archaeology and History: A Plea for Reconciliation.* London: Thames and Hudson, 1974.

Dyson, Freeman John. "Search for Artificial Stellar Sources of Infrared Radiation." *Science*, 131 (3 June 1960): 1667–1668.

Ezell, Edward C., and Linda Neuman Ezell. *On Mars: Exploration of the Red Planet, 1958–1978.* Washington, D.C.: NASA, 1984.

Federov, Yevgeny. *Polar Diaries.* Moscow: Progress, 1979.

Fimmel, R. O., and William Swindell. *Pioneer Odyssey.* Washington, D.C.: NASA, 1977.

Finney, Ben R. *From Sea to Space.* Palmerston North, New Zealand: Massey University Press, 1992.

Fox, William L. *Driving to Mars: In the Arctic with NASA on the Human Journey to the Red Planet.* Emeryville, CA: Shoemaker & Hoard, 2006.

Gillmor, C. S. "Science and Travel in Extreme Latitudes," *Isis* 85 (1994): 482–485.

Goudarzi, Sara. "Mars Orbiter Photographs Three Old Spacecraft," 2006, http://www.space.com/news/061205_mars_reconnaissance.html.

Gould, Richard A. *Recovering the Past.* Albuquerque: University of New Mexico Press, 1990.

_____. "The Archaeology of War," in Gould, Richard A., ed. *Shipwreck Anthropology*. Albuquerque: University of New Mexico Press, 1983.

Guodong, Du. "China's lunar probe *Chang'e 1* impacts moon." China View, March 1, 2009. *http://news.xinhuanet.com/english/2009-03/01/content_10923205.htm*.

Hall, R. Cargill. *Lunar Impact: A History of Project Ranger*. Washington, D.C.: National Aeronautics and Space Administration, SP-4210, 1977.

Handwerk. "Google Earth, Satellite Maps Boost Armchair Archaeology." *National Geographic News*, 7 November 2006.

Harrowfield, David L. "Historic Sites in the Ross Dependency, Antarctica." *Polar Record* 24, no. 151 (1988).

Hester, Thomas R., R. F. Heizer, and J. A. Graham. *Field Methods in Archaeology*. Mountain View, CA: Mayfield, 1975.

Heyerdahl, Thor. *Aku-Aku: The Secret of Easter Island*. London: George Allen and Unwin, 1958.

"India's Own Probe Also Found Water on Moon: ISRO." *Times of India*, 25 September 2009, http://timesofindia.indiatimes.com/news/india/Indians-own-probe-also-found-water-on-moon-ISRO/articleshow/5054436.cms.

Isbell, Douglas, and Mary Beth Murrill. "Jupiter's Europa Harbors Possible 'Warm Ice' or 'Liquid Water.'" *NASA Release* (13 Aug. 1996): 96–164, http://nssdc.gsfc.nasa.gov/planetary/text/gal_eur_water.txt.

Jones, Eric M. *"Where Is Everybody?" An Account of Fermi's Question*. Los Alamos, NM: Los Alamos National Laboratory Report LA-10311-MS, 1985.

Lyons, Thomas R., and Douglas H. Scovill. "Non-Destructive Archaeology and Remote Sensing: A Conceptual and Methodological Stance." In *Remote Sensing and Non-Destructive Archaeology*. Edited by T. R. Lyons and James I. Ebert. Washington, D.C.: National Park Service, 1978.

Nansen, Fridtjof. *En Ferd Til Spitsbergen*. Kristiania: Jacob Dybwads Forlag, 1920.

National Aeronautics and Space Administration. *Apollo 10* Press Kit. Release No. 69–68. Washington, D.C.: NASA, 1969.

_____. Apollo 10 *Mission Report; MSC-00126*. Houston, TX: Manned Spacecraft Center, 1969.

_____. *Space Settlements—A Design Study*. NASA SP-143, 1977.

O'Leary, Beth L. "The Cultural Heritage of Space, the Moon and Other Celestial Bodies." *Antiquity* 80, no. 307 (Mar. 2006).

_____, et al. *Lunar Legacy Project*. 2003. http://spacegrant.nmsu.edu/lunarlegacies/.

Richelson, Jeffrey T. "U.S. Satellite Imagery, 1960–1999." National Security Archive Electronic Briefing Book No. 13, 1999.

Ritchie, Neville A. "Archaeological Techniques and Technology on Ross Island, Antarctica." *Polar Record* 26, no. 159 (1990).

Sagan, Carl. *Cosmos*. New York: Random House, 1980.

_____. *Pale Blue Dot: A Vision of the Human Future in Space*. New York: Random House, 1994.

Schiffer, Michael. *Formation Processes of the Archaeological Record*. Salt Lake City: University of Utah Press, 1987.

Seaver, Kristen A. *The Frozen Echo: Greenland and the Exploration of North America, ca. A.D. 1000–1500*. Stanford: Stanford University Press, 1996.

Travis, John. "Deep-Sea Debate Pits *Alvin* Against *Jason*." *Science* 259 (1993).

Trefil, James. "Ah, But There May Have *Been* Life on Mars." *Smithsonian* 26, no. 5 (1995).

Van Gelder, Lawrence. "F.B.I. Revisits Earthly Theft of Moon Rock." *New York Times*, 2 December 1995.

Wadhams, P. "Sidescan Sonar Imagery of Sea Ice in the Arctic Ocean." *Canadian Journal of Remote Sensing* 4, no. 2 (1978).

Whitfield, John. "Shipwreck Network Launched: Three-Year European Project Aims to Safeguard Shipwrecks." *Nature News*, published on-line, 23 Jan. 2002.

Index